GLOBAL INVESTING FOR MAXIMUM PROFIT AND SAFETY

Also by Jerome Schneider

The Complete Guide to Offshore Money Havens

GLOBAL INVESTING FOR MAXIMUM PROFIT AND SAFETY

*Think Globally—Diversify Your
Investment Income to Take
Advantage of the Booming
Worldwide Economy*

JEROME SCHNEIDER

Prima Publishing

Library of Congress Cataloging-in-Publication Data

Schneider, Jerome.
    Global investing for maximum profit and safety: think globally—
diversify your investment income to take advantage of the booming
worldwide economy / Jerome Schneider.
        p.   cm.
    Includes index.
    ISBN 0-7615-1037-0
    1. Investments, Foreign.   I. Title.
HG4538.S344   1997
332.67'3—dc21   97-30461
                                                                    CIP

97 98 99 00 01 HH 10 9 8 7 6 5 4 3 2 1

Printed in the United States of America

How to Order:

Single copies may be ordered from Prima Publishing, P.O. Box 1260BK, Rocklin, CA 95677; telephone (916) 632-4400. Quantity discounts are also available. On your letterhead, include information concerning the intended use of the books and the number of books you wish to purchase.

Visit us online at http://www.primapublishing.com

*To those who seek the power to think globally and explore
opportunities that lie beyond America's borders.*

*Most of all, to my wife, J.C., who has taught me
about the importance of spiritual balance.*

This book is about global investing and international business opportunities. To get started, the author offers financial advice through workshops and one-on-one private consultation. For more information, Mr. Schneider invites you to contact him through his office in Vancouver, B.C. Canada at (604) 682-4000 or fax (604) 682-7700.

CONTENTS

ACKNOWLEDGMENTS

This book was written with the encouragement, support and constructive ideas of many people. I owe a debt of gratitude to many of my clients and colleagues who suggested that it be written. The members of my personal staff have earned a special thanks. In particular, I wish to express my appreciation to Max Benavidez and Kate Vozoff for their editorial direction throughout the project, and Brenda Nichols and Andrew Vallas for their professional assistance.

INTRODUCTION

This is a book about how to make money. It's also about one of the best kept secrets in America.

Most U.S. citizens don't know it, but international investment is no longer the exclusive domain of billionaires and Saudi Arabian oil barons. Quite the opposite. As this book goes to press, experts tell us that the global market has never been so ripe for the average investor to make profitable stock and bond purchases. Countries and consumers outside the United States are growing more sophisticated and richer by the day. Together those people produce four times the U.S. gross national product. They constitute 95 percent of the planet's population, and their number is growing 70 percent faster than the population of the United States.

Despite these facts, most Americans continue to limit their investment portfolio to U.S. companies, mutual funds, and Treasury bonds. The financial journals and magazines that dominate the domestic scene run articles every month, boasting of corporations that can offer remarkable investment gains of 10 to 15 percent. One such publication, the well-respected *Kiplinger's Mutual Fund '97*, recently ran a story called "The Twenty Best Funds in America." The author's goal was to offer readers a look at mutual funds that have excellent long-term records, retain seasoned managers, charge no sales fee, and sport ongoing annual expenses far below average. Sounds good.

As you look past this enticing introduction, however, you learn about funds that look for companies growing at 15 percent a year. One fund manager is proudly quoted as saying that he's willing to invest in companies growing as little as 12 percent annually. Given the choice between a company with lousy management in a solid industry and one with good managers in a dull industry, he'll opt every time for the latter because he's looking for "reasonable valuation."

Well, that's fine for that manager. His position on Wall Street is secure for at least as long as his wealthy clients— who already have megabucks in their portfolios—continue to see their sizable assets grow at a modest, "reasonable" pace. Why not? A 12 percent gain on millions of dollars would make even Donald Trump smirk.

But what about everybody else? What about people like you? And me? The truth is, most of this country's wealth is held by the smallest percentage of its citizens—the top 1 percent of America's ultrarich. That leaves, literally, tens of millions of people out in the cold—people with money to invest and a burning need to see that money grow. This book is meant for all of them. It's meant to provide them with information about the safe, lucrative, and relatively accessible opportunities that exist for them in established markets around the world as well as in the universe of emerging markets that want and need their investment capital.

Consider the Stomil Sanok factory, for example. Tucked deep in the sleepy southeast corner of Poland, it looks like a communist relic. But its shabby gray walls belie the bustling operation that's happening within as workers at high-tech molding machines churn out rubber parts for Fiat and the Daewoo Corporation. Never mind that its products are mundane and its sales are only $51 million. Stomil Sanok is one of the hottest investments available in Central Europe. Its profits grew 86 percent in 1996, and the company is expanding rapidly into Western Europe.

Consider Singapore business executive Charles Lee. For nearly thirty years he has lived with a heart irregularity that he can't control. At times his heart pounds furiously. Yet, because the palpitations come without warning and pass within minutes, doctors struggled for years to treat a disorder they never witnessed firsthand. Until recently. Last year Lee became a customer of Tele-Medical Services, a Singapore startup that provides sophisticated medical equipment to people with heart and respiratory conditions. Now, when an attack hits, Lee can call a control center and hook up his phone to portable equipment that can measure his heart rate. Cardiac specialists instantly see exactly what's happening and at last can offer appropriate treatment. The service isn't cheap, of course: $700 up front to buy the equipment and $90 a month for the monitoring services. Still, Lee argues that it's money well spent.

Health care companies throughout much of Asia see patients like Lee as the key to unlocking one of the world's most lucrative markets for private health care. In countries scattered throughout the Far East, years of brisk economic growth have created consumers eager to purchase everything from imported cars to car phones and designer handbags. Not surprisingly, these people also want better health care. And they're prepared to pay for it. Excluding Japan, Asians now spend $150 billion annually on heath care, and that figure is expected to soar by 70 percent by the year 2000. That means hot demand for private health care products and service providers like Tele-Medical.

Consider, finally, that in early 1996 most Egyptians shrugged at the news that President Hosni Mubarak had appointed Kamal Al-Ganzouri to the post of prime minister. A consummate bureaucrat, Al-Ganzouri was not seen as highly capable. Nobody expected him to wake up the country's sluggish economy or move ahead with a long-delayed program to privatize the hundreds of state-owned companies that made up more than a third of the Egyptian economy.

A year later the skeptics had changed their tune. The government had moved with surprising speed to surrender its dominant role in the country's financial life. As a result, the once sleepy Cairo Stock Exchange has become one of the hottest emerging market plays. Thanks largely to privatization, the trading volume of its most active stocks is eight times what it was two years ago. For the first time ever international fund managers are snooping around, like dogs on the scent of raw meat. "Egypt is more than hot," says Angus Blair, head of Middle East research at ING Barings Ltd. in London. "It's positively jumping all over the place."

These stories were not hard for me to come by. You don't have to look in obscure publications or read between the lines to see what's happening. The global market is booming. Even during the best years Wall Street harvests meager growth. Compared to its arid crop, international investments produce a cornucopia of high-yield equities and fixed-interest vehicles. A country-by-country study as seen in the Dow Jones Stock Index from *The Wall Street Journal* covering the period from late 1992 to mid 1993 showed a clear picture. The performance of U.S. stocks was typical: a 17 percent gain. Meanwhile, Singapore stocks showed a 26 percent gain. In Malaysia, it was nearly 43 percent. And in Hong Kong it was more than 44 percent. The advantages of investing globally are obvious. You simply have to open your eyes and look at them.

The question becomes: Why don't more people open their eyes? Why is the world of international investment still so small relative to its potential and the clear need among many U.S. investors to enliven their portfolios?

The answer, I think, has less to do with the reality of the global market and more to do with people's innate fear of the unknown. All investment involves risk. Risk of losing the money you put into an equity. Risk of choosing the right stock but at the wrong time. Risk of seeing your own mistakes, because nothing makes you feel as stupid as seeing your investment choices stand small in the shadow of the giant successes that you might have chosen if you'd only had a crystal ball to predict the big winners for this year or next.

Those fears are magnified for many people as they move further and further away from their home base. That's the case even on the domestic front. It's far easier for an auto worker in Detroit to invest in a company he knows (and perhaps even works for) than to put his money on the line to own part of an ostrich-breeding farm in northern California. It's easier for a yuppie in Silicon Valley to invest in a software project that's starting up in New Mexico than in a hypoallergenic cosmetic firm based in Manhattan. And it's easier for a divorced mother of three living in Boston to buy shares of a day care franchise that's established along the East Coast than to venture into North Dakota real estate. It's only human: The further you stray from where you live and what you know, the more unnerving investment becomes.

This basic human tendency makes it easier to understand people's reticence to get involved in the global market. In the more than twenty-five years that I've been doing international financial consulting, I've met thousands of fascinating investors—many of them intrigued by and attracted to the notion of diversifying into the global arena. Yet less than half of them ever act on those urges. I think the reason is fear. Fear that their money will simply vanish into some abyss that they imagine to be looming beyond their own national borders. Fear that fascist governments or inept, small-time bureaucrats running island tax havens will seize their money under the questionable laws that govern foreign countries. Fear as well that it will be impossible to monitor or fine-tune investment choices in a marketplace where nobody can communicate in English. We in the United States, after all, have a peculiar conceit when it comes to financial know-how. The French may hold top rank in the realm of culture. The Japanese in etiquette. The Italians in romance. But we have established a niche for ourselves as the world's best entrepreneurs. Many of us tend to take that role a little too seriously, hesitating to even involve foreigners in our asset development or management.

That's another reason for this book: It's a chance to walk you through those fears and, one by one, replace the anxiety brought on by the unknown with confidence that's born of accurate information and reasoned insight. I have been to almost every place I talk about in this book. I have read every book, manual, magazine article, and research study I mention. Certainly I don't want to paint myself as an expert on every financial market that exists today. Still, I am better informed about international investment than most of the people you could talk with about the subject. I want this book to assure you that the global option is viable. It's entirely legal. It's profitable beyond anything you could ever hope to achieve within the U.S. market. It protects your money from the overzealous greed of the U.S. tax system. And it allows you to operate with a level of financial privacy that has not existed in the United States for more than eighty years.

All of that is the good news.

The bad news is that the amazing benefits of international investment will not last forever. That's largely because every year the U.S. government takes another few steps toward limiting your right to make money abroad. New laws are enacted, new officials are elected, new regulatory offices are created—all in the effort to keep U.S. money within the jurisdiction of the federal (and state) government. Although the U.S. market cannot offer you the chance to get rich on Wall Street, Uncle Sam doesn't want you to go elsewhere to earn major profits. Why? Because every time you take one of your investment dollars and put it into a foreign bond or equity, you drain the flow of private money into U.S. corporate dominance. And the U.S. government has a lot invested (literally and figuratively) in the power and prestige of its multinational companies.

Examined from a slightly different angle, if you decide to invest in a promising New Delhi telecommunications company instead of in AT&T, you diminish the power of one of the most influential multinationals in the United States. And AT&T doesn't like rejection. Indeed, it pays a fleet of highly talented lobbyists some very big money to ensure that its place in the global economy remains unchallenged. Does AT&T want that startup company in India to succeed? Not on your life. Because AT&T wants to control telecommunications worldwide. It wants Indiana. It wants India too. Like all the major global players, AT&T wants it all. And it's big enough to close in around foreign competitors and eventually get exactly what it's after.

Fortunately for you and millions of other investors, even giants the size of AT&T can't do that overnight. It's going to take them time to get the job done. Quite a bit of time. Between now and then, you can take advantage of an open window to unparalleled opportunity. Infrastructure in China. Real estate development in Vietnam. Telecommunications in India. Food, fashion, and leisure pastimes—they all delight consumers in countries as diverse as Mexico, the Czech Republic, and Australia. Indeed, there are almost limitless unique products to sell and desirable services to offer in emerging markets around the world. And there's no foreseeable slowdown in the growing number of people who want to buy whatever their pocketbooks can handle in the way of trinkets and toys from Western culture.

Now is the time. The international market is full grown and ready for the rigors of real life. It's no longer considered the bastard child of communist dictators or barefoot peasants. By the same token, it's nowhere close to saturation. As you will see in this book, the heyday of sophisticated global investment opportunity is just dawning. That makes this a unique time for financial historians. And for you.

As best you can, remove any blinders you've grown accustomed to wearing when it comes to considering foreign investment. Open your eyes—to the words on the pages that follow and to the stunning reality they seek to introduce.

CHAPTER 1

THE GLOBAL BOOM

*When I think of Indonesia—a country on the
Equator with 180 million people, a median age
of 18 and a Moslem ban on alcohol—I feel I know
what heaven looks like.*

> — M. DOUGLAS IVESTER,
> PRESIDENT OF COCA-COLA

onsider the facts. This planet is now home to roughly 200 sovereign countries, and creative investors are forever finding new ways to make money in each of them. Yes, it's a big world out there. An $11.1 trillion world, in fact. That's the value of all the stocks in all the equity markets combined. And while it's true that the U.S. market makes up a hefty share of that figure, more than half of all existing stock originates from other markets.

There's little doubt that the international arena is the place to be. A look back at the state of the markets at the end of 1993 shows what I mean. Despite having a gain of 10 percent that year, the United States finished dead last among the world's forty-three major markets. At the same time, markets like Mexico and Hong Kong posted gains of more than 50 percent. In the face of such figures, you have to ask why the average American isn't taking better advantage of today's global investment boom. With international mutual funds promising better returns than they have in years, why do only 30 percent of the 63 million Americans who own mutual funds currently hold international funds in their portfolios?

The answer, I think, has a lot to do with our financial mind-set. We Americans are remarkably nationalistic. The United States is huge. Its influence is global, and historically its financial market has made a lot of people very rich. But that was then; this is now. The Dow Jones has moved beyond maturity. Yet investors continue to believe that a diversified domestic portfolio will take care of both their retirement and their children's inheritance. With blind confidence they stake their entire financial legacy on a market that perpetuates the economic status quo. The fact is that a minuscule segment of all U.S. investors control a preponderance of the market stock. In a very real sense the domestic market is closed. The most you can ever achieve there is a toehold in the bolted door to other people's affluence.

In contrast, the international marketplace is wide open and growing. The number of foreign-based U.S. corporate offices increases each year, and the international marketplace's pace of growth keeps accelerating in all sectors. Foreign firms have also made a serious commitment to global business. In fact, according to United Nations publications, there are already some 37,000 parent enterprises with more than 170,000 foreign affiliates earning in excess of $4.8 trillion annually on international ventures. Together these companies employ nearly 73 million people, fully 10 percent of the world's nonagricultural workforce.

The point is: The universe of financial opportunity is burgeoning even as high technology and telecommunications are putting all the world instantly at your fingertips. As recently as ten years ago I was among just a handful of consultants who wholeheartedly embraced the concept of international investment. At that time people feared both real and imagined problems. They worried about finding themselves at the mercy of uncooperative or even corrupt foreign governments. They wondered if, once outside U.S. borders, assets might simply vanish into a mysterious black hole, never to be retrieved. They anticipated a global marketplace in which few spoke English and even fewer understood American economics. The world beyond their borders was a terrifying obstacle course to be tackled only by the eminently prepared and the ridiculously foolish.

That left the international arena to be the playground of the megawealthy: corporate conglomerates, Saudi oil barons, billionaire industrialists, multinational corporations, and major brokerage houses. And play they have. Today international sales of Coca-Cola products account for 67 percent of the company's sales and 81 percent of its profits. By 1996 Merrill Lynch—one of the top-ranking brokerage firms in the world—was earning nearly one-third of its annual revenues from outside the United States. According to Merrill's chief executive, David H. Komansky, this is only the beginning. "The ability to have a truly global reach is going to be critical," he argues. "We are talking about something far in excess of originating outside the U.S. and distributing here. We are talking about originating in almost any foreign currency and being able to distribute products in almost any financial market in the world."

By making long-term commitments to large-scale foreign ventures, global giants like Coca-Cola, Merrill Lynch, and many others have irrevocably altered the rules of modern moneymaking. They have shattered the old myths about foreign governments, investors, and consumers. By replacing what was once a troubling information vacuum with solid, firsthand data about what international markets can offer, corporate giants of the twentieth century have given us a clear view of our complex investment universe. They've also drawn a detailed road map for individual investors who want to profit from all that the corporate giants have learned.

After twenty years' experience in international financial management, I am convinced that absolutely everyone can benefit from a global investment plan. The point is to find your personal "comfort level" within the foreign marketplace. Some people are meant to put most of their assets into international investment funds or foreign-owned businesses. Others would find such involvement an anxiety-ridden nightmare. To determine what will suit you best, you must begin learning about and pondering the size and scope of global moneymaking. This chapter is meant to help you do just that.

WHERE ON EARTH CAN YOU GO?

If the daily turbulence of the Dow Jones industrial average makes you jumpy, if overvalued investments have turned your portfolio slightly peaked, then think about doing what global investors do. Step back and look at the world as an investment supermarket in which domestic stocks are just one option. You can choose from among more than 300 open-ended global mutual funds whose managers pick stocks from around the world. You can trade in the foreign exchange market, taking day-to-day advantage of the world's strongest currencies. You can pursue possible venture partnerships with foreign businesspeople in virtually any part of the world. You can even establish a business abroad.

Your first step, though, is deciding where to put your money. With an entire planet's worth of nations to choose from, deciding can be a daunting task. Still, a lot of information is available to guide your selections. The bottom line is simple: Align yourself with companies that are heavily involved in the world's emerging markets. Experts tell us that by 2025 the earth's population will probably exceed 9 billion. More than two-thirds of those people will live in the Third World. Because of the improvements in global health care that we've already witnessed, the new emphasis on education that has taken root in these countries, and telecommunications bringing us closer and closer together, I predict that emerging markets will offer the most lucrative new investments in everything from infrastructure to pharmaceuticals and even leisure gadgets.

I am not the only one who thinks this way. Many experts agree that the best place to put your money is investments geared at developing nations because their markets are on such an upswing. Between 1990 and 1994 the economies of developing nations expanded an average of 5 percent, as opposed to the sluggish 2 percent growth among industrialized countries. Where that kind of explosion happens, money is sure to follow. It has. In 1993 total foreign investment in developing countries had hit $80 billion, and it's even greater today. It's been estimated that every year for the next decade the world's economically developing nations will need at least $200 billion in infrastructure investment alone!

China

Look for a moment at China. Not long ago we considered it a communist peasant state ruled by fascists and anti-American ideologues. To have considered investing in China during Mao Zedong's regime would have been tantamount to treason. Well, welcome to the late 1990s. In recent years the Chinese government has swallowed (with stony-faced silence) considerable U.S. criticism over its violations of human rights—all in the effort to keep and expand Western investment. Why? Because China needs it.

The World Bank estimates that, together with a number of smaller Asian countries, China will require up to $2 trillion in power plants, water systems, telecommunications systems, airports, highways, and other infrastructure investment by the year 2004. That's roughly $4 billion a week! The Chinese government isn't capable of supporting that enormous an effort. Only with huge infusions of foreign investment will China ever rise to the living standards of the twentieth century.

Glimpsing the possibility of almost limitless profit potential, international investors are standing in line to get involved. Non-Chinese pumped a cumulative $122 billion into the country between 1989 and 1995—and who can blame them? Since the late 1970s, when the government's economic policies took a definite turn for the better, China's gross national product has averaged an annual growth rate of nearly 10 percent. Forecasters expect it to easily maintain an 8 to 10 percent clip at least through the next decade.

Want some more investment news from the Far East? Between now and 2025 the Chinese government plans to increase telephone service twentyfold. It's their way, they say, of improving life for the two-thirds of their citizens who have never made a phone call. Think for a moment about the size of that market. Put simply, this means 15 to 17 million phone lines will be built every year for the next twenty-seven years. That's enough to make AT&T's top brass positively giddy! Indeed, that multinational giant has already partnered with the Chinese government to handle a hefty share of the work and, of course, reap a hefty profit. AT&T's goal, however, is far more ambitious. In its 1993 annual report AT&T explained that "this work could be the most extensive international project in our history." That's quite a statement coming from a company that leads the way in global business activity. It's an unequivocal endorsement of international investment and proof positive that money wisely put to work abroad can reap attractive profits.

East and South Asia

Similar though less dramatic activity is taking place throughout much of East and South Asia. Korea, Singapore, Taiwan, Malaysia, Indonesia, and Thailand all are experiencing profound social, political, and economic transformations. In

1970 one-third of all people in the region lived in what the World Bank called "absolute poverty." In other words, they had barely enough food to survive, and permanent shelter was not a fact of life. Today only one-tenth of East and South Asia can be termed absolutely poor. Quite an achievement under any circumstances, and all the more impressive when you realize that during that twenty-year period the overall population grew by 425 million.

The Philippines, once referred to as "the sick man of Asia," is also brimming with investment possibility. With a gross national product that jumped up 7 percent in 1996 and is expected to jump another 8 percent in 1997, the Philippines is poised for remarkable market activity. Much of the credit goes to President Fidel Ramos, the plainspoken West Point graduate who took office in 1992. Like a growing number of foreign politicians and officials, Ramos genuinely wants foreign investment. He has pursued it by giving his country a healthy dose of what any emerging market nation needs to raise living standards: honest, impartial institutions and an environment in which free enterprise can thrive. Under his administration the government has deregulated shipping, telecommunications, banking, and insurance.

Sure enough, foreign investment has snapped at the bait. Companies from the United States, Europe, and Asia have all made heavy commitments to Philippines-based ventures. For example, in early 1997 the island government awarded $7 billion in infrastructure contracts to two foreign consortia. One of them was the Bechtel Group, which has been hired to privately operate Manila's water system.

India

Over the next several years India may become an investment Mecca in its own right. A number of multinational corporations have already infiltrated India's economy. In early 1997 Rebecca Mark, chairperson and CEO of Houston-based

With international mutual funds promising better returns than they have had in years, why do only 30 percent of the 63 million Americans who own mutual funds currently hold international funds in their portfolios?

Enron International, spoke with *Business Week* magazine about her company's $2.5 billion Indian power project. "When [we] first came into India five years ago," she said, "everyone was looking China-ward, whereas Enron was ear-marking major investments for India. This year there was a total change. Most people who had gone into China were redirecting their focus to India." Although Mark may be a bit biased by her own professional involvement, her analysis contains a lot of truth.

Between now and 2025 China's population is expected to grow only slightly—from 1.2 to 1.55 billion. In contrast, according to the Population Reference Bureau, India's population is expected to swell from 900 million to almost 1.4 billion. Those numbers take on incredible significance when you consider the rapid growth of India's consumer market. Although 200 million Indians currently live in poverty, 40 million others enjoy high living standards, and another 150 million have significant disposable income. By 2005 middle-class Indians could number close to 400 million. Imagine the market that they'll create—for everything from chewing gum to four-wheel-drive vehicles.

To give a sense of the mind-set in India, I recently read that at Kodaikanal, in southern India, peasants assemble once a week at a central kiosk, where television links them through a small satellite dish to their favorite program, Robin Leach's *The Lifestyles of the Rich and Famous*. Of course, one can ponder the social implications of feeding uneducated peasants a steady diet of such conspicuous consumption, but such reflection will not reverse the tidal wave of consumerism. Foreign investment is no longer a possibility for India; it's an inevitability. The goal now must be culturally informed, respectful investment that helps Indians improve their standard of living even as it reaps sizable profits for stockholders, corporate enterprise, and mid-sized business.

Like China, India has a horribly substandard infrastructure and an increasingly demanding population. In 1960 India had just 250,000 kilometers of paved roads. By 1990 that figured had tripled to more than 750,000 kilometers. As the government grapples with how to build more roads, more electric power lines and plants, more telephone lines, and more sewage systems to serve millions of people who have never seen indoor running water, outside money and expertise will be critical. First under the leadership of Narasimha Rao, and then Prime Minister Devi, the government has introduced policies that lift the yoke of what used to be an all-pervasive national bureaucracy. To a great extent, India has implemented efficient free-market economic reform. Investors have responded by sending billions of dollars into the country.

Latin America

The story is much the same in Latin America. Mexico's 1994 currency collapse forced leaders throughout the region to face reality. Like it or not, they could no longer depend on foreign banks to bail them out of reckless national management. It was time to sink or swim. They swam. By deflating bloated bureaucracies and revamping welfare programs, they enacted budgets that matched national capacities. They also acknowledged for the first time that entrenched state enterprises were often inefficient drains on precious economic resources. Protectionist policies and excessive regulation were squelching competition and breeding both corruption and waste. Throughout much of Latin America, politicians and bankers acted with reason and speed. Liberalization, deregulation, and privatization became the building blocks of a new economic system that has attracted considerable foreign investment.

Most economists agree that a boost initiated by the North American Free Trade Agreement (NAFTA) has also contributed to setting this vast region on a long-term growth path. Overall domestic growth started heading upward by the mid 1990s—from 2.9 percent in 1992 to 3.3 percent in 1993. This growth may not seem impressive, but look at how it translates into terms that hard-nosed investors care about: The average return on 1996 Latin American bonds was a whopping 35 percent. That's ten times what U.S. Treasuries delivered. Shunned as too high-risk by all but the most daring, even up to a few years ago, Latin debt is now in such demand that issuers sold a record $50 billion in bonds on Latin markets in 1996.

The drop in interest rates within traditional Western markets is the driving force behind the success of these foreign markets. Investors searching for high yields must look beyond their own borders. Investors who not so long ago gave Latin debt short shrift now need to reconsider. Pension funds, insurance companies, and high-yield investors all are attracted by the tidy premiums Latin borrowers are paying. Mexico's latest ten-year bond, for example, pays 3.35 percentage points over comparable U.S. Treasuries. Even more remarkable, Mexico issued twenty- and thirty-year bonds in 1996. Shortly after the peso crisis such long maturities would have been considered ridiculous, but within the span of only two years everything changed! "People have been proven right to go back and invest in those markets," says David C. Mulford, worldwide vice chairman of Credit Suisse First Boston.

The hectic border between San Diego and Tijuana reflects the astonishing economic development that's taking place throughout much of Latin America. Until recently most San Diegans saw the world next-door mainly as a honky-tonk weekend haven for sailors and underage drinkers. Not anymore. Tijuana's population swelled nearly 6 percent between 1990 and 1995, and it's expected to double in the next fourteen years. The growing links between Tijuana and San Diego are visible at the border crossings, where commuting factory managers swell the traffic jams in twenty-three lanes heading each way. Separate truck lanes are clogged, too, with big rigs carrying everything from computers to coffee makers—all bound for distribution across North America.

Eastern Europe

Then there's the bonanza taking place throughout Eastern Europe. Remember when Ronald Reagan warned us not to underestimate the malevolence of the Evil Empire? The entire Western world feared the former Soviet Union—its uniformed military strutting through Red Square, its cruelty toward prisoners banished to Siberian salt mines, its Cold War stare and nuclear weapons. How things have changed! The small former Soviet nations cannot bark at the United States, much less bite us. They're utterly consumed by regional politics and religious antagonisms. Yet, for all their political strife, a few of these emerging markets are offering some of the world's best-performing stock markets. For example, from the end of 1995 through the end of January 1997, Hungary's market shot up 167 percent in dollar terms. Russia was up a phenomenal 247 percent.

So why, ask cautious investors, are these stocks still so inexpensive by European or U.S. standards? The answer is that Eastern Europe is really a reemerging market. Unlike Southeast Asia and Latin America, which are making the transition from agricultural to urban economies, Eastern Europe is already industrialized. That means today's investor need not pay to build factories to house profitable new industries. Therefore, these markets offer extremely good investments.

Even Russia has foreign money flooding into its stock market. Although many local investors are warming again to stocks (after a series of investment pyramid scams in the mid-1990s robbed many of considerable assets), foreigners still account for at least 90 percent of all trading. The Russian trading market is so active that Moscow's Credit Suisse Investment Fund recently spent nearly $1 million to renovate its skyscraper offices, and business is booming. The market surged 156 percent just during 1996, and another 60 percent during the first quarter of 1997. The entire phenomenon has Western analysts sitting on the edge of their seats. U.S. money managers like Franklin/Templeton and Pioneers are now competing with Credit Suisse and other local financial groups to sell Russian equity and bond funds to small investors worldwide. I can only imagine their smiles in the fall of 1996, when the World Bank's International Finance Corporation included Russia in its widely watched index of emerging equity markets.

CAN ONLY THE BIG INVESTORS PLAY?

Major U.S. corporations have been in on the global boom for a long time. Whirlpool is a perfect case in point. With $7 billion in annual sales of washers, dryers, and refrigerators (and more than a 30 percent share of the U.S. market), this corporation has made plenty of money in the United States. Unfortunately, the domestic market for Whirlpool's products is fairly saturated. Because most people here already have these appliances, domestic consumers do not represent a market with any real growth potential. So Whirlpool has been forced into the global market. The company started foreign business in Latin America as early as 1957. By the

1980s it had turned its attention to Europe. Everywhere it went Whirlpool made money. Now the focus is on Asia, where the company predicts an annual sales growth of between 8 and 12 percent for many years to come.

The global marketplace is full of stories like Whirlpool's—giant corporations that can pay researchers huge salaries to identify profitable foreign markets and then use their management structure and financial power to successfully promote their products abroad. But what about the smaller entrepreneur—the small or medium-sized enterprises that lack limitless resources but that would nonetheless like to take advantage of the international boom? Is there a niche for them?

Absolutely! In 1994 the Conference Board of New York surveyed 1,250 publicly traded U.S. manufacturing firms, trying to understand more about globalization trends. Of the companies surveyed, more than 90 percent reported direct foreign investment, foreign sales, or other forms of international activity. The Conference Board's conclusion was that the internationalization of marketing and manufacturing is now irreversible—even for relatively small companies.

In its survey report the Conference Board described the scenario by which most large and midsized businesses enter the global market. Basically, it found that the bigger the company, the more likely it is to approach the global arena one small step at a time. First there's a period of in-depth research, followed by the development of a few exports. Then an actual sales infrastructure is set up abroad. Finally, overseas production begins. This process is well documented by scores of corporate executives who have participated in one or more of these incremental steps. The results are, for the most part, impressive. Most multinational corporations do their homework, move slowly, and take few (if any) chances.

Frankly, none of the Conference Board's findings is too surprising, but the information the study gathered from midsized and small multinational businesses is intriguing.

> **S**mall and medium-sized businesses may not have the funds to undertake in-depth global research, but they can often beat their goliath competition by being faster and more flexible.

The Board found that these enterprises often take an alternative (and faster) route into the global arena. Put simply, they jump in even before they have enormous sums of money behind them. By initiating and conducting international activity well before they've reached the now famous $1 billion mark in annual sales, smaller businesses can compress (or even leapfrog) the many steps once assumed to be essential.

Large corporations are able to get mountains of information about any potential foreign investment. However, their enormous size can make them slow to act on new data, or so process oriented that even fabulous information fails to reach the right people at the right time. Small and medium-sized businesses may not have the funds to undertake in-depth global research, but they can often beat their goliath competition by being faster and more flexible.

Let me give you an example. My consulting firm helps investors internationalize their portfolios. A few years ago I met Floyd Sutcliff, a pistachio farmer from California's Central Valley. Twenty years ago Floyd was a wealthy guy, but by the time we met, the 1990s downturn in the U.S. economy had played havoc with his success. His profits were down and gave every indication of continuing this trend. In a brilliant attempt to resuscitate his assets, Floyd sold two of his three farms, moved to Canada, and built a well-diversified portfolio that included several international stocks. One of them was a sizable share of a small Filipino cellular phone company with plans to market its product throughout what was then Zaire, now the Democratic Republic of the Congo (DRC). A peculiar project, you might think. But not so odd once you realize that the DRC has no operational phone system whatsoever. Nothing. Floyd invested $1 million in the firm, and within twelve months his stock was worth $9 million. A 900 percent profit? You got it. And he didn't do it with help from AT&T or any other telecommunications giant. He made a brilliant investment in a small, never-before-heard-of electronics company that had one solid, creative idea.

The point of this story is simple: You don't have to invest in a major corporate enterprise; you don't have to hook your wagon to a multinational conglomerate that's been a cover story in *Fortune* magazine. You can make money in the global market by strategically investing in smaller companies that have done their homework and offer foreign consumers a product or service that they want and can afford.

WHO DOES THE GLASS SLIPPER FIT?

In the legendary fairy tale, Cinderella is the only maiden in the land whose tiny foot fits into the glass slipper. Overjoyed to have found his true love, the handsome prince marries her, and, of course, they live happily ever after. In a very real sense, small and midsized businesses of today are the global market's Cinderella. Often unassuming and even a bit simple, they have precisely the right qualities to complement the existing global market.

Major corporations are setting up offices and initiating foreign operations largely because they want to position themselves for the money they stand to earn in the future. Earn it they will, I'm sure, but only after significant social, economic, and cultural transformation occurs. Until then the multinationals are brilliantly biding time, establishing goodwill abroad, and securing a corner of what will eventually be a gargantuan market.

Take Ford Motor Company. With operations established in virtually every Third World country, Ford is an unquestioned leader in the global arena. But how many new car buyers are there in Managua, Prague, or Calcutta? Research reveals that of the 5.4 billion people on earth, almost 3.6 billion have neither the cash nor credit to buy much of anything. In other words, nearly 80 percent of the world's buying is still concentrated in countries that hold less than a quarter of the planet's population. In the mid-1980s there were thirteen people for every car in Brazil. Only one out of seventy-seven South Koreans had a car. And only one out of every 677 Chinese had ever driven.

The truth is, "big shoppers"—consumers able to afford everything from a backyard swimming pool to a university education—still amount to slightly fewer than 2 billion people. The universe of new car buyers is surely a fraction of this number. So the business development undertaken by Ford today will reap some minimal profits, but nothing compared to what it will reap in a decade (or two or three), when these developing economies have leaped solidly forward into the modern age.

Research also makes it clear that many people who can't afford the accoutrements of Western consumer culture still want them. In Korea young girls spend entire afternoons nibbling french fries, sipping Coke, and listening to American rock music at local McDonald's or Kentucky Fried Chicken restaurants. In Mexico City small children beg on the street for pesos to buy Frito-Lays and Ruffles potato chips. Why? Because they're entranced by TV ads. Frito-Lay runs as many as four consecutive commercials on local Mexican television. A 1981 survey of the National Consumer Institute in Mexico found that "grade school children spend more time watching TV than in school and have more knowledge of TV ads than of Mexican history." By 1990 more than one-third of all people in developing nations lived in cities where daily exposure to global products, through television, radio, and billboards, was inescapable.

For the smaller business this is wonderful news. It means that affordable products geared at the everyday lives of people throughout the developing world are likely to sell like hotcakes. Not irrelevant to this discussion is the fact that 40 percent of the people on earth are now under twenty years of age. So businesses geared at the likes, fashions, and follies of young people are likely to be big winners in the international market. Hard Candy undoubtedly will be.

A very new company based in southern California, Hard Candy was founded by Dinah Mohajer, a premed student who never intended to start a fashion empire. She just wanted some pale-blue nail polish to match her platform sandals. Unable to find any at the neighborhood beauty shops or department stores, she decided to mix the stuff herself. When she sported her jazzed-up toes around campus, "eleven girls stopped me one day and said, 'Oh, my God, that is so cute!'" recalls Mohajer. "So my sister was like, 'Are you retarded? You could make money at this.'"

She may talk like a ditzy Valley Girl, but Mohajer is anything but. As of mid-1997, Hard Candy was less than two years old and had projected sales of $20 million by year end. Now Mohajer maintains, "We're going to expand into a cutting edge cosmetic company with staying power for the long

You can make money in the global market by strategically investing in smaller companies that have done their homework and offer foreign consumers a product or service that they want or can afford.

haul." With a new CEO who has done time with Rockwell International and a smattering of cosmetics companies, the nail polish manufacturer has set up shop in various locations throughout Europe, Japan, Taiwan, and New Zealand. Their hope is that teenagers worldwide will react like American girls have: with an unquenchable thirst for Sky Blue, Mint Green, and some sixty other shades with names like Trailer Trash, Gold Digger, Jailbait, Porno, Scorn, and Manic. "It's like totally not retarded," boasts Mohajer. Translated: "We're going to be rolling in dough!"

Hard Candy and thousands of other small to medium-sized businesses are set to clean up internationally because they can do what the huge conglomerates cannot: get in, sell fast, and get out when the market evaporates. In their book *Boom* Frank Vogl and James Sinclair offer an insightful analysis of precisely this phenomenon. They explain that a United Nations survey of smaller enterprises around the world found four main areas in which such firms (and their investors) can enjoy competitive advantages over large transnational corporations in the international arena:

1. *They can take advantage of production opportunities left open by large companies.* In other words, they can make what the big guys forget (or never think) to make. Like Hard Candy. Where was Estée Lauder, Chanel, Clinique, or Revlon when it came time to capture the teenybopper market? Obviously they were out to lunch—which allowed Dinah Mohajer the chance to slip right into a profitable market spot. She and her investors will benefit handsomely from filling that little niche.

2. *They may possess technologies that have been phased out by large firms but for which there remain distinct regional markets.* I read recently about the booming comic book industry in China. Reportedly, 80 percent of all children's books sold

in China are foreign cartoons. In China's one-child culture parents are extremely concerned about giving their child the best possible chance for success—a major part of that success being good, wholesome values. The imported (mostly Japanese) comic books are thought to depict too much violence, sex, and "immoral" values. But no culturally sensitive alternative is available. A clever publisher could easily fill that market void and make a mint for itself and its investors.

3. *They have advantages in downscaling technologies to small markets, in making production more labor intensive, and in adapting to local factor proportions.* That just means that small businesses—because they are not entirely automated and computer controlled—tend to be more labor intensive. By offering jobs (even low-paying ones) to local residents, they often engender great community affection and consumer loyalty. The best global investors look to place their money with companies that take precisely this approach.

4. *They can gain cost advantages by having highly flexible and simple organizational structures—in fact, flexibility of management represents the smaller company's greatest source of competitive advantage.* Remember Floyd Sutcliff? He invested in a small operation. In fact, the entire company was run by two brothers from Manila. One was an electronics engineer trained at the California Institute of Technology. The other had an MBA from Harvard. Whatever supplemental talent they required to run the business they subcontracted out on a project-by-project basis. This allowed them to keep costs down and sidestep the needless delays that accompany an entrenched, calcified management base.

The best global investments are sometimes made in a small or medium-sized company that aims to meet an everyday need of people with limited financial resources but with a burning desire to buy, rent, borrow, or otherwise possess a trinket from the industrialized world.

The bottom line is this: The best global investments are sometimes made in a small or medium-sized company that aims to meet an everyday need of people with limited financial resources but with a burning desire to buy, rent, borrow, or otherwise possess a trinket from the industrialized world. If, on top of all this, the company markets a product geared at young consumers with a bit of money in their pockets (or backpacks)—all the better!

Now Is THE TIME

In this chapter I have tried to lay out a clear picture of the international market. It's big (and growing bigger). It's young (and not likely to age much over the coming decades). It's filled with eager consumers who want nothing more than to possess the fashion, food, and fun that they associate with the United States. Beyond the borders of this country rests a virtual cornucopia of moneymaking opportunity. The emerging markets, in particular, are surging forward. Whether your personal taste for international activity attracts you to something as traditional and timeless as

Timex stock or as trendy and exhilarating as Hard Candy's teen cosmetics, the time to act is now.

Major financial players have inhabited the international arena long enough to have tested the waters. Have no fear; you are not about to venture into uncharted territory. By the same token, global investment and business operation are still in their infancy. Western speculators, executives, and financial houses have barely scratched the surface of what's there to be had. Over time, of course, the markets will "mature"—just like our domestic markets did long ago. Don't wait for the parade to pass you by. The late 1990s offer you a unique window of opportunity. Open it, and jump through.

Chapter 2

Masters of the Game

*When you have tremendous conviction on a trade,
you have to go for the jugular. It takes courage to
be a pig.*

— Stanley Druckenmiller,
senior advisor to George Soros

Some people are intimidated by greatness. I myself am
fascinated by it. I'm the kind of guy who loves watching George Foreman in the ring, Julia Child in the
kitchen, Robert De Niro on the screen. Most of all, I love listening to and learning about the masters of global investment—those brilliant, often eccentric, individuals whose
ability to make money places them in a league of their own.

It fascinates me that the success these rare investors
enjoy far exceeds the sum of their intelligence, courage, and
network of contacts. Countless other speculators out there
are every bit as bright, gutsy, and connected but never approach quantum wealth. Something else distinguishes the
successful from the legendary. I don't pretend to understand
it completely. I do think, however, that it has something to
do with their love of the game. When most of us get involved
in an investment project, we keep our eyes rigidly focused
on the bottom-line outcome. Either the investment will
make us money or it will cost us money. The more I learn

The more I learn about the giants of the global marketplace, the less they seem like the rest of us. They have a unique ability to forget about the money.

about the giants of the global marketplace, the less they seem like the rest of us. They have a unique ability to forget about the money (or perhaps never to think about it much in the first place).

I am reminded of my wife's good friend Rob. A highly placed music industry executive, he also collects vintage pottery and regularly sells his early California pieces for upwards of several thousand dollars. To maintain his rather impressive collection, Rob spends what seems to me an inordinate amount of time scouring the city's antique shops and estate sales looking for pieces that he can pick up and turn around for a handsome profit. A few years ago my wife and I spent an afternoon with him as he made the rounds through local dust piles and junk stores. By the end of the day I was exhausted, dusty, and frustrated by the fact that he'd found nothing to buy but a wicker lounge, which he planned to use on his own back deck. Drained by the entire ordeal, I asked him how he can stand such days. "Oh, I guess I just enjoy the search," he replied.

The major players in today's financial market must also "enjoy the search." It's more than the money for them. It's the satisfaction that comes from letting gut instinct lead the way. Granted, instinct alone isn't enough. In fact, that's the difference between speculators and investors: Speculators go by gut feeling only and hope for a profitable outcome. Investors, in contrast, let their instinct point them in the right direction and then compile all the data they need to tell them whether their gut feeling is worth pursuing.

In the hope that you, too, might enjoy a glimpse into the investment styles and personalities of these exceptional people, I want to describe some of the more interesting global masters. Some famous names are in the pages that follow, but also a sampling of lesser known men and women. You'll see that each of them has a very particular investment and entrepreneurial style. Each of them operates in a specific corner of the investment universe. And despite the fact that they all pursue their moneymaking in different ways, each is utterly convinced of the infallibility of his or her basic approach.

So sit back and prepare to be entertained, because everyone mentioned in this chapter is worthy of a full-length biography. I must say up front that I don't discuss them so that you can run out and emulate them. In fact, if there's anything to be learned from a panoramic view of the Who's Who in modern investment, it's that you reap only modest profits by copying somebody else's methodology. Real success goes to the originals. My intention is to get your creativity flowing by showing you how it flows (sometimes even floods) through the veins of the masters of the game. Then you can mix and match their various secrets to devise the investment plan that suits you best.

EVER SUREFOOTED, WARREN BUFFETT

The offshore investment phenomenon has grown so diverse (and sometimes so complex) that the beginner can wonder where to begin. How do you wade through all the options and make sound decisions? For newcomers to the global market, Warren Buffett serves as a beacon light in what may at first appear overwhelming waters. No nonsense. No risk. That's the Buffett approach to making money. His amazing success is a testament to just how profitable that approach can be.

Even among the giants of modern investment, Buffett stands alone. Starting with just $100 in 1956, he has amassed an estimated $21 billion—one of the most amazing fortunes of the twentieth century. We've seen oil magnates, real estate moguls, shippers, and robber barons at the top of the money heap, but Buffett is the first person ever to attain such quantum success through nothing more than an uncanny knack for picking stocks. It's become almost a cliché to point out that if you had invested just $10,000 with him when he began in Omaha, Nebraska, in 1956 and stuck with him, you would now be worth in the neighborhood of $95 million. If you'd given him only $1,000 in 1969, you'd now be sitting on a cool million.

Remarkably, Buffett, often called the "oracle of Omaha," asserts that his incredible wealth results not from any special talent or even well-honed investment technique but from a blend of fundamental analysis, calculation, common sense, and patience that anyone can imitate. The key, he says, is to identify the real value of any business venture and then, when you can buy into a project that's worth more than what is being asked for your involvement, invest as much as you can in it and wait for time to prove you right. "Time is the friend of the wonderful business," he once said, "and the enemy of the mediocre."

Fred Carr, celebrated head of the mutual fund with the same name, once remarked that every stock he held was for sale every morning, along with his shirt and tie. Yet another fund manager is on record for arguing that it isn't enough to study stock prices week by week or even day by day; they must be studied minute by minute. There is no minute-by-minute valuation in Warren Buffett's world. He doesn't have a stock ticker in his nondescript Omaha office. Nor does he have a computer terminal. ("I am a computer," he once remarked when asked about this glaring office deficiency.)

Instead, Buffett spends his time methodically reviewing annual reports (the fewer the number of pictures and charts, the better) and financial statements, looking for stocks worth more than their asking price. When he finds one, his commitment is total and virtually permanent. He doesn't maintain an eclectic portfolio. Would you believe that 80 percent of the gains in his holding firm, Berkshire Hathaway, come from just six issues? Not one of them ranks among the top fifty performers of the past twenty years. Nevertheless, the last time Buffett disposed of a major position was 1986.

If you fear speculation and want to begin by dipping just a foot into the international ocean, then Buffett is a perfect role model. A Midwestern realist through and through, he's not one for picking up European companies on the cheap or pursuing partnerships with Japanese developers. Instead, he likes to invest in U.S.-based companies that coordinate their own offshore profit making. If you'd like to follow his example, then remember four of Buffet's investment rules as you shop for companies that will provide you with this indirect approach to the global market:

1. *Pay no attention to economic trends or forecasts and disregard other people's predictions about the future course of stock prices.* Buffett loves to tell a parable about the stock market's irrationality. In 1963 a scandal at a small subsidiary of American Express drove down the price of the company's shares. Buffett was curious just how bad the problem really was. He spent an evening with the cashier at Ross's Steak House in Omaha, looking to see if people would stop using their green American Express cards. The scandal didn't seem to give a single diner indigestion, so Buffett seized the opportunity to buy 5 percent of the company for $13 million. He later sold the holding for a $20 million profit.

2. *Focus on long-term business value, on the likelihood of profitability down the road.* In the fall of 1988 Buffett started buying stock in Coca-Cola.

Why then? The company's story, after all, was hardly new. Indeed, in 1938 a *Fortune* writer had looked admiringly at Coca-Cola's prospects but decided that it was probably too late to buy. What's more, Buffett's investments generally hinge on values that can be tabulated from a balance sheet, but this venture was different. Trading at thirteen times expected 1989 earnings, about 15 percent higher than the average stock, Coke certainly was not a natural fit for his portfolio. Still, he liked very particular things about the company. It was a simple business that had had pricing power and—with the most famous brand name in the world—a virtually foolproof insulation against competitors. Most important, Buffett insisted, it had earning power. It was like getting a Mercedes for the price of a Chevy. In other words, Buffett couldn't compute Coca-Cola's value, but he could see it.

3. ***Always stick to stocks you can understand.*** Some people have said that the most distinguishing trait of Buffett's investment philosophy is the clear realization that, by owning stock, he owns a business, not pieces of paper. The idea of buying stock without understanding the company's operating functions—including its products and services, labor relations, raw material expenses, plant and equipment, capital reinvestment requirements, inventories, and receivable and working capital—is inconceivable to him. "Always invest within your circle of competence," Buffett insists. "It's not how big the circle is that counts; it's how well you define the parameters." He practices what he preaches. He invests only in simple, understandable businesses. For instance, he's on record as saying that if a venture involves high technology, he admittedly will not understand it and therefore is not interested.

4. ***Never buy stock in a company that requires a change in management.*** Buffett never buys a

company if he has to supply the management. The business must be prepared to operate with an extraordinary degree of freedom and is preferably run by the same family members who managed it before the Berkshire purchase. Here's a perfect example. In early 1986 Bob Heldman, chair of Fechheimer Brothers (and a longtime shareholder of Berkshire Hathaway), wrote Buffett explaining that Fechheimer was a venture that might be of interest to him. The two men met, and by summer Buffett had added another business to his collection. Fechheimer manufactures and distributes uniforms. The company traces its roots back to 1842, and the Heldman family has been involved since 1941. The family wanted to continue running the company, but they needed capital. To get cash from Berkshire and still retain partial ownership was their ideal. Buffett paid $46 million for 84 percent of the capital stock. Yet, to this day, he's never visited its headquarters in Cincinnati, nor has he toured any of its plants.

THE THRIFT SHOPPER, SIR JOHN TEMPLETON

For the slightly more daring investor, John Templeton's story offers an exceptional balance of caution and daring.

Having worked his way through Yale University (and earning a Rhodes Scholarship to boot), Templeton displayed his particular investment style from the start. In 1939, when he was twenty-six years old and nearly penniless, he felt certain that war was imminent and that it would pull the United States out of its economic depression. When the upswing began, he reasoned, all stocks would increase in value, and the "rejects" would ultimately prove to have been the best bargains. So he borrowed $10,000 from his employer and asked a stockbroker to purchase $100 worth of every stock that was selling for no more than a dollar per share.

The broker was more than a bit perplexed by the peculiar request, but he agreed to handle the transaction. A few days later he called Templeton to report that he'd picked up $100 worth of every stock that cost one dollar or less so long as the company wasn't completely bankrupt. Templeton's response was immediate and impassioned. "No, you don't understand!" he said. "I want them all!" It was back to work for the broker, and when his assignment was done, John Templeton had acquired a junk pile of stock in 104 companies—thirty-four of which were bankrupt.

This story highlights two basic elements in Templeton's investment approach. First and foremost, he argues, it's wise to be a bargain hunter. Like a garage sale addict, the clever investor is willing to rummage around through what everyone else has thrown aside, looking for the wonderfully rare, the beautifully special, the diamonds in the rough. To be good at this treasure hunt, he says, you must be able to evaluate the "neglected factor" that will change things for the better. You must wear glasses different from those worn by all the ordinary people who don't like what they see.

I remember the Abrams, clients of mine who made a sizable fortune in California real estate. During the early 1980s, when properties were just beginning to go for more than they could possibly be worth in Los Angeles, this middle-aged couple started purchasing the ugliest fixer-uppers I've ever seen. I'm not just talking about houses that needed a few cosmetic improvements. I'm talking about junkers that offered little more than rusty plumbing and leaky roofs. "But it's all location," they used to laugh. They'd buy properties for almost nothing, and, thanks to their unique ability to visualize what a place would look like after you knock down every nonessential wall and cut as much window and skylight space as zoning will allow, they turned around and sold them for a nifty profit. Today, enjoying an early retirement, they're an example of this Templeton dictate: See what others cannot see; like what others find unappealing.

The second element at the heart of Templeton's investment approach is this: You must hold stocks for an average of four years. In his view they need that much time to show that they were in fact a bargain. In other words, a lemon can't be turned into lemonade in an instant. It takes time. Templeton ought to know. He held those stocks that he bought in 1939 for four years. When he sold the kit, it brought him $40,000—four times his initial investment!

Another critical feature in Templeton's style is that he's extremely global. His investments range over many markets. He's every bit as financially connected to Japan as he is to the United States, Canada, Switzerland, Germany, Holland, Belgium, Australia, or South Africa. What's more, he got involved in the international marketplace way before almost everybody else. For example, he became interested in Japan in 1962. He recalls that you could buy even the leading companies at half or a third of their real earnings at that time, with the benefit of extensive hidden assets that never showed up on the balance sheet. Most American and European investors couldn't (or wouldn't) believe their eyes, so the bargains persisted. Templeton had a field day.

Although Templeton claims that growth rates are slowing somewhat in Japan, his own financial involvement there continues. In fact, of all the companies he owns, the one he claims to have most confidence in for the long term is Ito Yokado, a supermarket chain. It has proved very profitable for him already, and, he maintains, it should produce a handsome 30 percent annual growth rate for a good ten years because supermarkets are just getting started in Japan. When he bought the chain of stores in 1980 they sold at over twenty times their earnings—making this deal a departure from his usual bargain. Still, if his hunch is right about just how valuable Ito Yokado will be in another few years, then this deal may still prove him a master at the bargain basement approach to offshore investing.

Templeton also points out that when he first invested in Japan, the average Japanese investor liked only the big names. They trusted what they'd heard about. They hadn't heard about small specialty growth companies that were still in a dynamic phase of development. The Japanese also gave more weight to the six-month earning outlook than to six-year prospects. This cultural bias allowed Templeton to clean up. He acquired several small firms and watched them grow to the point that they could be sold at a substantial premium over the giants. For the intelligent investor of today, this aspect of Templeton's style can be the secret to similar international profits. All you have to do is identify offshore markets in which local investors shy away from small companies. With careful analysis and a nose for bargains, you may well pick up firms that will sell for big profits in only a few years.

This love for small ventures characterizes Templeton's investments almost everywhere. He doesn't particularly like large, familiar names. A well-established small company with fat profit margins selling for a low price tends to be his favorite investment. Likewise, he doesn't like to work through big brokerage firms. He maintains that if a stock is so out of favor that it's a bargain, then major brokerage houses (with considerable overhead and salespeople to pay) really can't dare to get involved with it. That, in fact, is why he sold his enormously successful holding company in 1968. Its size made it impossible for him to "play" in the market the way he liked. He now runs a very small fund out of his home in Nassau, and he gets involved in dozens of little firms that his clients have never heard about. In 1994, for instance, the fund's portfolio contained 220 different names.

One other ingredient in Templeton's success that should be added to any international investment plan is that he is almost always on his own in the early stages of profit making. To buy what others reject and sell when others get a craving—that's the essence of the master investor's art, according to Templeton. You must be able to live content as you go against the herd, even though the herd instinct is the strongest human emotion. This calls for a solitary thinker.

THE ECONOMIC PHILOSOPHER, GEORGE SOROS

Even among the exceptional, George Soros is special. Sometimes called "the world's greatest money manager," he personifies global investment. He understands that making money is anything but a provincial activity. It is happening everywhere, all the time, and if you pay attention to the ups and downs of financial markets all over the world, you stand an excellent chance of making money all over the world.

Soros was born in Hungary and spent his early childhood in the upper middle class Jewish community of Budapest. The start of World War II didn't change much for him. In fact, there's a story that at age nine he read a newspaper appeal for aid to Finland and rushed over to the newspaper office to make a donation. By 1944 the Nazi threat had grown far more immediate, and he spent the remainder of the war hiding—sometimes literally tucked away in a cellar, other times using non-Jewish identification papers. It's a reflection of his particular brand of eccentricity that Soros would later remark that his entire experience of the war was thrilling, and he described this period as the happiest years of his life. Perhaps it made him feel like James Bond, oblivious to danger and immune to the fears that he saw in those around him. In a very real way these were the traits that have made him one of the most successful investors of the century.

In all that you hear and read about Soros, what inevitably emerges is his love of the intelligentsia. He once wanted to be an economics professor and even now is something of a financial philosopher—publishing complicated theories to explain how the world's markets work. But in his early twenties even his degree from the London School of Economics didn't help much in the job market. His first job, which he hated, was selling handbags at a resort in northern England. Later he took a job as a trainee for Singer & Friedlander—the only investment bank that responded to his letter and résumé. The general consensus is that he was fairly much a failure in the job. But the experience excited him. He felt comfortable in the world of stocks and bonds. In 1956 he moved to New York City and immediately went to work for F. M. Mayer, and his luck definitely started to change.

Remember that forty-five years ago it was quite unusual to know the European markets. Soros knew them like the back of his hand. What had earned him little more than mediocre standing in London made him the immediate darling of Wall Street. By 1963 he was working at Arnhold & Bleichroeder, one of the few American houses trading heavily in foreign securities. This was a natural home for Soros. While other brokers in the firm stumbled over how to pronounce the names of European firms, Soros knew the owners. Though his beat at Arnhold was trucking, his colleagues recall that he steered the conversation at every opportunity toward the larger, global scene. Soros has never missed the forest for the trees.

Perhaps the most intriguing thing about Soros is that he has developed a complete theory on how to get rich in the international market. It's difficult to summarize the theory because it's quite complicated and a bit obtuse. But at its core his theory argues that everything in life—including the world's financial markets—has good times and bad. When things are bad, they're bound to make a turn for the better. When everything is going well, a downturn is inevitable. The secret, Soros insists, is to read the signals and decipher when a transformation phase is about to begin. When it starts, run against the dominant current, and you'll make money.

As you might suspect, Soros doesn't rely much on annual reports or financial statements to tell him when change is about to happen. He's far more interested in people's perceptions of these so-called objective assessments. He is convinced that just as facts have an impact on what people believe, people's beliefs alter facts. In the real world, he explains, the decision to buy or sell is based not on any perfect knowledge of the marketplace. Instead it is based on investors' expectations. "The major insight I bring to understanding things," he once remarked, "is the role that imperfect understanding plays in shaping events. Traditional economics is based on theories of equilibrium, where supply and demand are equal. But if you realize what an important role our imperfect understanding plays, you realize that what you are dealing with is disequilibrium. . . . That's really how I make my money: understanding the revolutionary process in financial markets."

If Soros is right, then it's essential that an investor grasp the role that misconceptions play in shaping events. Sometimes, he theorizes, the difference between what's really happening in a market and what people think is happening is very small. Such situations shouldn't concern the smart speculator. Occasionally, though, great disparity occurs between what is actually taking place and what people think is happening. These situations should interest you very much. Why? Because they initiate what Soros calls "boom/ bust sequences." Flawed perceptions cause markets to feed on themselves, he argues. In other words, investors work themselves into a blind frenzy, a "boom" mentality. But, Soros reminds us, what goes up must come down. So instead of doing what everybody else does, shrewd investors do the opposite. With the pendulum's next swing, they profit in the face of widespread loss.

This is exactly what Soros did in betting correctly on the collapse of the tremendously popular British pound. In 1992 it was becoming increasingly clear that a number of European currencies were significantly overvalued in relation to stronger ones. This fact, coupled with the British recession, led the brightest speculators to smell blood. Soros was among them, and he did in a big way what lots of them did on a smaller scale. Through a long chain of events, he wound up staking $10 million (perhaps the largest bet ever made) that the British government would be forced to abandon the Exchange Rate Mechanism, the new Western European monetary system, and would essentially go broke. He was right, and when the dust settled, he had earned nearly $2 billion—a billion from the pound's collapse and another billion out of the subsequent chaos that swept through the Italian and Swedish currencies as well as the Tokyo stock market.

Of course, even Soros knows that his theory doesn't work every time. He's been burned. Sometimes the market just won't cooperate—even when he's bet brilliantly against a tidal wave of speculation. Still, Soros insists that he is always looking for impending boom/bust sequences. When he believes he's found one, he makes a very aggressive effort to exploit it for as long as there's money to be made. "It's like shooting fish in a barrel," he told one of his advisors. "As long as the barrel holds up, you keep on shooting fish."

THE B-STRING PLAYERS

Compared to Buffett, Templeton, and Soros, even otherwise impressive investors can appear a bit mundane. However, I warn you: Don't underestimate the success of the B string. They're growing in number and following a whole new set of investment rules. They like to make money the new-fashioned way. They let their international involvement earn it.

Ronald Lauder is a perfect example. Son of the legendary cosmetic queen Estée Lauder, he was once the U.S. ambassador to Austria. He has used the contacts and experience he gained in that position to create one of the most successful investment projects in Eastern Europe. In 1996 his Central European Media holding company outpaced Viacom, Time Warner, and even Disney. Its stock value jumped

50 percent that year and has doubled since going public in 1994. Over the last three years its revenues have nearly tripled, to $138 million.

Lauder got the idea for Central Media as he watched the appetite for cosmetics grow in the newly liberated Central and Eastern European countries. It occurred to him that as people began buying better cosmetics, cars, toothpaste, and even dish detergent, television advertising would blossom. In 1993 he bought his first TV license, allowing him to broadcast in Prague and Berlin. Raising $62 million in an initial public offering the next year, Central Media added licenses in Hungary, Romania, and Slovenia. A subsequent offering raised another $213 million, which bought licenses in the Slovak Republic, Ukraine, Poland, and Germany.

The venture's success is due, in large part, to Lauder's insight into local regulators. "Every other company came in and talked about how these countries would become part of a vast worldwide network," explains Lauder. "That was exactly the wrong story. What they wanted was to be their own country—and there we were unique." At a Central Media station in Prague, only a third of the programming is imported from Hollywood. Another 20 percent comes from Europe, Canada, or Australia. That leaves half of the airtime open for local shows like *Taboo*. This program features a different anonymous guest each night—on one occasion an extremely obese woman; on another, a teenage murderer. From a darkened booth, they take questions from the audience. At the end of the show, they choose whether or not to reveal their true identity. "About a third do," says Vladimir Zelenzy, the general director of the station. *Taboo* attracts more than a million viewers every night, 10 percent of the Czech population.

With a stock market value of $800 million, six times its revenues, Central Media is not a cheap investment. Yet with profits that are likely to grow rapidly for several years to come, it may still be a fabulous bargain. Why? Because, to quote Judy Thomas, regional manager of DMB & B

Europe (an advertising agency that's already placed $10 million worth of commercial time in the Czech Republic for clients like Texaco and Coca-Cola), "Central Media really understands what viewers want. It sounds simple, but there are so few television stations that actually do."

But Americans aren't the only ones who grasp the concept of international investment. Take, for example, Ananda Krishnan. He's a third-generation Sri Lankan Tamil from Malaysia. He comes from a tiny minority group in a country that makes little room for cultural diversity. Yet he's already extremely rich and out to make his country a powerhouse from India to Taiwan.

Twenty-four hours a day Malaysian censors monitor imported Western television channels like MTV, HBO, and even NBC to ferret out anything offensive before letting programs air on local stations. Overseeing it all is Krishnan, a fifty-eight-year-old oil tycoon and real estate developer recently turned communications executive. He owns Astro, the government-sanctioned censor and watchdog of the public interest. With an estimated worth of more than $1 billion, Krishnan claims he's just getting started. He wants to create a business empire—a network of satellites, digital television, telecommunications, original film and television programming, and even online banking and gambling by phone. The goal is to have millions of customers from Taiwan to India by early in the next decade. If he can pull it off, he'll be rich beyond belief and will produce a showcase for the Malaysian government, which has bent over backwards to accommodate him.

Like Ronald Lauder, Krishnan believes he can accomplish what has eluded even the seasoned media companies because he understands local culture and the values that hold it together. He clearly intends to provide Asian alternatives to the Western media. "Asia is not going to sit down and lap up U.S. programming," Krishnan asserts. To give viewers a viable alternative, he has live-action and animation studios in Malaysia, the Philippines, and Vietnam, all of them working overtime to produce shows that will be culturally sensitive and morally acceptable to conservative Asian audiences. He's also purchasing thousands of hours' worth of programming from Chinese and Malay producers.

For all his bravado, Krishnan hasn't rejected all things Western. In fact, technology from the United States was essential in developing one of Astro's newest offerings, a digital service that allows consumers with special satellite dishes and decoder boxes to receive twenty channels. By next year Krishnan also aims to introduce, through a U.S. subsidiary, banking, stock-trading, home-shopping, and Web-surfing technology for the Astro system. He also envisions Malaysian students taking American university classes via Astro. Next on his list: pay-per-view movies, Internet services, maybe even a children's channel. (Question: How would Bert and Ernie sound in Malaysian? Answer: Profitable.)

Of course, more and more women are making a mark for themselves in the global arena. It is my experience that offshore markets are often more open than Wall Street to women investors. I read recently that half the attendees at a trading conference in Singapore were women. At a similar seminar in the United States you'd be lucky if 10 percent were women. According to Mei Ping Yang, vice president and proprietary trader for Goldman Sachs, "That's because Singapore is a very unusual country. It's always had something of a meritocracy."

Yang is not an investor, strictly speaking. She's a trader, so she's not working with her own money. Still, she's among a handful of Wall Street people to watch because she has such international experience. Born in Singapore, she also lived in Malaysia for ten years. She once served as a portfolio manager in international investment advisory with Bankers Trust, where she was responsible for discretionary foreign currency exchange overlay for $1.3 billion in high-net-worth portfolios and another $400 million in institutional global fixed-income portfolios. She knows her stuff and isn't afraid to stake big amounts on foreign ventures, provided the prospects look promising. By her own estimation, Yang has handled up to a half billion dollars at a time in the international currency markets. "In the beginning I juggled $5 million," she says. "At a certain point it was all the way to $500 or $600 million. But I think one of the ways I've coped with that aspect is never to think of the money in absolute terms."

One would expect such a player to be pushy. Wrong. As described in Sue Herera's *Women of the Street,* Yang is quiet and reserved. She actually describes herself as "pathologically shy." Yet she also has the utmost composure—which gets to the heart of what I find most interesting about her. Yang has a fascinating and unique perspective on what it takes to be a confident investor. "The ingredient you must have is self-knowledge," she says, "because what you will find, and what I found in trading, was a journey to find myself, to know myself." That's because, for better or worse, investing is a solitary game. Yang recalls working for one man at a bank in Norway. "After my having worked there just a week or so in trading, he said, 'Here, you can do this, trade under my limit.' It could have been devastating, because if I'd really bombed out, it could have created a lot of problems. Still, I never really had a mentor in that situation. It was just, 'Here, go ahead, do it, kid.'"

Like a lot of seasoned market analysts and investors, Yang is humbled by her involvement in international finance.

Buffett's pragmatism. Templeton's innovation. Soros's guts. Throw in Krishnan's cultural sensitivity, Lauder's foreign connections, and Yang's humility. You come up with a perfect prescription for financial success.

"Some people say, 'I beat the market.' I would never say that. I would rather say, 'I worked with the market,' because let me tell you something, you never really beat the market; and if you try to beat the market, it will beat . . . you."

Yang prefers to say that she respects the market. Is it her friend? "A friend," she muses, "perhaps a very bad spouse on occasion."

FINDING YOUR PERFECT FIT

Buffett's pragmatism. Templeton's innovation. Soros's guts. Throw in Krishnan's cultural sensitivity, Lauder's foreign connections, and Yang's humility. You come up with a perfect prescription for financial success. Can you ever hope to embody all these qualities? Not if you're a mere mortal. Still, there's a lot to be said for learning how the legends of our time do it. Knowledge is power, they say. That's especially true when it's knowledge of the highs and lows of a genius. What my Uncle Jake does to make or lose money in the stock market has never taught me much. That's because Jake's fate has more to do with luck than with the just rewards of intelligent investment. But when the giants of the offshore markets do it right (or wrong), I learn a lot about what's more (or less) likely to prove profitable—at least over the short term.

Watch. As you study the world of international finance, you'll begin to notice patterns. Conservative styles. High-risk styles. The people who like to make money fast and run; the people who prefer to play the tortoise in a race against the frantic hare. I wish I could tell you what works best, but the truth is, it's kind of like dating somebody. It's not whether your companion is objectively desirable or not. It's about the chemistry between the two of you. Either it's there, or it isn't. Investing works a lot like that. It has to feel right. So listen to everything, be intrigued by anything, but feel obli-

Things change. Never be afraid to change with them—that's the real lesson to be gleaned from the masters.

gated to nothing. Remember that what feels right today may be all wrong tomorrow. Investments aren't static. They're alive. Things change. Never be afraid to change with them— that's the real lesson to be gleaned from the masters.

I have even come up with a term for this invaluable lesson: the *international investor dynamic*. This dynamic— the subtle movement that governs and affects investment decisions—is something you learn with experience. Sure, you need to have a "feel" for the situation at hand. And you should have as much information as you can gather. But you also need to understand the rhythm of the game. That's why the only way to become a master of this most fascinating of all sports is to begin investing in the international world of finance. I hope to see you there in the arena along with Soros, Templeton, and the rest of the world's greatest investors.

CHAPTER 3

SOMETHING FOR EVERYONE

International Mutual Funds

Life has taught me you'd be smart to trade a
whole lot of talent for just a little bit of luck.

— ORSON WELLES

Remember when all fledgling professionals got U.S. stock options for their graduation gifts? Loving relatives and family friends generously gave a few shares of Hewlett Packard, Bechtel, or General Electric—then the building blocks of a solid investment portfolio. Today such stocks are next to obsolete. Up against the profit and excitement available through global investment, "they have all the appeal of shag carpet." That's the way Wade Paxton put it when I met him three years ago.

Wade had recently graduated cum laude in engineering from the Massachusetts Institute of Technology (MIT). Hardly what you'd imagine in the way of a technonerd, he came into my office looking like a rock musician—black jeans and T-shirt, an oversized trenchcoat, and the clunkiest leather boots I've ever seen. It was only August, a matter of weeks since leaving MIT, but he had already accepted a position with a software design firm in Silicon Valley. Before heading west he wanted to make some intelligent decisions about the cornucopia of certificates of deposit (CDs) and U.S. corporate shares he'd received at graduation. Wade suspected that he could do better in foreign markets than he could on Wall Street. He just didn't know how much better; and he didn't know how to transfer his "paper assets" overseas.

I told him then what I'm telling you now: You're wise to be skeptical about a lifelong investment partnership with the domestic market. Despite the economic recovery we hear so much about these days, the domestic market consistently trails behind emerging markets all over the world. Many U.S. citizens are worried, too. Married couples wake up in the dead of night, terrified that the savings account they've nurtured for decades and their collection of low-growth CDs will fail to ensure a comfortable retirement. Divorced and single women—who suffer a definite disadvantage in the U.S. tax system—wonder how they'll ever manage to pay their monthly rent, much less save enough to buy expensive stock. The baby boomer generation has already begun marching into middle age with a Social Security system that's forever on the verge of crisis. Even people in their twenties have started to realize that if they want to retire before the age of ninety-nine, they had better start thinking in terms of compounding interest.

Given these facts, the domestic market hardly deserves your loyalty or forbearance. You don't need to be limited by the lackluster performance of U.S. stocks. You can refuse to let Uncle Sam regulate and curtail financial investments— especially since he openly admits that he'll offer you painfully little support down the line. You can do what Wade did: Take a significant percentage of your available assets and invest them in foreign markets that promise far more impressive profits, far lower taxes, and virtually no invasive government regulation.

International funds come in many designs and are structured to do many different things, but they all aim to maximize your investment returns while limiting the risk you incur. Like funds that handle domestic stocks, they are common funds managed by professional investment managers. Like domestic funds, they have financial professionals on staff to conduct in-depth research and make day-to-day investment decisions. Like domestic funds, they capitalize on the fact that collective investment is a cost-effective way to build a diversified portfolio. They offer a third benefit, however, that domestic funds cannot: They operate within financial markets that perform more impressively than that of the United States.

U.S. mutual funds have been investing in the international arena for decades. Even foreign-based mutual funds are no longer new. The first ones were established in the early 1970s by fund management companies in England to service nondomestic fund management fund subsidiaries. These funds were quickly utilized, however, by expatriate non-tax-paying investors and foreign subsidiaries of U.K. firms. By the late 1970s and early 1980s the funds had become a safe refuge for individuals and corporations with sizable assets in countries where turbulent political changes made markets and currencies unstable.

By the early 1990s the foreign investment industry was taking off. In 1993 and 1994, for example, when markets starting booming throughout Latin America and Hong Kong, nothing less than $53 billion poured into these funds. What happened? The number of international funds grew. To be more precise, U.S.-based funds with international holdings doubled to an impressive count of 366. And the number of offshore mutual funds jumped to around a whopping 5,000! The trouble then was that foreign stocks were expensive. They traded, on average, at nearly forty-seven times their previous year's earnings, while domestic stocks were trading at about half that amount. It was enough to squelch the interest of even adventurous U.S. investors.

Since the mid-1990s investment profits from foreign markets have shot through the roof. According to the *Wall Street Journal's Smart Money* magazine, U.S. stocks are now trading at 19.3 times their earnings, foreign stocks at 18.7. Not surprisingly, the number of funds has grown even larger. The current total is 903 internationally oriented, U.S.-based funds, and more are being established every year. Says Henry Gross, a managing director of Chase Global Asset Management, "Next year, or in two or three years, in Europe and Asia, the potential for earning growth is much greater than it is in the United States. And therefore the potential for price appreciation is greater."

The verdict is in: Over the long run you will benefit from exposure to the international market. Since 1970 the Morgan Stanley European, Australian, and Far Eastern (EAFE) index has risen at an average annual rate of 12.9 percent, while the Standard & Poor's (S&P) 500 has risen at 12.3 percent. Compounded over time that 0.6 percent spread makes quite a difference. If you'd invested $10,000 in the EAFE index twenty-seven years ago, you'd now have $264,100 in assets. That same $10,000 would have climbed to only $227,500 if invested here in the domestic market. Even the well-regarded (though somewhat fiscally conservative) *Kiplinger's Mutual Fund '97* concluded that "it makes sense to put as much as one-third of your money into foreign stock funds."

I want to give you a mini-primer on international mutual funds to introduce you to their benefits and inherent risks. Once Wade Paxton got this information, he built a portfolio that combined low-risk/small-win guarantees with high-risk/big-win potential. I encourage you to do that, too. But I don't want to steal the thunder from my own story. Instead, let's walk you down Wade's investment path one step at a time.

What Have They Got to Offer?

Just like domestic market funds, the international fund arena is full of choices. How can you pick those that will serve you best? According to Robert Milroy, a well-respected fund analyst, the best approach is to decide on how aggressive you can allow your portfolio to be. "Just be conscious of your objectives," Milroy advises. "Invest aggressively for long-term goals and conservatively for short-term needs." He adds cautiously, "The more aggressive you are, the greater risk you assume. That's the nature of all investment, domestic or international." In other words, it takes time to make a lot of money.

Equity Funds

As of 1995 international equity funds accounted for 25 percent of all the world's equity funds. These funds invest all their assets in non-U.S. stocks. They must be distinguished from global stock funds, which reserve the right to invest a portion of their assets in U.S. stocks. Both international and global funds primarily purchase shares of publicly listed companies, so their value rises and falls with the fortunes of the companies they partially own.

For the average individual investor (excluding, of course, the high-risk thrill seeker), international and global equity funds are on the relatively high-risk end of foreign investment. That's because there is no guarantee that the companies selected by any fund's manager will do well. If they don't, your assets shrink. Still, for the past seventy years—through wars, crashes, a depression, recessions, riots, and assassinations—stocks have far outpaced every other form of investment in average annual return. The secret is patience. The long-term direction of every stock market ever studied is up, but the less time you can wait, the less of your assets you should place in funds that favor stocks. For those who need to turn a profit in less than three years, equities are generally thought to be too high risk. Even the most promising companies need more than thirty-six months to prove themselves.

Many foreign equity funds specialize in the stock markets of a particular country or region. Perpetual American Growth, for example, invests mostly in North American companies, while Jardine Fleming Pacific Securities favors the markets of East Asia. Some funds are even more specific, like GT Chile Growth. As its name suggests, it concentrates exclusively on shares of Chilean companies. A growing number of funds deal in the emerging markets. Others invest mainly in smaller companies or the shares of companies in a particular field (for example, Alliance International Health Care or GT Telecommunications). In general, the more diverse the fund's investment sphere, the lower your risk. If the Chilean market goes into free fall, GT Chile Growth is in deep trouble. A fund with more diversified holdings at best would lose nothing; at worst it would lose only a part of its portfolio.

Most international fund managers take what's called a "top-down" investment approach. They're continuously looking at how the world's various markets are likely to perform and adjusting their portfolios accordingly. They may favor a hefty investment in Asia this year, and smaller commitments to firms in Eastern Europe and Latin America. By the middle of the next year they may restructure—moving more into Latin America and less into Asia. By spreading investors' money across many markets, this approach reduces the risk of major loss. Even if a particular market does badly overall, money is working profitably elsewhere to lighten the economic blow.

The alternative, "bottom-up" investing, is slightly more speculative (and consequently more potentially profitable). Here the fund manager disregards any emphasis on geographic balance. Instead the focus is on hand-selecting a group of specific companies that appear ready for major growth and profit. I prefer this approach, but only if I know the fund manager and trust his or her talent, track record, and gut instinct. It's analogous to your relationship with a physician. Top-down investment managers are a lot like general practitioners: They don't cure cancer, but they don't try risky treatment, either. Bottom-up managers are like cutting-edge medical specialists. I can't imagine anything more reassuring than the care of a fine specialist. By the same token, the wrong one can do far more harm than a mediocre family physician.

Wade was intrigued with the idea of trading some of his U.S. stock for foreign equity. He kept the Coca-Cola shares that he'd received because he was impressed by the scope of their foreign business, but he dumped everything else. Since the U.S. market had already started its mid-1990s ascent, he actually had earned a meager profit in the short time he'd held the shares. After careful research and advice from the consultant I encouraged him to call, Wade went with two international funds. One specializes in the Eastern European market; the other focuses on Asia. His reasoning was sound: Instinct told him that the Eastern bloc nations would make him a tremendous amount of money. Even if they didn't, he could count on the Asian markets to produce very respectable gains.

Money Market Funds

At the opposite end of the risk spectrum are money market funds that invest in debt securities with very short (not more than ninety-day) maturity dates. Most of the debts come from governments, but some come from bank certificates of deposit, bankers' acceptances (debts arising from international trade transactions), and unsecured corporate IOUs. Basically, these funds function like a savings account but pay a higher interest rate.

There's virtually no risk involved so long as the fund invests only in the securities of stable governments. Obviously, some governments have defaulted on debts before. Remember the U.S. federal budget crisis in early 1996? At that time people were predicting that the United States could default. But it didn't, and, in general, major economies never do. You can take on some risk if you venture into less stable national debt and/or corporate debt. (You also stand to make a bigger profit because money doesn't come cheap to high-risk borrowers. When they do pay their debt, it comes in with handsome interest tacked on.) Like equity funds, international money market funds vary. Some invest globally; others specialize in a particular region or country. The more diverse their investments, the lower their clients' risk and the lower their likely profit.

Because Wade was structuring his portfolio to make money over the long haul, he decided to skip money market funds altogether. "I'd rather take the money and buy lottery tickets," he said. "At least that way I've got some chance of earning a major profit." Given Wade's age and his investment goals, I can understand the move. Sill, the guarantee of even a little bit of money feels a whole lot better than the knowledge that your lottery card didn't have a single winning number.

Fixed-Interest Stock Funds

Fixed-interest stock funds are the next most popular form of international investment after equity funds. They invest in a wide range of bonds—mostly Treasury bonds and corporate and municipal bonds—with a maturity date of three years or more. Theoretically, they're relatively low risk. We're repeatedly told that the only trouble would be if the bond issuer ultimately could not repay. As with money market funds, we hear that even that risk drops almost to zero if the fund is lending to a stable government. If, however, it extends

money to a developing nation or a corporation, your investment is slightly more jeopardized. Also, like money market
funds, the more you're willing to risk, the better an interest
rate you'll earn if and when the debt is paid.

Wade decided to purchase foreign bonds through a
number of these fixed-interest funds. Again, he spread his
risk by buying bonds in both high- and low-volatility markets. His personal favorites were Mexican and Australian
bonds, but he had many of the traditional standards—Swiss,
German, and Hong Kong.

Short-Term Bond Funds

Halfway between money market and fixed-interest stock
funds are short-term bond funds. I say "halfway" because
they hold investment instruments with maturities of between ninety days and three years. They are also a midway
point between money market funds (which are just like
bank deposits) and fixed-interest stock funds (which are
long-term investments) in terms of risk and profitability.
They're essentially safe but produce slightly better returns
than money markets. Frankly, there aren't a lot of these
vehicles out there to be had. If you find one, it's likely to be
with an investment manager who's heavily tied to the European markets, because that's where these originate. My feeling: If you're willing to sacrifice the tiny ounce of safety that
these short-term bonds force you to give away, you'd probably be better off to go straight to fixed-interest or even equity
stocks. That was the advice I gave Wade Paxton. He took it
and stayed clear of this vehicle.

Convertible Bond Funds

Another word for these investments is *debentures*. They're
unsecured loans to corporations that the bond holder can

choose to exchange for ordinary shares in the companies. They're a little like stock and a little like bonds. When the price of stock in the company exceeds the conversion price of the bond, then the bond's value will tend to move in line with the price of the underlying shares. But should the share price fall below the conversion price, then the bond acts like a traditional bond—paying interest and having a limited life span. Over time this makes them perform less profitably than equities but better than fixed-interest stocks.

Debentures are not easy to find. I've found only thirty of them (based mainly in Japan, the Far East, England, and Switzerland). They appeal to a great many international enthusiasts because they allow for investment growth but prevent excessive risk. They give you a stake in a rising stock market while protecting you from the bad times, when the bonds continue to pay out interest.

Wade wanted to dabble in debentures, so I put him in touch with a client of mine who owns a private bank in Vanuatu. Although my client actually lives in Hawaii, his bank conducts business with customers worldwide, many of them in Japan. Using the South Pacific bank as an intermediary, Wade made contact with a Japanese house that could purchase debentures. I suggested that he forego this vehicle in exchange for more international equity. I find stock easier to monitor. But that's what makes the world go 'round: personal preference.

Mixed and Umbrella Funds

If you're a beginner and prefer to leave the basic asset allocation decisions up to a fund manager, you may be interested in mixed funds. They don't specialize in any one kind of investment. They attempt to balance riskier holdings with lower returning fixed-interest vehicles to produce a portfolio that offers reasonable return at a relatively low risk. Some, geared more toward the riskier end of the asset spectrum, have a higher-than-average proportion of equity holdings. Others play it safe by carrying mostly bonds and money market instruments.

There are a number of umbrella funds from which to choose. These are composed of subfunds or compartments, and you can select your preferences. You can switch between subfunds without incurring a fee. However, it's rare for an umbrella fund to combine high-performing managers across the range of equities, bonds, and money markets. Also, make sure that your preferred funds contain a good selection of subfunds. If you aren't offered much choice, it's hardly worth restricting yourself to the umbrella format.

It's interesting that Wade didn't opt for an umbrella fund. It would seem the perfect way for him to enter the global arena. I think he made other choices because he wanted to take a more hands-on approach to managing his portfolio. He didn't want to pass along decision making to a fund manager, no matter how capable.

For comparison's sake, I should mention that I have several clients who have done extremely well with umbrella funds. One of them is Chloe Valencia. Everything her name implies, Chloe is flamboyant, exciting, and irreverent. When I met her, she was on husband number five, and their relationship was pretty shaky. Living off a sizable inheritance from her Chicago industrialist father, Chloe had done very little of substance with her life. Still, she had managed to follow the three rules her dad lived by for seventy-six years: In business, never spend your own money, never cheat a friend, and always protect what's yours as you would a newborn baby. That last piece of advice probably accounts for Chloe's diligent efforts to ship a significant share of her assets offshore, where they could generate impressive enough profits to sustain her very expensive lifestyle. Alimony alone ran her close to $200,000 a year! Through umbrella funds Chloe found a way to let somebody more responsible and better versed in foreign markets do all the work for her.

Speculative Funds

A number of more speculative international vehicles exist for the daredevils among us. For example, warrants let you sign up to buy shares in a foreign company at some future date and at a price that's fixed at the time the warrant is issued. That means that for a relatively small initial investment you get the option of a future stake in a company's equity. Some warrants expire in one or two years' time, while many are for five or ten years. Others are perpetual. Huge sums can be made or lost by investing in warrants. Warrant funds are best left to the seasoned international investor. Even if you're willing to take on a bit of speculation, I would encourage you to limit warrants to a small percentage of your portfolio.

Specialist funds, which invest in a narrow range of assets, also tend to pose significant risk. There are commodity and natural resources funds, which invest in companies that operate in commodity-related industries (like mining) or that hold physical assets such as gold bullion or other precious metals. There are also real estate funds, which invest in the shares of companies that hold property or work in property-related industries.

Derivative investment funds concentrate on futures and options. Futures are shares or commodities bought or sold for future delivery. Shares have a current price; they also have a price for delivery at some future date. These two prices are usually different, depending on market expectations. A fund may buy a future without ever intending to take on the related asset. Instead, the goal is to rely on price changes that will make it lucrative to sell prior to the delivery date. Options work in a similar way. They give you the right (but not the obligation) to buy or sell an asset at a fixed strike price within a specified period. The danger in all these investments is pretty much the same: Should the market perform badly or the company head south, you can be left sitting on a giant heap of nothing.

Although Wade Paxton was attracted to risk, he knew his own limits. He decided that at least for the first few years he'd leave the truly speculative vehicles to the seasoned investors. A smart move.

What's Better: Talent or Luck?

One of the reasons investors (global and otherwise) fear risk is that they associate it with irresponsibility and a lack of knowledge. There's a Puritan streak in us all, warning us that only fools rush in to speculative ventures. We assume that the more talented and experienced players don't need to incur risk. "Risk is for chumps," we imagine them chuckling to one another as they sit at the exclusive table of plenty.

Guess what? Risk is inherent in all investment. At the most obvious level that means there's always the chance that the market in which you invest will decline and diminish the value of your holdings. But risk has many faces. There's also the risk that inflation will eat away at the purchasing power of your money; the risk that the issuer of a bond you own might default; even the risk that your judgment will prove to be poor, that you could have made a better investment than the one you chose.

In a desperate attempt to accomplish the impossible and eliminate risk, I see a lot of investors cheat themselves out of what they could have had—if they'd only dared to try. International investors are not immune to such wastes of time. Especially as they approach the global arena, they decide to "protect" themselves by avoiding the potential profits of foreign equities in favor of low-earning money market funds. I think this is a misguided attempt at self-preservation and is in itself a risk—a risk of lost opportunity.

Even bonds, the lowest-risk vehicle available, are subject to an omnipresent interest rate risk. Using U.S. dollars to clarify my point, imagine that you have a $1,000 bond

Risk is inherent in all investment. At the most obvious level that means there's always the chance that the market in which you invest will decline and diminish the value of your holdings.

paying 6 percent and maturing in two years. If prevailing interest rates rise by even 1 percent (and we all know that they can rise more than that in two years), then the 6 percent that your bond earns suddenly becomes less attractive. A buyer might be willing to pay only $982 for your bond as compensation for accepting less-than-optimum income. There's also the length of maturity to consider. The longer the time until the bond matures, the more violent a downturn you can suffer. A five-year bond would fall to about $959 under the same circumstances, a twenty-year bond to around $894.

Of course, the whole reason to invest in international bonds is to tap into their higher interest rates. But no matter where on earth you invest or in what currency you hold your assets, you are vulnerable to the possibility that interest hikes will lower the value of your investment. Selected wisely, bonds usually eliminate the chance of total economic loss, but that's a far cry from a complete guarantee against risk. All investment entails risk. When you put your money to work in one vehicle rather than another, you risk the possibility of making the less profitable choice. If you later realize that you would have done better had you made a different choice, you've lost the money you originally stood to gain. I say a loss is a loss. Bonds can't eliminate the chance of loss any more than equities can. (And they don't offer an equal chance at profit, either.)

Having said all this, I must join all the experts in urging
you to follow Wade Paxton's example: Reduce your risk by
diversifying. How diversified should you aim to be? In my
view, it does not follow that if some diversification is a good
thing, then a lot is better. The average equity fund holds
about 100 stocks, so an investor with ten funds in a single
investment category is exposed to up to a thousand different
stocks. The problem is that quite often the same stocks will
be represented across the range of funds, resulting in redun-
dant transaction costs and reducing your overall investment return.

Obviously, one international mutual fund is an inade-
quate holding for most investors, particularly if it's a
specialty fund focused on a single country or industry. So
minimize your portfolio duplication (and the related excess
costs) by spreading your interests across several categories.
You might include one aggressive fund focused on shares of
Japanese firms that have had a hard time but now seem set
to make a profitable recovery, plus a few European funds
investing in large blue chip companies. Similarly, a spread
of emerging market funds is unlikely to produce over-
laps; regions suffering setbacks will probably be offset
by others showing strong performance. If you have a fascination with a specific fund category, you can choose a
handful of funds that employ different management styles.
Because one is aggressive and the other more conservative, they're likely to favor companies with markedly differing circumstances.

Tips for Getting Started

Let's suppose that you're interested in pursuing an international mutual fund involvement. How can you get started? I
urge you to do some reading. Don't use this single chapter of
one book to serve as your only guide. The universe of inter-

national funds is so big that there are several books to help you. I think the best is Milroy's *The Micropal Guide to Off-shore Investment Funds*. It's updated every few years, so the most recent edition will give you the most current information available. Not insignificant is the fact that it's written in language that's easy for anyone to understand. Not all the guide books can make that claim.

In the meantime, I suggest that you answer the following five questions. When you're done, you'll have created the beginnings of your own strategic investment plan.

One: Where Should Your Fund Be Based?

You can choose to have your fund managed by a mutual fund investment manager working for one of the U.S. funds. This remains the common practice. There are now 903 of these U.S.-based funds. That's an awful lot of funds to choose from, but you can narrow the field considerably by eliminating those with a track record of less than five years. I discourage you from getting tied up with a fund any younger than that. Now you're down to 167 funds. You can slash that number in half by deciding whether you want a single-country (or region) fund or a more broadly focused fund. Both approaches are viable. I find that it's largely a matter of personal taste.

As an alternative to the U.S.-based mutual fund, you can buy into an "offshore fund," one of the thousands of common funds managed by a professional investment manager and based in one of the world's tax havens or low-tax areas. These offshore funds definitely offer added wealth protection—whether from punitive taxes, creditors, or excessive changes due to legal damages. Also, offshore funds can invest in absolutely anything they want. Domestic funds can't because they carry the burden of government-designed restrictions, which the Securities Exchange Commission (SEC) monitors strictly.

Since offshore funds don't come under the jurisdictional authority of the SEC, they legally circumvent the commission's overzealous review. What's more, they escape the high cost of processing and reporting, and these savings are passed along to their investors. (This is not to say that there is no consumer protection with offshore funds. Indeed, most offshore financial centers are very careful to guard their good reputation. That means they use only reputable investment managers and keep a diligent eye on their activities.)

As a diehard internationalist, I strongly favor the offshore mutual fund format. Even the best domestic investment managers are based here in the United States. It's true that they travel a great deal and work diligently to keep abreast of the economic, political, and social developments in the foreign markets they handle. Still, a foreign-based mutual fund and the manager who runs it have a firsthand, bird's eye view into everything that's happening in that nation, region, or specialized industry. It's my feeling that no amount of homework, jet lag, or second-language studies can compare to an offshore fund's very real advantage.

Offshore funds will not accept U.S. clients directly, because if they did, they would come under the jurisdiction of the SEC. This means that if you want to go this route, you'll need to work through an offshore intermediary. This entire topic will be explored more fully in Chapter 8, but for now let's just say that with even a modest investment,

The world twenty years from now is going to be a very different place, and emerging markets are one way to capitalize on the economics of the coming world order.

you can participate in an offshore venture that allows you entrance into any mutual fund anywhere in the world.

Two: How Broad a Geographic Spread Do You Want?

When deciding on your global spread, understand that almost all portfolios reflect the regional prejudices of the investor. Asian investors tend to keep most of their money in Asian shares. Private U.S. investors have so much to choose from in their home market that it can be difficult to drag them into the international market. If you're a bit skittish at first, you might want to venture into just the foreign stock markets in England, Europe, and Japan. These markets are extremely liquid, have the most shares to choose from, and are situated in countries with secure governments that have good regulators and stable currencies.

After you've acclimated to global investment, I would urge you to move quickly into the emerging markets. Do not overexpose yourself to them, because they do imply a relatively high risk. Still, every week another article appears in a major daily or financial monthly, extolling the profits to be made in the developing world or those that have until recently been dominated by communist regimes. The world twenty years from now is going to be a very different place, and emerging markets are one way to capitalize on the economics of the coming world order.

Three: When Should You Enter (and Exit) a Market?

With every new market "discovery" comes a surge of new releases—even when a number of reputable funds are already operating in the market. New launches can be tempting, but when you buy in, don't lose sight of your overall portfolio. Don't let it get too weighted in any one direction. As a general rule, you should wait until a fund's shares have been on offer to the general public for at least one year before buying.

It's also critical that you be aware of economic factors when planning to enter a new market. Prevailing interest rates are a good indication of opportunity. If they start to pick up, it is probably a bad time to commit yourself. Money is already beginning to tighten up, and the economy is overheating. Investments made at this time are likely to prove poor. If interest rates have peaked, then it's a great time to buy because when interest rates start to decline, the value of stocks and bonds will rise.

When you think about trying a new market, take time to learn the country's gross domestic product (GDP) and money supply. GDP tracks the growth of a country's economy by measuring the increase in the value of its goods and services. Growth economies offer you a better bet for long-term investment exposure. Yet when too much money is circulating in an economy, it's a warning of approaching inflation and rising interest rates. That means you should stay out for now.

When to sell? That's a tougher question. Of course, only an idiot would argue that you should never sell. Still, it's fair to say that fund investments should be assumed for the long term. Is that too vague? Then let's quantify it: You should hold an investment for at least five years and know that during that time it will have various ups and downs. An element of volatility is unavoidable. There are, of course, good reasons to sell. But usually they have less to do with a fund's current performance and more to do with a sense that the stock market is sliding. So long as the overall market is continuing to hum, you should probably deal with anxiety by reducing the percentage of equity funds in your portfolio and increasing more stable sectors like money market, fixed-interest, or mixed funds.

Four: What Kind of Fund Charges Should You Expect to Pay?

Charges vary, and, unfortunately, there's no single international system of charges to help you decide whether the fees incurred are fair in a relative sense. What's more, offshore funds in particular do not require that their investment managers reveal every charge in their promotional brochures, nor do they impose maximum fees chargeable to investors. For all these reasons, I hesitate to give you any standard rule, but it is fair to at least break down the fees into a few general categories:

- *Initial fees* are essentially the cost of admission. They are often a percentage of the amount you invest—perhaps 5 percent. If you're looking to enter with $5,000 (the low end of an average entry investment purse), then your fees would be $250. Be careful that when you invest you know whether this start-up fee is deducted from the assets that are actually put to work for you.

- *Annual charges* arise once you hold shares. For a typical international equity fund the annual management fee is usually about 1.5 percent, for a bond it's about 1 percent, and for an emerging market equity fund it is likely to be as high as 2 to 2.5 percent.

- *Switching charges* are incurred when you switch your categories of stock distribution in an umbrella fund. You usually don't have to pay a full new initial fee every time you change; you may just be charged a flat fee to cover administrative handling.

- *Performance fees* most often affect more speculative investments. In some funds you must pay a manager 10 to 20 percent of the increase on the net asset value of stock once it reaches a certain profit benchmark.

Don't forget to enlist plain old common sense when trying to envision your investment charges. For example, a fund investing aggressively in Far Eastern equities will undoubtedly cost more than one investing in U.S. dollar deposits because it's more complicated and expensive to manage.

Five: How Do You Purchase an International Investment?

Before you fork over so much as a dime, it's important to read the prospectus and annual reports of any potentially attractive fund. Be sure about its investment philosophy, goals, asset selection, and portfolio management style. These materials should be easy to order by letter, phone, or fax. If they're not, a giant alarm should go off in your head. Be smart; move on to another fund.

The next step is a conscious, methodical examination of the fund's track record. As everyone knows, a spectacular past performance does not guarantee future profit. Still, it's about all you've got to rely on. Experts disagree about what time period you should use when making judgments about a fund's general performance. I believe you should review results over at least three years.

When you're ready to buy, you can decide to handle the purchase yourself. Just use the application that came with the promotional package you requested. It will ask you to clarify whether you're paying by check, draft, or electronic transfer. You'll need to supply your name and address. If you invest through a trust or company vehicle, the person authorized to deal must also supply their name and signature. As we've already established, there can be purchase restrictions that prohibit or limit the holding of shares by any one person or company. They're imposed so that the fund will not be deemed a public issuer within the United States

> International mutual funds are simply a re-
> flection of this very exciting new global sys-
> tem. They allow their owners to benefit
> from the ups in every market even as they
> protect them from the slumps.

(and therefore subject to the rules and regulations of the
SEC).

You can also opt to use an advisor—someone to help
you choose the funds that best meet your needs and are
within your risk tolerance. This consultant will also handle
the actual purchase process for you. It could be your banker,
your accountant, or a dedicated financial advisor. (Be sure to
make all checks payable directly to the investment company,
not the advisor.) I highly recommend that you find yourself a
professional advisor. Hire someone who knows the ropes
to help you maneuver through the obstacle course. It will
be well worth the money you spend.

IT's A SMALL, SMALL WORLD

Today it's entirely reasonable to be born in one country, be
educated in another, work in a third, have clients mainly in
a fourth, have suppliers based primarily in a fifth, own a
vacation home in a sixth, and plan to retire in a seventh. Our
world is no longer made up of self-sufficient political or
economic states. Instead it's an interlocking system of co-
dependent groups. International mutual funds are simply
a reflection of this very exciting new global system. They

allow their owners to benefit from the ups in every market even as they protect them from the slumps.

As you consider investing in one or more of these funds, I encourage you to remember this: The past several years have proved that economies can change at quite a clip. Mexico was on the verge of financial extinction less than a decade ago. Today it's enjoying a financial boom. Russia, once the cornerstone of the totalitarian Soviet regime, is now considered by many analysts to offer the best investment market anywhere. The most successful investors recognize the impermanence of any one market's profit potential, and they learn to enjoy the art of moving assets first here, then there—wherever the financial outlook is most promising.

CHAPTER 4

GOT A YEN FOR SOME BUCKS?

Trading Currency in the World Market

Show me the money!
— CUBA GOODING, JR., AS ROD TIDWELL
IN *JERRY MAGUIRE*

Early in second grade I established a little business for myself. Known for having the best bagged lunches on planet Earth, I figured out one day that several of my classmates would happily swap some pretty cool stuff for one of my double-dutch chocolate brownies, a thermos of chicken noodle soup, or one of my mom's submarine sandwiches.

Being a natural capitalist, I quickly set up shop on the playground where we ate. I'd trade a brownie for two baseball cards, my soup for somebody's chips, or a sandwich for one of those silly pens with a hula dancer who shakes her hips when you move the cap back and forth. It was a thriving business, and everyone was happy with the arrangement. My "customers" would rush off to gobble up their tasty purchases while I spread out my precious booty and just smiled.

Things went along like this for a few months, and then my older sister started making the school lunches. I don't know what possessed my parents to allow this ridiculous turn of events, but it ruined my business! Suddenly I couldn't get a decent trade going to save myself. My sandwiches became nothing more distinctive than peanut butter and jelly on egg bread. The soup disappeared completely. Even the brownies didn't bring much of a price anymore. I guess that when consumers sour on you, they discard the good with the bad. I would glimpse the contents of my brown paper bag each day and sadly long for the good old days.

If you translate this story into grown-up terminology, you have an almost perfect analogy for the simplest laws of currency. Throughout that school year I had the same daily staples in my lunch bag (let's call them *currency*). As long as Mom prepared them, they represented real culinary skill (we'll call that *intrinsic value*). They were highly desirable; kids were willing to give me some pretty cool stuff for them. In fact, I think I often got more for my goods than they were really worth, because once the word got out, everybody ran to be first in line to make a purchase (that's referred to as *buyer psychology*). But when events shifted, through no fault of my own, my currency reflected less refined cooking skills and became virtually worthless almost overnight. Had somebody invested in my little business, they would have shared in my early profits. Likewise, when things turned bad, they would have lost right along with me.

Put in overly simple terms, currency is nothing more (or less) than the total of what a nation produces. When that nation is politically stable, making products and generating services that are perceived to be of value, its currency is valuable. When instability strikes or the fickleness of consumer tastes change, then its currency reflects that decrease in its overall value. For international investors these principles offer a marvelous opportunity to shop the world for currencies of particular worth. Owning them can make you rich. The trick is to accurately wager when their values are about to decline so you can trade them for others that will perform better in the global market.

In making these wagers, the best investors realize that nothing stays the same (at least, not for long). Rising U.S. interest rates, Japanese trade surpluses, a new government in Canada, devaluation of the Mexican peso, movement up or down in the U.S. budget deficit—all these factors affect the relative value of different currencies. Also, a change in the worth of one nation's currency can sometimes have a very significant effect on currencies throughout an entire region, and the effect can be felt almost immediately. For example, the U.S. dollar took a bad beating on December 28, 1994, as immediate fallout from the Mexican peso market pushed the value of the dollar down. Traders around the world expressed their lack of confidence in the dollar by dumping it like water from a sinking ship and buying the deutschmark and Japanese yen. Looking west from Tokyo, of course, it was a great day: Yen futures rallied 250 ticks within twenty-four hours!

The international currency markets can be seen as one enormous melting pot. Culture often separates us. Politics divide us. Religion sometimes alienates us from each other.

The international currency markets can be seen as one enormous melting pot. Culture often separates us. Politics divide us. Religion sometimes alienates us from each other. Still, in a large and ever-changing blend of current events, currency puts us all in a relationship with one another.

Still, in a large and ever-changing blend of current events, currency puts us all in a relationship with one another. Of course, that relationship is in constant flux because global supply and demand are constantly changing. Indeed, that's what makes currency so fascinating (and so worth the effort to understand). It is the perfect reflection of all that is going on in the world at any moment.

For years the world's currency markets were thought to be the exclusive domain of the largest banks and multinational corporations. Nothing could be further from the truth. In fact, currency trading is perhaps the single most democratic of all investment vehicles. Mutual funds typically demand a minimum entry purchase. Foreign real estate and joint partnerships also require an intimidating financial outlay. Not so with currency investment. Assuming you live in a city, you can walk into just about any major financial institution in your neighborhood and purchase foreign currency. Or you can buy an interest-bearing CD in almost any denomination—Australian dollars, British pounds, French francs, Japanese yen, Mexican pesos, or Brazilian reals. That means that with as much or as little money as you wish to commit, you can invest in the most potentially lucrative economies anywhere in the world.

LEARNING TO TIGO

It's one thing to put your assets to work abroad. It's another to do it successfully. To make your portfolio truly desirable, you have to learn the principles of what I call *TIGO*—trade, invest, and get out.

The base currency of your portfolio is the one in which you originally make an investment and the one into which your profits will ultimately be realized: U.S. dollars for Americans, for example. However, realize that when you invest internationally, you must expose yourself to other currencies. Buying any asset in another country—whether it's stock, certificates of deposit, real estate, or goods and services—means using the currency of that country. At some point your base currency must be converted into the currency in which the foreign share can be bought. Once you hold that asset, its value is susceptible to change not only when it's traded on the market but also when (and if) the strength of the currency in which it is denominated happens to change.

Let me illustrate my point with two stories. The first is fictional; the second is fact. If you invest $1,000 in a U.S. bank CD paying 12 percent interest over one year, then after twelve months you will have $1,120 to show for your effort. If instead you choose to invest that $1,000 in a CD paying the same interest rate but denominated in Compuvanian miggots (an imaginary currency from a make-believe country), you would get back the same $1,120 only if the exchange rate between the U.S. dollar and the Compuvanian miggot remained steady throughout the entire one-year life of the contract. If the exchange rates fluctuates even the slightest bit, your Compuvanian investment will prove to have been a better or less desirable investment than what you could have made at your neighborhood bank in the United States.

If the miggot appreciates 10 percent (a tenable thought)—from $0.20 to $0.22 during the course of that year—then you would actually get back $1,232—the same $1,120 representing the principal and interest on the CD, plus a $112 bonus representing the exchange rate adjustment. Instead of 12 percent interest, you'd receive slightly better than 23 percent! If, however, the miggot depreciates against the dollar by that same 10 percent, you would get back only $1,008—a net interest rate of less than 1 percent. The new exchange rate would eat away nearly all the interest paid.

In truth, exchange rate fluctuations have at least as much to do with making money globally as your choice of actual investments. Here's a true story to show you exactly what I mean. At the end of World War II most currencies around the world were pegged to the U.S. dollar under the 1946 Bretton Woods Agreement. The Swiss franc was fixed at a rate of about 4.3 francs to the dollar. Through the decades that followed the underlying value of the Swiss franc far exceeded this established relationship to the dollar. When the Swiss broke ranks with the rest of the industrialized world and allowed the franc to float (that is, sink or swim in the marketplace without any predetermined value) in 1971, it immediately jumped upward against the dollar. How far did it jump? From an official rate of $0.23 in mid-1971 to almost $0.36 by mid-1973. Then it remained fairly well in line with its genuine value until the end of 1977, when investor demand pushed it to $0.65 in only eighteen months—well above its intrinsic value. For U.S. investors at the time the Swiss franc offered a tremendous investment vehicle. Its value against the dollar allowed lucky banks and individuals to nearly triple the value of their assets.

Unfortunately, the honeymoon didn't last. By the early 1980s the franc was performing sluggishly as it began retreating back to its underlying value. Those same investors who had watched the value of their Swiss investments climb up and up and up suddenly watched the ball drop down and down and down. The smart ones undoubtedly saw the writing on the wall early on, cashed in their francs for dollars, and took them somewhere else to play. The less lucky investors got swept up in the market current and lost a healthy chunk of the profits they had earned just a few years earlier. Ironically, fortune investors'—both good and bad—were linked to the same market reality: currency exchange rates. When you buy money for less than it turns out to be worth down the line, you make money. Conversely, when you buy currency just before its value plunges, you take a bath.

Currency is the key to international investing. Savvy investors know this, and foreign interest rates tend to reflect prevailing investor sentiment and expert predictions. For example, you'll always earn better interest on a volatile (sometimes called "soft") currency—one that has the analysts guessing. Why? Because if its value falls, you'll be left in the loser's seat. High interest rates are used to tempt speculators, those willing to take the risk of losing in exchange for the chance to win big. For example, a bond denominated in a currency that analysts expect to decline over the term of its life will offer much higher interest than one denominated in a currency that's expected to appreciate. After all, who would buy a bond that experts predict to be on its way down in value? High interest is the only way to compensate for an anticipated drop in currency exchange.

Still, it's amazing just how often the experts are wrong. In 1977, for example, corporate bonds in both Spain and England were paying several points above the average of most industrialized nations. Spain paid 11.58 percent, and England paid 11.88 percent. Only France paid more (12.09 percent). Clearly there was a hunch worldwide that the peseta and pound were about to decline, but that hunch was wrong. The yields adjusted for the U.S. investor show that the Spanish bonds ultimately paid only 7.01 percent, while the British bonds paid 26.44 percent—the highest yield of any country that particular year. The experts underestimated just how far the peseta would fall and were blind to the pound's incredible impending climb.

So, while expert opinion can be a useful tool in determining when and where to spend your investment dollars, I'd like to tell you something my grandfather used to say: "That's only their opinion, and an opinion is like a rear end. Everybody's got one." Ultimately you're on your own. Using all the opinions available to guide you, using independent research materials, and trusting your gut, you have to know where to go to trade for the most potentially profitable currency. You have to invest as much as you can in that currency. And you have to develop a skill for knowing just the right moment to get out—that moment being the twilight zone between peak market performance and the absolutely inevitable downturn.

As a basic concept TIGO sounds simple. (I want it to.) But don't kid yourself. What sounds easy on paper can become extremely challenging in the real world of global finance. Why? Because not every trade—no matter how good it looks up front—will be a "winner." Even the giants admit to winning on at best perhaps 40 percent of their trades. The key is to cut your losses short, let your profits run, and never work with funds you can't afford to lose.

Historically, the most stable currencies have been the German deutsche mark, the Swiss franc, and (despite its recent troubles) the Japanese yen. You're wise to spread yourself across as many of these as you can. That way you avoid the worst consequences of a major loss should one single currency take a sharp, quick downturn. By holding foreign assets, you insure your portfolio against the possibility of your own currency depreciating relative to others in the global market.

I find that most people make the bulk of their purchases in their home country using their domestic currency. There are many reasons for this myopic approach. In part it's the result of the U.S. government (through its watchdog, the SEC) making the pragmatics of foreign investment both cumbersome and complex. Equally important, people are accustomed to working with their own currency. To begin trading foreign currencies, you have to understand what makes one denomination more valuable than another one. Beyond that, you have to accept this basic investor rule: Diversity is the key to high return, and it brings with it a degree of protected risk.

If yours is one of the major world currencies, then you're fairly safe with this conservative approach. You'll have better years and less profitable ones. Still, hard currencies are not prone to devastating devaluation—at least not overnight. Weaker ones, however, can be extremely vulnerable. For example, you should not rely on the South African rand or Mexican peso with much confidence. If your base currency is fairly weak or has proved to be highly volatile over recent years, then it would pay for you to keep much of your portfolio in foreign assets denominated in more stable foreign currencies. If your base currency is strong, then you have the luxury of choosing. You can stick close to home, taking few risks and counting on respectable (though fairly unimpressive) profits. Or you can use the principles of TIGO to place a portion of your money abroad, trading it in for currencies that you believe will do better than your own.

WHAT A LITTLE INFLATION CAN DO

Powerful people have a powerful impact on currency value. When a new president is elected in the United States, the stock market typically reacts based on global expectations of that person's ability to strengthen or weaken the value of the dollar. When a small country, like El Salvador, holds its first free and open election in decades, ushering in what the world perceives to be a new era of political stability and economic growth, the value of its currency can jump far and fast. It's interesting that these fluctuations are based on nothing more than general consensus. Still, that consensus opens a door—sometimes for just a short time—to making a lot of money very quickly.

I had dinner with some friends at their home in Manhattan a few weeks ago, and their eleven-year-old daughter opened a lively round of conversation by asking all of us who we considered to be the most powerful person in the country. One person believed it to be the president. Another speculated that it was Peter Jennings. I never hesitated. "Alan Greenspan," I argued, "because he controls the money. Whoever controls inflation controls the nation." I've thought

It's interesting that these fluctuations are based on nothing more than general consensus. Still, that consensus opens a door—sometimes for just a short time—to making a lot of money very quickly.

about our friendly debate a number of times since that evening, and while I wish I'd made my point more eloquently, I still stand by my opinion.

Richard C. Young, a currency analyst who gained international recognition during the 1980s, once asked, "What central factor controls the value of currencies one to the other over the long haul?" His answer: "Inflation." "Everything else," he said, "ultimately proves to be of secondary concern." Any country that controls inflation controls the strength of its currency. Look at Switzerland. Its inflation is low, and its currency is strong. Look at Argentina. During the 1970s, when inflation was running into the triple digits, the peso plummeted. In 1974 there were five Argentine pesos to the dollar. At the end of 1980 there were 1,977 pesos to the dollar. And by the end of 1982 it took more than 50,000 pesos to equal one dollar!

Now look at England. By the early 1990s inflation was crippling its entire economy. It was clear to almost everyone that the pound was significantly overvalued in relation to stronger European currencies, yet the government's only way to keep speculators at bay was to refuse any urge to raise its unrealistically low interest rate and devalue its currency. For former Prime Minister John Major the problem took on increasingly nightmarish proportions until September 1994, when the pound's value sank so low that sterling was sold, said one dealer, "like water running out of a tap." England's money was worth next to nothing.

To show the profound link between inflation and currency value, let's return for a moment to the make-believe land of Compuvania, a computer-exporting nation. Let's pretend that for decades it has maintained a solid trading relationship with Chevroland, a country that makes and sells automobiles. The relative value placed on these items in the marketplace says that ten computers are worth one car. In Chevroland the car sells for 10,000 rosos; Compuvania sells each computer for 250 miggots. The exchange rate, then, is four rosos to one miggot.

Let's imagine for a moment that over the course of the next year Compuvania inflates its currency by 20 percent. The number of computers produced does not change, and Compuvanian citizens continue to place the same value on the equipment. Still, because there are now 20 percent more miggots running after the same number of goods, the price of all domestic goods will jump by about 20 percent. A computer now costs 300 miggots.

How does this Compuvanian inflation affect trade between Compuvania and Chevroland? Remember, in terms of underlying value, nothing has changed: One car is still worth ten computers. But when the car exporter goes to his bank and exchanges 10,000 rosos into miggots at the old exchange rate, he'll have 2,500 rosos. That will no longer be enough to buy ten computers. Due to Compuvania's inflation, he can purchase only eight computers (with a little change left over). Do you think he'll still be willing to trade one of his cars for eight computers? Not on your life! He'll want more miggots for every car—20 percent more—so that he can continue to trade one car for every ten computers. The exchange rate shifts to one miggot equaling 3.2 rosos.

There you have it: the clear relationship between the inflation of a currency and the decline in its exchange rate against the money of a more stable nation.

Granted, other factors beyond domestic inflation can impact a country's economic health and therefore the strength of its currency. For example, if Chevroland's president were to be assassinated and the nation thrust into even short-term political chaos, its currency could drop—perhaps lower than Compuvania's. Or the demand for its cars could go down when a new Japanese compact becomes the international rage—again deflating the value of the Chevroland roso. Still, inflation is at the heart of any currency's value because that value is determined by supply and demand. And inflation determines supply.

These basic economic principles of inflation and currency value form the foundation of an all-important rule of international investment. If you're considering a long-term foreign investment—real estate or business acquisition being two prime examples—then take time up front to examine the money supply and inflation data on the country in which you would be involved. If its domestic currency is vulnerable to a recent history of up-and-down inflation, you should probably look elsewhere. Of course, if you go ahead, and your luck is good, inflation will stay low long enough for you to make a substantial chunk of money. (But, even then, remember the last tenet of TIGO: Know when to get out. Even the most bullish markets in the world will turn sour at some point. When you perceive that the roar of the bear is just around the bend, it's time to take your profits and move elsewhere.)

One way to circumvent the worst of a rapid downturn is a technique commonly referred to as "hedging." Although most investors see it as new phenomenon, hedging was actually initiated in 1949 by Alexander Winslow Jones. Noting that some parts of an economy did very well while others did poorly, Jones devised a creative scale of investing. Using his guidelines, a very bullish investor might "go long" (bank on the strength of a particular currency) with 80 percent of his assets but "go short" (bet on the weakness of that same currency) with the remaining 20 percent. The point, Jones argued, is to vary your risk. So, in essence, you put most of your money into markets that you believe will do well, but you hedge your bet by investing some smaller portion of your money into markets that will benefit in the event that your hunch is wrong.

Despite the fact that market analysts and financial writers frequently mention the notion of going long or short, I meet many people who have trouble grasping the concept. Here's a silly fairy tale to help explain it. Once upon a time there was a beautiful princess with long, golden hair. Although her silken tresses were the envy of every young maiden in the land, she found them unruly and hot against her neck. She longed for some way to relieve her discomfort.

It so happened there was a handsome young shoemaker in the village who heard about her trouble. He believed he could help (and make a bundle while he was at it). He took a small, soft circle of leather, punched two small holes directly across from each other on the outside rim of the orb, and slipped a sturdy oak twig through the holes. He called his tiny invention a "barrette." Of course, being just a poor shoemaker, it took him days to gain audience with the princess. But when at last she saw him and learned how his gadget could lift her hair up and off her back, she was delighted! She wore the barrette both day and night, and the shoemaker was very proud.

It didn't take long for word to spread throughout the land: Barrettes were wonderful! Indeed, all the maidens wanted several for their very own. Fortunately, the shoemaker had suspected this might happen. Without telling anyone his plan, he had purchased many extra leather hides from the trapper and piles of extra twigs from the forester. Late at night, after his cobbling work was done, he industriously made hundreds of barrettes. When it came time for the village fair he had them to sell—for several gold coins a piece. By the end of the fair all were sold. So he made more. And more. And still more—all from his cheap supply of leather and twigs. Barrettes could be seen everywhere throughout the land, and before long the shoemaker had become a very rich man. Now able to afford velvet robes, strong white stallions, and a castle of his own, he confidently asked the princess to be his bride. She said yes, of course, and they lived happily ever after with the fortune he'd accumulated.

Get it? By "going long" on leather and twigs, the shoemaker beat the public to its rush for barrettes. Because he correctly speculated that barrettes would become increasingly valuable in the short term, he bought his supplies while they were still cheap and saved himself the increased cost of buying them after their sellers knew how valuable they had become. Did the young man take a risk? Definitely! What if his barrettes had been a flop? He would have been out the entire cost of all those supplies. He would have had tons of leather and twigs, and nobody to buy them.

In the real financial world, going long implies the same risk. Had I stockpiled Japanese yen during the early 1990s, thinking they would increase in value (and earn me a handsome profit when I sold), then I would be in quite a pickle right now. The yen has fallen dramatically in recent years, and it's expected to continuing falling. I'd be sitting on a mountain of yen that I couldn't trade to anybody informed.

I recently read an article by Thomas L. Friedman in the *New York Times*, proposing a captivating argument for what may be the biggest "hedge" of the late 1990s. Will the fifteen members of the European Union get their act together and actually agree by 1999 to dump the French franc, the Italian lira, and the German deutsche mark in favor of a single Eurocurrency? The European Monetary Union (EMU) is without question the most ambitious proposal in political economy since the Bolshevik Revolution. For fifteen independent nations to hand over complete financial power to one supercurrency is unprecedented.

Friedman builds a clever argument for going short on the deutsche mark if you believe that EMU will achieve its goal, long on the deutsche mark if you think it will ultimately fail. Why? Because if the project goes belly up, everyone in Europe will rush to put their money back in the strongest currency around, the deutsche mark. Friedman speculates

that EMU will happen because the most powerful states-
man in Europe, Chancellor Helmut Kohl of Germany, has
staked his entire career on the project. Seeing it as the
means to a unified Europe and a stronger Germany, he is
waging the battle of his professional lifetime. And, argues
Friedman, "Mr. Kohl is such a dominant figure in Europe that
it's hard to bet against him."

Still, Friedman hedges on his argument by admitting
that EMU has a tough row to hoe because it's asking for a
single Eurocurrency before there is a single Euroeconomy.
Think about it: If one small EMU member experiences a sag-
ging market, it's bound to use all the standard remedies. It
will lower interest rates, use fiscal policy to pump money
into its economy, and depreciate its currency. But what if,
as that country is tanking, another EMU market booms to
the point that it begins to worry about inflation? It's going
to want to raise its interest rate. Yet under EMU there would
be just one central bank in Europe with one interest rate policy. How would it deal with one nation's need for a weak
Eurocurrency and another's desire for a strong one?

Put simply, if EMU works, the European Union will be
stronger than ever. If it fails, Western European alliances
could unravel quickly. If that happens, you'd be smart to do
what the hedge fund masters will undoubtedly do: Go after
the weakest currencies first, dragging them off into the forest, until all that's left is a rock-solid German deutsche mark.
As Friedman so aptly comments, "It won't be pretty. But you
can bet on it."

INVESTING WITH THE COMEBACK KID

Now is a very good time for U.S. dollar investors. Since 1995
the dollar has jumped 45 percent against the yen and 25 percent against the German deutsche mark (two of the more
stable currencies in the international market). Many experts

predict continued appreciation for at least the short term. For example, money is pouring out of Japan into higher yielding, fixed-income markets—the United States being first and foremost among them. Let's face it: With very little good news coming out of Tokyo these days, there's not much to beckon domestic investors back from Wall Street, where their money is doing quite nicely.

At the most obvious level this is a good time to spend U.S. dollars in markets where their rate of exchange allows you to get a real bargain for your money. Let me offer a few suggestions. The Turkish lira fell from 43,478 to 100,000 per dollar between spring 1996 and spring 1997. That's a whopping 130 percent decline. Think about what that means for dollar-dealing investors! They can pick up almost anything at less than half the price it would have cost them just a few months ago! The Venezuelan bolivar is another currency in trouble against the dollar. Between 1996 and 1997 its exchange rate dropped by 56 percent. There have been less dramatic (though still significant) drops in several other currencies: the Austrian schilling, Belgian franc, Danish krone, Ecuadorian sucre, Finnish mark, French franc, Greek drachma, Dutch guilder, Portuguese escudo, South African rand, Spanish peseta, and Tahitian franc.

If nothing else this is a great time to vacation abroad. While you're there it's a great time to purchase all the Italian clothes, French wines, and German luxury cars that you've always wanted but felt were priced too high. Foreign business executives will love you for it.

Consider Solange Gestas, for instance. She's the chief executive of a 152-year-old firm that makes copies of nineteenth-century furniture. Tucked away in the Pyrenees mountains of southwestern France, her company depends heavily on U.S. buyers. She started targeting the U.S. market in the mid-1980s, when the American economy was booming and a rising dollar made her products affordable to many American buyers. Then came a stretch of lean years. Discretionary money dried up, and a weak dollar made the frivolities of faux antiques less than compelling. Luckily for Gestas, the tide has turned. Today, with the dollar once again enjoying a comeback, U.S. buyers represent nearly half of the furniture maker's $3 million in annual sales.

Or take Daimler Benz, where years of restructuring seem to be paying off on the export side. In the first three months of 1997 sales of Mercedes-Benz automobiles to the United States jumped 26 percent. Swiss pharmaceuticals giant Roche is feeling the same benefits of a strong dollar: First-quarter sales in 1997 to U.S. buyers were 18 percent higher (in Swiss franc terms) than they had been the year before. The pattern is the same for many European exporters. "We can only clap our hands at the strong dollar," says Nestlé Vice President Francois-Xavier Perroud. Indeed, he should be clapping. Earnings growth at the global food maker has rebounded to double digits after several years in which a strong franc depressed returns.

Before we get too carried away by all the U.S. dollar can do these days, it's important to utter that very unappealing word *inflation*. It can do some horrible things to the power of any currency. For example, inflation in Venezuela ran at an estimated 103 percent in 1996. Given that fact, it was no great advantage in 1997 that the dollar could buy 56 percent more than it had the year before. Similarly, the dollar's gains of 37 percent against Ecuador's sucre and 130 percent against the Turkish lira came during national inflation rates in those countries of 25 percent and 80 percent, respectively. Granted, bargains were still available, but not to the extent that exchange rate listings alone would have suggested. The secret is to wade through the figures—dry and dull as they can be—to find those foreign markets that offer you the biggest bang for your buck.

What about when the inevitable happens and the dollar takes a nose-dive? I'm not trying to paint a picture of doom and gloom. The dollar is never going to be a worthless currency. Still, it has known tough times before, and money moves through cycles. That's why even now, when the outlook on Wall Street is bright, smart dollar investors have committed a portion of their assets elsewhere. How have they done it?

Some investors might have foreign cash socked away under their mattress. This is not the best way to own foreign assets, but it is one way. Believe it or not, I know some people who take pretty much this approach. They simply walk into their local bank and purchase bank notes or traveler's checks denominated in a foreign currency. There are no minimums for this sort of transaction, so they can buy as much or little as they like. If you decide to go this route, then realize that you'll need to pay the bank a commission to trade these notes—first into a foreign currency and then again to trade them back into dollars. The commission isn't the biggest problem, though. More important than that, why just hold foreign money when you can use other investment vehicles that allow you to earn interest on your purchase?

To take advantage of interest, you'll need to hold an interest-bearing account at a foreign bank. Savings accounts have very few restrictions, so you can cash out at your leisure and then move on to a different bank in a different country using a different currency. But you'll earn higher interest if you purchase a foreign bank certificate of deposit.

The dollar is never going to be a worthless currency. Still, it has known tough times before, and money moves through cycles. That's why even now, when the outlook on Wall Street is bright, smart dollar investors have committed a portion of their assets elsewhere.

Be aware, though, that you're often charged heavy penalties for early withdrawal. In some countries no early withdrawal is allowed; you're locked in for the term of the deposit. So consider your goals. If you want to be able to move money at a moment's notice, you may want to avoid even a CD—not to mention the constraints of longer-term investments like real estate or business acquisition.

To help avoid frustration down the line, I recommend that you follow five currency trading rules. The first is perhaps the most important.

1. *Choose to work with a money manager.* To go it alone is possible, but it's risky. Unless you've had considerable experience in the international market, it's best to get help from a savvy consultant. There are increasingly more of these professionals out there; if you know one, give that person a call. If you don't know one, then start by asking your tax accountant or attorney to recommend one. These folks deal with money every day, and they're probably familiar with someone who can guide you through the process.

2. *Always trade short-term movements in line with the long-term trend, not against it.* This may be the conservative approach, but the global market makes very little room for brilliant mavericks.

3. *Always trade a weak currency against a strong one, not two weak or two strong ones against each other.* The reasoning here is that you'll never make much headway if you're swapping among equally valuable (or equally low-valuable) currencies. It's sort of like trading a Macintosh apple for a Golden Delicious. What's the real gain? If you're going to trade an apple, trade it for a watermelon—or whatever you consider a truly more appealing fruit. Using currencies instead of apples

to make my point: There's little point in trading Czech koruna for Ecuadorian sucre. Their relative values are too similar. Better to trade koruna for German deutsche marks.

4. ***Avoid trading currencies within the same "block," or cluster of currencies that tend to act in unison.*** The two major blocks are the U.S. dollar and German deutsche mark. In the case of the U.S. dollar block, the major players along with the U.S. dollar are the Canadian dollar and the Japanese yen. The German deutsche mark block includes (along with Germany) France, Belgium, and the Netherlands. The reasoning behind this rule is much like the previous one: If a currency is moving in unison with several others, the benefits of a trade within that block are negligible.

5. ***Trade with the central banks, not against them.*** Of course, these institutions may not always forecast moves correctly, but their massive buying power can often make a move. When they do, you don't want to be swimming against the tidal wave they create.

THE KING MIDAS TOUCH

Remember the legend of King Midas? He begged the gods to grant but one wish: that everything he touched might turn to gold. His wish was granted, but as he watched his food, clothes, bed, and throne transform at the slightest touch of his fingers, he prayed to the gods that they would reverse his fate. Two morals emerge from this story. The first is (as every wise mother tells her children): Be careful what you wish for because it almost always comes true. The second is (to quote John Stuart Mill): "There is nothing more originally desirable about money than about any heap of glittering pebbles."

To understand currency is to glimpse not the sight of sparkling gold bullion or the twinkle of gems in the sunlight. Rather, it is to grasp the fundamental laws of exchange. Trade has been at the root of every human culture since recorded history began. People have traded fur pelts for seashells, corn for firewood, even land for trinkets. Some of these deals have been even trades; a few have been bargains. My goal with this chapter has been to explain the basic principles by which trade has been transformed from that simple, hand-to-hand exchange of everyday necessities into a global electronic game of supply and demand, and to encourage you to consider the opportunities that exist for finding bargains all over the world. It is true that at any time of the day or night someone, somewhere, is trading currencies. You can too. All it takes is some careful research up front, a good consultant to ease the process, and the nose for a bargain. So start sniffing!

CHAPTER 5

THE TOP TEN GLOBAL MARKETS

What's Hot and What's Not

The '90s have become the international dogfight.
— PETER MOORE, SENIOR VICE PRESIDENT,
REEBOK INTERNATIONAL

It used to be that the U.S. dominated the world economy, so it was appropriate for U.S. investors to ignore the rest of the world," explains James J. Atkinson, Jr., director of California-based Guinness Flight Global Asset Management Ltd. "But you can't make that claim anymore."

Atkinson is right, of course. In a study conducted by the large mutual fund group T. Rowe Price, analysts compared the performance of the S&P 500 index with the EAFE index (which covers eighteen foreign countries and more than a thousand companies in Europe, Asia, and the Far East). They found that between 1982 and 1992 investors who allocated 100 percent of their assets to the S&P 500 averaged an annual return of 16.04 percent. Those with all their assets invested in the EAFE averaged a 17.39 percent return. Similarly, a country-by-country study covering the first eight months of 1993 showed a clear picture of just how dramatically the global landscape has changed. Overall market gain during that period was 17.5 percent in the United States. In Singapore it was more than 26 percent, and in Malaysia it was nearly 43 percent!

The challenge for individual investors is to put money into the right foreign markets at the right time. With so many places from which to choose and such diverse opinions circulating on each of them, how do you pick? One way is simply to follow the herd and lap up the international "flavor of the month." But the "in" choice is not always the right choice. Some fads prove to be worth the hoopla; others bomb out even before the ink dries on magazine pages touting their supposed potential.

What follows is my review of ten so-called hot markets. I've included some just because their tremendous popularity and reputation invite careful scrutiny. Others are here because I believe they offer exceptional opportunity. The financial world changes so much so quickly that it's difficult to say if these ten will still be the darlings of global investment gurus by the time you read this book. Some may be nearly obsolete by then.

MARKET CRITERIA

To help you evaluate my assessments (and to provide you with a rating scale for your future analyses), I will apply four basic criteria to each market. I encourage you to learn these criteria, because, while the global environment will undoubtedly change again and again, these standards are fixed and, in my view, offer you a permanent and reliable method for distinguishing the good from the bad.

Does the Foreign Country You Are Considering Have a Strong and Free Government?

A free market and political stability are critical ingredients in any wise global investment, because without them there cannot be any chance for economic security. We are living in fascinating times. Many countries that spent decades burdened by the weight of fascism and complete government control are now taking their place among the world's free nations. Eastern Europe is the most obvious example. Fourteen small nation-states are working overtime to open their economy to free trade and the boost that can come only from Western investment. Plenty of opportunity comes from this. Still, it's important to be wary of nations that put the cart before the horse. Without a strong and responsible government to support economic reform, even the most ingenious financial dreams are likely to become nightmares. In my reviews, you'll see my effort to balance the allure of clever investment ventures against the political landscape in which they must be managed. The markets I rate most favorably offer good business concepts within relatively stable political environments. As you venture into the global arena, always place your money in such markets.

We are living in fascinating times. Many countries that spent decades burdened by the weight of fascism and complete government control are now taking their place among the world's free nations.

Is the Currency in the Market You Are Considering Strong with a History of Exchange Rate Stability?

If you plan to eventually convert your investment profits from the foreign market currency back into U.S. dollars, you will be subjected to currency risk exchange. Any currency that fluctuates too much or remains under constant threat of devaluation will magnify that risk. Conversely, a strong foreign currency helps you minimize your risk. As I explained in Chapter 4, the investment world is already tuned in to this fact. The interest rate earned on CDs in markets with solid currency and stable exchange rates will be lower than the interest rate earned in volatile markets. Still, there is room for intelligent strategy. The trick is to make the right (informed) guess on which currencies are likely to perform well and exchange profitably. My reviews give a few of my own best hunches. I encourage you to learn as much as you can about this subject. The better you understand currency, the better your "guesses" will be.

Is the Company You Are Considering Strong and Stable?

Too often investors rely solely on the reputation of the foreign market they're considering and forget that foreign stocks are subject to the same economic and industry-related risks as their domestic equivalents. Granted, those risks have a great deal to do with how the country's economy is behaving, but they also have something to do with the performance of the firm itself. To reduce your investment risk, I encourage you to put your money only into companies that offer a proven track record of steady, controlled growth or a new product or service that's poised for widespread popularity. As you'll see later in this chapter, I sometimes mention specific companies that I consider to be good bets over the short term. How have I identified them? Through endless information gathering. Books, newspapers, magazines, business lunch conversations—there are countless ways to keep tabs on promising foreign companies. I suggest you learn to like every one of them. Only political campaign managers believe that too much knowledge can be dangerous. Like virtually every financial consultant, I prefer the motto "Knowledge is power."

What Major Sponsorship Backs the Foreign Market or Company You Are Considering?

I'm no George Soros, no Warren Buffett. To my credit I'm smart enough to recognize that fact. I'm humble enough to happily follow in the footsteps of people I've identified as better at the game than I am. You should take a similar approach to global investment. If you hear about somebody who's exceptionally skilled in a particular market or within a specific industry, seriously consider attaching your money to that person's choices. Some idols are famous, and their whims are fairly easy to follow. Less recognized geniuses are out there too, though. Find out who they are. If you like a conservative approach to global investment, there are certainly methodical masters to emulate. If you lean more toward an aggressive investment style, you can stand in the shadows of maverick moguls. You'll notice a few individuals mentioned in this chapter. I include them because they are people I've come to admire. They may not rank in your top ten. That's fine. The point is, you don't have to reinvent the wheel every time you decide to enter another foreign market. Just watch what your heroes do and step in time.

EAST ASIA

Some of the world's most phenomenal investment opportunities are in Asia, mostly within industries that I call the "three Ts" (transportation, telecommunications, and technology). Here are a few examples of what I mean:

- South Korea is investing $13.4 billion in a high-speed train link between Seoul and Pusan and will spend another $50 billion on thirty new power plants, including seven nuclear plants. All of this—along with the design and construction of a new $5 billion airport in Seoul—will happen between now and the year 2000. Firms tagged for these contracts will make a mint.

- Over the next few years Malaysia will spend $9 billion on infrastructure, Indonesia will spend close to $12 billion, and the Philippines some $4.5 billion.

The short-term financial outlays are mind-boggling. The Asian Development Bank estimates that Asia will spend $1 trillion, just by the year 2000, on energy, communications systems, and transportation. Many analysts question whether Asia can afford to build all this infrastructure. Other astute experts have asked: Can it afford not to? Clearly, the answer is no. That paves the way for some extremely exciting business partnerships between Asia and the West.

It is not just through Asia-oriented use of the U.S. stock market that you can make money in the Far East. Asia's stock, bond, and futures markets are experiencing tremendous change and growth. In 1987, for example, Asia's stock markets (excluding Japan) were capitalized at $195 billion. Today that figure exceeds $1 trillion. It's no wonder that institutional investors, companies, and individuals from virtually every nation are plunging headlong into this, the world's fastest-growing financial market. Ten years ago only a tiny portion of U.S. equity went into Asia. By 1993 U.S.

equity investment in Asia hit $12.9 billion—a third of that year's $40 billion total! Similar volumes of cash poured in from Japan, England, and Europe.

Of course, not every Asian country offers an equally attractive investment environment. Here's my assessment of today's most talked-about options.

Japan

Mention Asian investment, and people instantly think of Japan. It's understandable. It wasn't that long ago that the Tokyo exchange dazzled the financial world with a long series of economic triumphs. Well, things have changed. In Japan people talk about the economy "before the bubble," "during the bubble," and "after the bubble" (when a lot of investors lost everything). The "bubble" to which they refer happened in the late 1980s, when industry overinvested and financial institutions loaned too much money. Everyone was lending and spending. In 1990 prices went berserk, and the bubble burst. Real estate and stock prices took a nose dive, and Japan entered a deadly deflation spiral. By 1995 the stock market was 63 percent below its high and still overvalued. Property prices were down by 50 percent. While the government has made noises about controlling the problem, no foreseeable relief is in sight. Many researchers predict, in fact, that by the year 2000 the average Japanese investor will have lost more than the average American investor did in the 1930s.

"Is Japan finished?" asks Edith Terry in *World Business*. "The Japan of the bubble economy was as unbalanced in its way as the former Soviet Union, forced to devote most of its human and material resources to creating national wealth. Faced with pressure for change, bureaucrats and politicians are falling back on hoary Japanese values, such as collectivism and obedience, rather than taking bold action. If that continues, a nation obsessed with becoming number one will have to settle for a position considerably lower on the list." The Japanese economy, she says, is emerging from nearly a decade of recession "as a misshapen monster—a dinosaur's body with the head of an ostrich."

Bottom line: For the average investor eager to profit by Asia's financial boom, there are far better choices than Japan.

My rating: *A Poor Choice at This Time.*

Indonesia

In the spring of 1997 seventy-five-year-old President Suharto was again reelected by Indonesian citizens. After thirty-one years in power, that victory is likely to be his last. His once-inspiring record of economic modernization is now tainted by widespread resentment over corruption, flagrant nepotism, and harsh treatment of popular opposition figures.

Over the past few years violence has become common-place in Indonesia. For example, just weeks before the presidential election, in the province of Central Java, the officially sanctioned Islamic opposition party put up dozens of its signature green flags. Almost immediately workers for Suharto's party, Golkar, tore them down and covered the town with their emblematic yellow—splattering canary-colored paint over government offices, tree trunks, curb-stones, and other public property. The Islamic party ripped down the yellow flags, and then rampaging mobs from each side trashed freshly painted buildings. One Islamic leader was hospitalized. At least one Golkar member was killed. Hundreds went to prison.

With Suharto now officially authorized to rule for another term, perhaps tensions will subside. I don't think they will. Even if the crude violence is contained, Suharto's basic problem will remain. A retired general, accustomed to autocratic rule, he must begin to build a more democratic society or risk destroying the economic miracle he performed for Indonesia during the 1970s and 1980s. Sadly, reform advocates have met with nothing but resistance from the president and his inner circle. In fact, in early 1997 nine prodemocracy students drafted a new national constitution and for that offense received prison sentences of up to thirteen years. Suharto's six grown children continue to incite the nation by using their family connections to corner Indonesia's best business deals.

Suharto is hoping that his past achievements will keep a majority of ordinary Indonesians on his side. Perhaps. Per capita income has jumped from $50 to $1,370 under his political rule. Annual inflation has dropped from 600 percent to 7 percent. Paved roads, sleek express trains, international flight routes, and cellular telephone grids are now a part of everyday life. Foreign investors have socked some $176 billion into the country's privatized ventures. Still, it all totters on a precipice of disaster. Suharto has disappointed and angered the domestic and foreign business communities by reneging on earlier promises to open up the economy and eliminate corruption. "People don't really trust the government," complains Bank Indonesia Governor J. Soedradjat Djiwandono. "Any time we say anything, everyone asks, 'Is that true?'"

Bottom line: One thing is clear—Indonesia is on the brink of dramatic (and probably violent) political change. The best scenario would have Suharto spend his final years creating a democratic legacy. That is unlikely, and even if it happened, it would bring about temporary economic instability. If, as is more likely, he continues to rule without mercy until he drops, 200 million Indonesians will be left to cope with the violent aftermath of his social and financial mistakes. That would spell investment disaster for any foreigner whose assets are tied up in Indonesian interests. It is certainly true that down the line Indonesia will turn around. When it does, a world of opportunity will open to foreign investors.

My rating: *A Poor Choice at This Time.*

Malaysia

Perhaps the greatest lesson to be learned from Asian markets is the enormous benefit that privatization gives to any economy. The value of privately owned, profitable companies (as opposed to state-owned and state-operated ventures) is that they keep fixed costs low in order to earn the highest possible profit.

Malaysia has learned that lesson very, very well. Some 120 of the country's businesses have been privatized since 1983. The results are economic growth, efficiency, and nearly a zero rate of unemployment. The country saves $24 billion a year—more than $2 billion in salaries and pensions alone. At the Kelang Container Terminal cargo takes less than three days to clear; it used to take eight. There's a wider choice of television and radio programming, and a huge reduction in power outages makes it possible for people to enjoy both. There is steady telephone service. And the privately built North-South Highway has shaved ninety minutes off the six-hour drive from Kuala Lumpur to Singapore.

"To say that Malaysia is a model to developing countries is an understatement," claims Khoo Eng Choo, the managing

Perhaps the greatest lesson to be learned from Asian markets is the enormous benefit that privatization gives to any economy. The value of privately owned, profitable companies (as opposed to state-owned and state-operated ventures) is that they keep fixed costs low in order to earn the highest possible profit.

partner of Price Waterhouse in Kuala Lumpur. "Privatization in Malaysia is more advanced and more widely applied" than in almost any other emerging market. Harvard economist Jeffrey Sachs agrees. "Malaysia has proven that privatization works."

The man most responsible for this grand economic achievement is Prime Minister Mahathir Mohamad. As John Naisbitt puts it in his insightful book *Megatrends Asia*, Mahathir took his country "across the great divide." Those who governed before him believed that national economic interests (especially those of ethnic minorities) could be properly supervised only by the state. Mahathir proved them wrong by designing and implementing an affirmative action plan that sets aside a significant share of privatization opportunities for indigenous Malays.

Mahathir has also created a new pattern for Asian privatization efforts by ensuring a continued role for the Malaysian government as either shareholder or regulator. Raising money has never been the goal of his privatization program. "It's never been a fund-raising exercise," explains Finance Minister Anwar Ibrahim. "We let the private sector take the lead, and the government acts as a check and balance."

In this kind of stable political environment private industry can live up to its purpose of making money by providing useful products and services. Investors around the world would be wise to put their money to work in those Malaysian corporations that have been participating in the country's successful expansion. Corporations like IJM Corporation, for example. IJM is well respected for completing its projects on time and within budget. Major contracts include a $22 million industrial estate in Kedah State and two power plant expansions for state-owned Tenago Nasional Bhd.

Bottom line: Malaysia can be a smart investor's dream if that investor has the help of an experienced and savvy money manager. Strategically situated, Malaysia offers a base camp for dealings with three of the world's largest future markets: China to the north, India to the west, and Indonesia to the south.

I give it a giant thumbs-up and my highest rating: ***Proceed without Fear.***

Thailand

Just three years ago Thailand was the investment darling of Asia. Not anymore. In early 1997 the government announced measures to shore up the country's troubled financial sector, and many analysts hoped the economic slide might stop. So far not much has improved. Not only is the downturn still serious, but the economy isn't likely to experience rapid growth even when the crisis is over. "We have to forget about enjoying an 8 percent growth rate," argues Finance Minister Amnuay Viravan. "Those days are gone."

Thailand's fall from favor shows how even a rising star can tumble due to bad management and corrupt policies. It all began with an inspired plan to make Bangkok a financial hub. The plan sounded great when the bankers talked, and it even looked pretty good on paper. The plan ultimately failed, though, because it addicted the Thai economy to cheap foreign money. Here's the story.

In 1993 the government let a handful of foreign and local banks make loans in U.S. dollars and other currencies. The proponents of this approach said that having loans booked in Thailand would allow the country to become a regional financial center for neighboring economies. In reality most of the $50 billion in foreign loans went to local companies. With the minimum set at just $500,000, almost any Thai business could secure a loan.

The country's financial problems were aggravated by numerous Thai companies raising even more funds through public stock offerings. Shares were snapped up by a horde of foreign investors eager to get in early to an emerging market they believed would take off economically. In three years, for example, TelecomAsia and Thai Telephone & Telegraph raised $4 billion to add more than 4 million phone lines throughout the country, but signed up only 2 million new subscribers. The company and its stockholders were left holding the bag.

Former Prime Minister Banharn Silpa-archa made another mistake. He let several of his cronies meddle with institutions as important as the central bank, which had traditionally been respected for its independence. Regulators stood by as the Bangkok Bank of Commerce collapsed and the property bubble grew bigger. Concedes the former finance minister, "Had we been more vigilant in terms of monitoring and supervision, it would have been better."

Thailand's new government has made solid moves to correct the country's economic woes, but they are too late. The new premier, Chavalit Yongchaiyudh, is requiring banks and other financial institutions to set aside $2 billion in reserves to cover bad loans. He also pledges to cut the budget deficit by reducing spending by some $4 billion. And in 1996 the central bank introduced rules to discourage short-term borrowing (which fell from 86 percent of total loans in 1995 to 73 percent by the end of 1996).

Bottom line: Although some investors expect the Thai market to rebound, the economic crash of the summer of 1997 has left its mark. The baht has lost a third of its value, and a sense of crisis still hangs over the economy. I advise extreme caution. Even when the worst is over, the government must address the problem of valuing its currency. If the U.S. dollar keeps rising against the yen and other currencies, pressure will build for a further devaluation of the baht. The initial drop attracted a pack of wolves among which were some major currency speculators. Amidst the crisis the speculators came in and made matters worse by shorting the baht. This would be good for exporters, but with $80 billion in foreign currency loans still outstanding, many Thai companies would be hard hit. That could give the central bank little choice but to defend the baht and prolong the financial misery. In my view, Thailand needs a lot more time. If by mid-1999 or early 2000 the environment has continued to move toward more political and economic stability, then invest.

My rating: *A Very Poor Choice at This Time.*

Vietnam

The Vietnamese market has received a great deal of publicity lately. And no wonder! It offers a fascinating (and somewhat perplexing) investment environment. Since 1992 its population has grown by a third, to 75 million people. A hefty 70 percent of them are twenty-five or younger. Vietnam's economy has been growing fast, too. Growth was 9 percent in 1996, and inflation is now comfortably under 10 per-cent annually.

All this is good news for investors, as is the fact that the Vietnamese are positively mesmerized by all things Western. Bowling alleys are the rage with countless young consumers, who hope for a strike with balls emblazoned with Coca-Cola logos as they listen to piped-in rock-and-roll hits. This postwar generation is not concerned (much less bitter) about the country's war-torn past. Everything from McDonald's burgers to jobs with foreign companies serves as happy links to the outside world.

This small Asian country is a dramatic illustration of the shift from a government-controlled to a market-driven economy. In 1978 the government closed all private businesses, and restrictions remained in place until 1986. Between 1989 and 1993 private business created 4.7 million new jobs. The number of entrepreneurs applying for business licenses increased from seventy-six in 1991 to 4,403 in 1993. Just eight years ago there were only twenty-two registered private companies in Ho Chi Minh City. As John Naisbitt points out in his excellent book *Megatrends Asia,* there are now 2,600 private companies, plus tens of thousands of small shops. In 1994 BMW began assembling cars in Vietnam, which has a 95 percent literacy rate and a strong work ethic. In Germany the auto company pays its workers $30 per hour, 50 percent of which goes to government-funded welfare programs. In Vietnam BMW pays workers $1 a day.

GE, AT&T, Coca-Cola, Citibank, Boeing, Motorola, Caterpillar—a who's who of U.S. multinationals are chomping at the bit, eager for a chance to invest in the numerous opportunities already available and the many others that are assumed to be just around the corner. For their part, the Vietnamese couldn't be happier about foreign investor involvement. Products like Coke, Pepsi, Marlboro, and Colgate already enjoy widespread brand recognition as holdovers from the war. Having experienced domination by Asian neighbors, Vietnam wants to maintain a strong Western presence in its markets.

Bottom line: There are major problems to keep in mind as you choose your investment vehicles. Incomes are unevenly distributed. In fact, 51 percent of the population still lives below the poverty line. Many critics believe that the public administration is ineffective. The legal framework is unreliable. The banking business is precarious. And people's personal savings are a lot lower than in other Asian countries. All this suggests that investments made without adequate research can produce disastrous results. Still, the switch to a market economy is being carefully nurtured and sustained in Vietnam. I believe that with so many young consumers so anxious to emulate a Western lifestyle, the country will become a wonderland for careful investment shoppers.

My rating: ***Proceed with Caution.***

WESTERN EUROPE

It used to be that most European investment amounted to a high-interest savings account in a Swiss bank. Not anymore. Since 1995 Europe has created six new secondary stock markets, including the Brussels-based European Association of Securities Dealers Automated Quotation (EASDAQ), London's AIM, and four Euro New Market (NM) member exchanges. Within two years some 178 companies had gone public on these exchanges, raising nearly $2.8 billion in equity. Another 170 businesses are expected to go public by the end of 1997.

Most of these public offerings involve high technology. Unlike U.S. tech stocks, which seesaw up and down notoriously, most of Europe's new tech issues consistently outperform market averages. For example, the total value of shares listed on France's Nouveau Marche rose 59 percent during the exchange's first thirteen months—outperforming the nation's CAC index of top forty companies. More than half of that trading came from non-French investors, mostly from Britain, the United States, and Switzerland. "We are finally seeing the infrastructure to support high-growth technology companies," says Robert Hook, managing director of Prelude, an investment company based in Cambridge, England.

While the money raised in Europe may be just a drop in the bucket compared with what NASDAQ currently raises every year, the trend toward smaller market involvement marks a dramatic shift in the Continent's equity culture. For the first time young technology firms can turn to local exchanges to fuel their growth. And investors who used to search for up-and-coming stock mainly in the United States and Asia are learning to investigate Europe. No wonder many of Europe's money managers have started to call these stocks "the next emerging market."

Not all the news is good, though. The tale of online service company Infonie is not unusual. The first listing on

France's Nouveau Marche, Infonie stock plunged 66 percent in just one year—a reflection of the company's eagerness to go public before it was truly ready for the challenge. Price volatility is another problem. Perhaps at the root of all the trouble, European banks still lack in-depth research expertise in technology. In America an investment bank is likely to keep an entire team of analysts employed full time just monitoring developments and opportunities in technology software. By contrast, European banks sometimes commit funds without adequate knowledge upon which to base their decisions.

Still, I encourage you to watch these new markets consistently and carefully. As you interview various money managers, ask them what they know and how they feel about the new exchanges scattered throughout Western Europe. If they don't seem fluent in the subject, keep looking for a better informed consultant. Two highly publicized countries, Germany and Sweden, seem promising enough to rate here.

Germany

Germany is the hottest topic in the Western European investment community. Straddling two worlds—between the industrialized Continent and the newly liberated Eastern bloc—Germany is something like a set of Siamese twins. One of them is strong and, without even knowing it, saps the meager energy of the other. But don't underestimate the tinier twin. Now free to nurture itself and freely direct its own development, this runt may prove itself capable of financial independence and outstanding achievement.

One investment arena in which Eastern Europe offers exceptional opportunity is highly specialized fine handicrafts. At Lange Uhren, in a sleepy town called Glashutte, craftsmen like Frank Wolf lovingly assemble some of the world's most exquisite timepieces. They create gold and platinum beauties from 360 individually handmade parts, often spending forty hours to complete just one watch. Top-end models sporting the name A. Lange & Suhne fetch up to $87,000!

Just eight years after the fall of communism a small number of East German companies are creating sumptuous luxury goods that would make any proletarian rebel turn in his grave. Rekindling Germany's legendary tradition of fine craftwork, they produce everything from handblown glass globes to intricately engraved rifles and sell them to extremely rich customers from Tokyo to Manhattan. "Every watch we make already has a buyer," says Lange Uhren's president, Hartmut Knothe. And those buyers fork over substantial sums each year to own one of the manufacturer's limited items. Sales in 1997 hit $18.5 million, up 30 percent from the year before.

East Germans are extrapolating from the craftsmanship model and have learned to layer elegance on top of even mundane items. For example, underwear maker Bruno Nanani once sold nothing but utilitarian bras and boxer shorts. In 1992 marketing expert Wolfgang Jassner bought a stake in the company. He changed the name; worked to create a youthful, athletic image; and started selling sexier cotton and silk undies. Now customers happily pay $35 and up for a pair of Bruno's briefs, and the company's profits have shot right through the roof.

Beyond this fun look at how Eastern Germany is contributing to the nation's sputtering economy are solid indications that the country is set for economic vitality. The immediate momentum behind its strength is exports, up nearly 11 percent from just a year ago and still accelerating. Real interest rates are now the lowest in more than a decade. What's equally important for international investors, Germany is finally getting serious about eliminating the insider trading that for decades has excluded all but a small cast of unscrupulous characters.

For example, prosecutors in Frankfurt are hot on the trail of up to 100 insiders who may have illegally traded shares in SAP, a high-flying, $2.3 billion software company. It will be interesting to see what happens, because investors all over the world hold SAP shares. That makes the case internationally relevant and gives the country's young securities oversight agency a chance to prove itself. German authorities still don't have the full power of the law behind them. They have no police powers and cannot seize evidence, pass judgment, or assess fines. Instead, they must pass cases on to local prosecutors who handle criminal investigations.

If Germany can fully implement its cleanup campaign, there's every reason to expect that other European nations will follow. The incentive to protect ordinary stock owners is growing as companies learn how to raise capital in the furthest corners of the world, and as struggling markets learn how to compete for new investors. Countries where enforcement has been lax—like England, Italy, and Switzerland—will come under more pressure to squelch questionable trading.

Bottom line: All this together paints the picture of a potentially robust and wholesome investment market. It's true that Germany is struggling to weld together its two halves. But the country is led by Helmut Kohl, one of the sharpest politicians in Europe. The deutsche mark is a strong currency, and it will get stronger should plans for a single Eurocurrency fall through. The market offers opportunities ranging from conservative corporate stock to creative and high-risk partnerships with revived craft houses. A securities protection agency is in place and appears raring to go. Germany is a reasonable investment environment for investors who want to begin cautiously adding some international flavor to their portfolio.

My rating: ***Proceed with Caution.***

Sweden

There's a man to watch in Sweden named Percy Barnevik. After recently stepping down as CEO of Asea Brown Boveri (ABB)—one of Sweden's premiere brokerage houses—he signed on as chairman of Investor, the giant holding company controlled by Sweden's Wallenberg family. Barnevik admits that his goals for Investor are even grander than those he had for ABB, where he pioneered as a global manager and created what many consider the model of a stateless company.

For the moment Investor's concerns are mostly in Sweden, but that's likely to chance under Barnevik's leadership. He thinks the company could become a world power, and he envisions it adding major ventures in the United States, emerging markets worldwide, and perhaps Eastern Europe. His plan is to acquire minority stakes in non-Swedish companies and then influence them by helping to select new CEOs and offering ongoing management advice. This is precisely the way he manages his stable of Swedish interests, which have a combined market capitalization of some $100 billion. Barnevik believes the approach can work globally. He says, "If you are prepared to put in time and effort to improve performance for everybody, the shareholders are often very happy with that."

Barnevik argues that it is essential to establish beachheads in emerging markets. "If you want to be a global player in twenty to thirty years," he says, "you had better be a strong domestic player in countries such as China, India, and Indonesia." He has the personal connections to become just that (and take his stockholders along with him). With access to political leaders like China's new premier and Poland's president, he can circumvent some bureaucratic red tape and get reliable information straight from the top.

Smelling dazzling international stock is not Barnevik's only talent. He's also a proven wizard with Swedish blue chips, and he's made it clear that he'll be taking a close look at these Investor holdings, where 20 percent annual returns hide some poor performers. He promises to "relentlessly push for higher targets and instill a mentality of continuous change."

Bottom line: Sweden is a small market, but Barnevik is a giant. The krona is a reliable currency. The federal government is solid and receptive to outside investors. It may not be a place for permanent financial residence, but I'd say that Investor is ready to take off. (And that's the best time to buy in.) So, while it's putting a lot on his shoulders, I'd say follow Barnevik and keep tabs on his success.

My rating: ***Proceed with Caution.***

THE EASTERN BLOC

You know why global investors smile at the thought of Eastern bloc investment? Because in 1996 most brokers were scared of Russian stocks. Elections were coming up, and many speculated that Boris Yeltsin would lose. One bold fund manager, though, chose to take a chance on Lukoil, the huge Russian oil company. "He was paying 30 to 40 cents a barrel for proven reserves," muses one analyst. "With Exxon, you pay $6 to $7 a barrel." The Lukoil stock shot up nearly 150 percent in less than a year! Profit like that is nearly a once-in-a-lifetime bonanza.

Under the gray skies of Moscow, within the brown brick buildings of Bucharest, throughout the streets of Prague, from Budapest all the way to St. Petersburg—new financial markets are emerging and offering careful investors a toehold into tomorrow's stocks and bonds fortunes. New gas stations and bright supermarkets pop out along the roadways. Hotel rooms that once cost $130 a night now rent for half that much again. Well-dressed business executives, until recently an endangered species, snap orders into cellular phones at chic cafes that serve expensive international fare.

This new world was born out of political upheaval and misery. It has been less than a decade since the Soviet Union collapsed, but time enough for a few select markets to emerge as special. However, this is dangerous investment terrain. Fortunes can be made as well as lost in the rollercoaster ride that Eastern European vehicles withstand on an ongoing basis. Let's look at some of the most publicized markets and see how they measure up.

Czech Republic

Thanks to Hollywood the Czech Republic has enjoyed a lot of interest among global investors these past few years. By pushing low costs, good locations, and a skilled workforce, the country captured forty Western movie units in 1993 alone. Their films included *Pinocchio;* Sigourney Weaver's *Snow White in the Black Forest;* and *Immortal Beloved,* starring Gary Oldman as the musical master Beethoven.

But success spoiled the Czechs. It caused them to lose themselves to a classic American trait: greed. "Advance teams would come out, find locations, accommodations, catering crews, agree on prices, then go home to rustle up the dough," says South African director Winner Bauer. "When they came back six months later, they'd find the contracts had been ripped up and folks were demanding ten times the price." It all came to a head when actor and producer Tom Cruise arrived in Prague to make the $50 million action flick *Mission: Impossible.* Calling the outrageous cost hikes "blackmail," Cruise nearly pulled out before finally paying up. The word on the street quickly turned sour, and by 1996 only ten full-length films were made in the Czech Republic.

This is not a large country or a hefty market. The loss of their one big moneymaking idea has left the Czechs slack-jawed and teary eyed. In the effort to revive Hollywood's interest, they have proposed the formation of an independent film commission that would impose a uniform standard of professional ethics. But the lax government is reluctant to underwrite the commission's $2 million annual cost.

However, the tightfisted government is helping the film industry by allowing corporations (Czech or foreign) to write off contributions to the arts. The reason is advertising. Government incentives pay for themselves in tourist revenue. "Look what *Crocodile Dundee* did for Australia, or *Braveheart* for Scotland," says Karel Kasal, locations chief of Barrandov Studios. Tourism quadrupled in both countries after the films were released.

Bottom line: All of this does little to impress me. I believe the Czechs blew it, and while there's certainly the chance that they'll revive their economy, I doubt that it will happen via Hollywood film studios. The government and local business need to develop plans for new profit-making ventures. So far they seem unable to do that. Like an addict who needs to bottom out before he can see the need for genuine transformation, the Czech Republic will probably spend some more years trying to recapture an industry that's moved on to other, better pastures. In the meantime, I feel sorry for foreign investors who allow themselves to be swept up in the fantasy that Czech investments will profit from Hollywood's deep pockets. If this is what the Czechs have to offer, then I say forget it.

My rating: *A Poor Choice at This Time.*

Romania

Barely a day has gone by since early 1997 that the Romanian government has not passed some new decree. Usually, it reflects new Premier Victor Ciorbea's drive for economic stability through privatization of industry. Some fifty companies a week are being privatized even as I write, including giants like Romtelecom and Tarom Airlines. Ciorbea pledges that the restructuring of communist-era enterprises will be accelerated and privatization laws amended. Companies will be "sold off for a dollar if necessary," says one senior official. Investment laws are also being changed to boost tax breaks and otherwise grease the wheels for foreign investment, which amounted to nothing more than $2.2 billion before Ciorbea came into political power.

The Bucharest Stock Exchange (BSE) reopened in 1995 after a gap of nearly sixty years. For the first year it was a gothic sight: fully modernized rooms, brand-new computers, mugs of steaming coffee, and not a single trader to be seen. That changed in late 1996, when the BSE got help from the U.S. Agency for International Development, which provided tips on how to function more like the NASDAQ. The result has been sharp jumps in trading. Activity has been further fueled by RASDAQ's listing of about half the 6,000 companies sold thus far through Romania's privatization campaign.

For Romanian citizens there's good news and bad news in all this. Ciorbea has taken the reins and is likely to get the economy back on a steady course. That kind of basic structural change doesn't happen for free. So far polls show that cash-strapped citizens support the government, despite the fact that gross domestic product will fall about 3 percent in 1997 and inflation will run at a staggering 100 percent. Perhaps the people understand that the premier's austerity package is the price that must be paid for past mistakes and future safety.

Bottom line: For global investors Romania is a market worth monitoring. I agree with James Oates, a strategist for Union Bank of Switzerland in London. He maintains that "this market will take off. It's just a matter of time." My advice is to wait a bit longer, until Ciorbea (elected in early 1997) has had three years to prove he can fulfill the dreams he has outlined for the country. If at that time you see reasonable progress and continued privatization, I would move to invest.

My rating, if that day comes: **Proceed with Caution.**

Russia

After careful research, clearheaded investors are likely to notice that some Russian cities and regions are in much better fiscal shape than the deficit-ridden federal government. Moscow, for example, rakes in revenues from vast real estate and business holdings, including a stake in the chain of local McDonald's restaurants. Nizhny Novgorod, an industrial region in the Volga River basin, has become a magnet for foreign investment under Governor Boris Nemtsov.

Most of the action is coming from the issuance of Eurobonds. In the second half of 1997 Moscow raised close to $500 million through Eurobond issues—almost entirely from U.S. and European investors. The city received solid marks from Western bond-rating agencies, and that helped officials line up Credit Suisse First Boston Corporation and Nomura Securities Company to manage the issue. The money will be used to finance revenue-earning projects, everything from commercial buildings to high-tech company startups.

"The appetite for exposure to Russian municipals is quite strong," says David Boren, vice president for economic and market analysis at Salomon Brother Inc. in London. High-yielding government debt is in short supply worldwide, and Russia's municipal Eurobonds are expected to yield more than 9 percent. That makes good investment sense for outsiders and for Russia's local governments, which need cash to repair infrastructure and ignite private industry expansion. The domestic market for ruble-denominated municipal bonds is limited and expensive, with interest rates running close to 30 percent. Although Moscow issues more than $1 billion in these domestic bonds each year, the city is eager for a shot at cheaper foreign financing.

To placate lingering concern over Russia's volatility and the high risk that runs alongside it, Moscow has promised to establish a "pledge fund" to hold highly liquid assets such as real estate and stocks that could compensate bondholders in case of a default. However, if the action seen through 1996 and 1997 can be taken as any indication of future enthusiasm, foreign investors looking for a way to diversify don't seem to need much encouragement. "Moscow's borrowing program can become a model for other regions in Russia," explains Mechislav Klimovich, chairman of the city's Capital Market Development Committee. Along with other experts, he expects municipal Eurobond issues to reach $1.5 billion a year.

Bottom line: I always hesitate to encourage investment anywhere in the Eastern bloc—unless there's a track record of economic stability and solid vehicle performance to support it. Russia is not stable, but there is considerable evidence to suggest that parts of it are doing well and poised to do even better. Moscow is just that kind of region. Careful and methodical research to confirm that the area you've identified is a good one is essential.

My rating: *Proceed with Caution.*

PRESCRIPTION FOR GLOBAL SUCCESS

There you have it. Not all the markets earn high marks, but if they did my rating system wouldn't be worth much. That brings me to an important point. In the rush to gain global exposure, don't let yourself be sold a bill of goods by slick consultants, fund managers, or international investment experts. I'd like a hundred-dollar bill for every armchair investor I know who proudly boasts about having personal

> **S**tart out with reputable help. Always make it your business to investigate even the most trustworthy tips. Diligently stay on top of changes within the global marketplace so that you can respond accordingly. That's a prescription for success, and I've never seen it fail.

assets tied up in foreign stock or bonds. When I ask where they have their holdings, they'll beam and say, "Thailand," or, "Japan." Who am I to burst their bubble? But let's be honest: Either they've been too busy to notice that the parade passed by (quite a while ago) or they've been swindled by some fast-talking investment advisor.

Don't you let either of these things happen to you. Start out with reputable help. Always make it your business to investigate even the most trustworthy tips. Diligently stay on top of changes within the global marketplace so that you can respond accordingly. That's a prescription for success, and I've never seen it fail.

Now, with all that said, let's tackle the investment dragon: China.

CHAPTER 6

CHINA

The Big Dim Sum

The Cold War is over, and the Chinese won.
— JOHN NAISBITT, *MEGATRENDS ASIA*

B igger than anything yet tackled by even the largest multinational giants, desperately in need of both products and services that can bring it up to speed within the context of twenty-first-century economics, and exasperating as only something so elusive and alluring can be— China is where even the most seasoned investors tread lightly. It is where smart beginners stand quietly on the sidelines, learning what succeeds, what fails, and what mysteriously disappears into the murky waters of cross-culture partnership.

By the most recent count, mainland China's population is about 1.2 billion. That's the equivalent of five United States of Americas. And that's why China is so important to investors worldwide. For anybody with anything to sell, a potential market of more than 1 billion people is exhilarating.

China is where even the most seasoned investors tread lightly. It is where smart beginners stand quietly on the sidelines, learning what succeeds, what fails, and what mysteriously disappears into the murky waters of cross-culture partnership.

Car manufacturers are a case in point. China is now hard at work developing what it calls the "people's car," an affordable compact meant to appeal to the world's largest untapped car market. When China recently invited the world's top car makers to submit their concepts for the vehicle, virtually every major name responded. Even the likes of Porsche and Mercedes Benz—hardly known for their bargain basement vehicles—asked to be considered for the job. Why all the flurry of activity? General Motors spokesperson Michael G. Meyerand summed it up beautifully: "China is such a potentially huge market that if only 1 percent of Chinese people could afford cars, that would be 12 million. That's roughly our market size of Europe."

There are big obstacles to profitable investment in China, however. The government, while more open than ever before, is still a communist regime. That means business deals sometimes fall through at a moment's notice for no logical reason. Standard practices and assumed protocol that define business in the Western world are not inherent in the Chinese economy. After signing an "agreement of principles" to build cellular telephone systems in Tianjin and Beijing with China's state-owned Unicom Corp., U.S. phone operator BellSouth at its own expense worked up numerous plans, trained more than a dozen Chinese employees, and hosted several visits by Unicom's CEO, Zhao Weichen, to the United States. Still, negotiations to actually close the deal dragged on. Then Zhau sent a letter demanding a $10 million cash advance within one week or the negotiations would cease. BellSouth cut its losses and got out but never recouped its money. BellSouth isn't the only company to have such losses in China. Some of the smartest corporate executives and individual investors from around the world have been left holding the bag when Chinese bureaucrats and businesspeople have walked away from costly partnership plans.

This fickle streak isn't confined to high-technology deals. I have a friend named Charles Lei who manages development for Disney, and it took him nearly a year to sell *Pinocchio* and *Snow White* to the Chinese market. The delay was caused largely because anything having to do with news, information, art, or entertainment goes through the Ministry of Propaganda, even kids' movies. The Ministry bureaucrats debated for months about whether or not *Snow White* might be subversive. Only after reviewing the script and watching the film ad infinitum did they give approval to distribute the films. This kind of delay would cripple business in the West, but it's commonplace in China.

Beyond the totalitarian nature of the Chinese political system, some of the trouble boils down to a very basic difference between Western and Eastern values. I don't pretend to understand the Chinese. In fact, they consistently confound me. I remember a story about a Chinese taxi driver who looks out his car window and stares admiringly at a Rolls Royce passing him on the street. "I may never sit in that car," he says to himself, "but my son will." John Hung,

For anybody with anything to sell, a potential market of more than 1 billion people is exhilarating.

an expatriate Westerner who has lived for a long time in Hong Kong, offers an insightful comment on the story. "Westerners have a strong entitlement mentality on a wide range of things," he explains. "They insist on their rights, whereas Asians aspire."

All of this takes on very concrete (and oftentimes frustrating) consequences for Western investors and their corporate dignitaries doing business with the Chinese. Westerners want to do business, and they want to do it now. Perhaps our youthful exuberance is showing. The United States, after all, is less than 250 years old. The American perspective stems from a people who ascended to global preeminence in far less than two centuries. To be right, bold, and aggressive— these are the cornerstones of the American self-image. No wonder we push so hard. No wonder we view any delay as obstruction.

The Chinese, in contrast, want to do it when they perceive the time to be right. With a national history now approaching 5,000 years and a population larger than that of any other nation on earth, they're willing to wait. And why not? Time and sheer numbers are undeniably on their side. Equally important, China has reinvented itself many times. The mighty have fallen and risen again like a phoenix. It is understandable, then, that the Chinese place less importance on the here and now. Understandable, too, that they view us as heavy-handed. Like an ancient sage dealing with a young pupil, China isn't ruffled by our investment or political demands. At best it's amused by us, at worst roused to anger like a strict disciplinarian.

Put all of these facts against a backdrop of modern economic reality, and you begin to see why investors are willing to put up with almost any dismissal or disrespect. China's economy has doubled in just the past six years. The country has averaged more than a 10 percent growth rate per year for the past several years. There is such wealth within China that by 1995 foreign trade totaled $280 billion. That was nearly a 20 percent increase over the previous year. The average Chinese family's standard of living is bursting out of survival into consumption. While Americans spend close to half their income on housing, health care, education, and transportation, the Chinese spend only about 5 percent of their income on such necessities. Where does the rest go? That's the question that intrigues investors of every stripe and political persuasion. Experts predict that the Asian middle class could number 1 billion people in less than fifteen years, the greatest share of those people being Chinese. That translates into roughly $8 to $10 trillion in spending power—a figure that easily exceeds today's total U.S. economy!

As Paul Sheng, head of investment banking at Lehman Brothers Asia, has so aptly put it, "The worst nightmare for all of us, the bankers and the operators and the equipment suppliers, is: What if things sort themselves out and you're not there?" With the billions to be made by every investment sector on earth, the thought of being excluded from the party that may take place is terrible.

So Long, Hong Kong

On July 1, 1997, Hong Kong officially rejoined China. In a globally televised extravaganza history happened: A thriving capitalist state, long the colony of England, was voluntarily and peacefully handed over to a communist government. What will this ultimately mean for investors already committed to Hong Kong? And for the thousands more who might eventually consider a portfolio involvement in this city that has sometimes been called "the world's freest economy"?

One thing is certain: Hong Kong will change. The question is how. Analysts fall into two camps on the issue. One group believes that the financial center will wither quickly— a victim of totalitarian bureaucracy and corruption. Others remain confident that Hong Kong's long history of economic vigor will force the mainland Chinese to keep a hands-off policy when it comes to investment law and policy.

I believe both visions are extremes. I think we'll see something between the two: a Hong Kong that continues to serve as a robust financial center but that also reflects the philosophy of the nation that controls it. One reason for believing Hong Kong will retain much of its current financial ambiance is this: Hong Kong already makes money for wealthy investors from the People's Republic of China (PRC). With a corporate tax rate of 16.5 percent, Hong Kong is a far more attractive investment and savings environment than mainland China, where taxes are exorbitant. As Colin Bradbury, Hong Kong regional analyst for Jardine Fleming Broking, said recently in an interview with *Barron's*, "The basic message here is that a lot of what is commonly called 'foreign capital' that's going into China isn't really foreign. It's PRC money from one source or another that has been kept offshore for whatever reasons. This money is sent back to the mainland as investment opportunities arise."

Some of the world's richest people live in China. In fact, the Chinese dominated *Forbes* magazine's 1996 list of East Asian billionaires outside of Japan and Korea. These people run things in China, just as the rich run things everywhere. For them Hong Kong is a close, convenient money haven. It would hardly be in their best interests for it to succumb to the political pressures or restrictions of a communist regime. What is not in their interest is not going to happen because Chinese society is run according to the unwritten laws of *guanxi*—connections—between individuals, family dynasties, corporations, and politicians. Corporate interests have even more to say about how things are run in China than in the United States.

In China power operates more behind the scenes than it does elsewhere. For example, in late 1996 politicians, scholars, and journalists around the world wondered who would be selected to run Hong Kong after the British government left. Then local businessman Henry Ying-tung Fok specu-

Chinese society is run according to the unwritten laws of *guanxi*—connections—between individuals, family dynasties, corporations, and politicians. Corporate interests have even more to say about how things are run in China than in the United States.

lated publicly that the job would go to Chee-hwa Tung, and people knew the die was cast. Why? Because Fok has such strong *guanxi* that his "hunch" carries almost as much weight as divine vision. He has done big favors for people within the government, and therefore he's owed big favors. He saved the communists during the 1950s, when Western nations imposed a trade embargo against China for its support of North Korea during the war. In his late twenties at the time, Fok broke the embargo, using boats and trucks to smuggle much-needed medicine, spare parts, and other supplies from Hong Kong into the People's Republic.

By the end of the war Fok was extremely rich, and he has spent the past forty-five years getting even richer. Each step along the way has brought him more *guanxi*. A distinguished member of Hong Kong's economic elite, Fok helped draft the Basic Law, an agreement between England and China that laid the groundwork for the 1997 handover. He is also a member of the NPC, China's highest lawmaking body. In promoting Tung, Fok put his power behind someone who owes him favors. In 1986 the Tung family's shipping business was on the verge of bankruptcy. At the last minute Fok stepped in with a $120 million investment that resuscitated the firm and put it back in the black.

Fok is part of a small inner circle that maintains financial ties with both mainland China and Hong Kong. Along with this handful of other Chinese businesspeople who wield big-time *guanxi*, he will help shape the future relationship between the communist government and its reclaimed financial center. Fok and the rest are not politically motivated. In fact, as *Forbes* magazine pointed out in late 1996, Fok realized that "he could exercise all the power he wanted through his man, Chee-hwa Tung, while maintaining the very low profile he craves." Fok's interest is money, and to continue generating the amount of it he wants, he needs Hong Kong. You can bet he'll use every ounce of influence he's got (and he's got plenty) to protect himself from any financial threat—even one that comes from his own government.

When making predictions about Hong Kong's future, also keep in mind the city's existing economic woes. The truth is, the city's famed competitive edge has already dulled and would have required significant sharpening even without the recent political change. Despite the optimism of its fans, Hong Kong has been withstanding year after year of slower-than-expected growth, rising outflows of capital, and a serious shortage of technotalent and creative business management. As Raymond Ch'ien, managing director of food processor Lam Soon and an outspoken local leader, has said, "If Hong Kong dies, it will be caused by suicide, not by China."

I couldn't agree more. It seems to me there are at least four huge crises looming on Hong Kong's horizon:

Crisis 1: Real estate costs are suffocating Hong Kong's business base. Nothing is a bargain in a town where a room at a second-class hotel runs close to $400 a day. Developers are paying record prices for land. Prime office space now costs more than comparable accommodations in Tokyo. Admits Victor Fung, chairman of both the investment bank Prudential Asia and the Hong Kong Trade Development Council, "We are known in the international business community as an expensive place to operate. That is hard to deny and harder to change." It's ironic that this should be the case, since the city itself owns all the land. About 30 percent of Hong Kong's annual revenue comes from auctioning off land and collecting fees from a handful of property developers. It would seem the city has overdone a good thing. "Hong Kong is in the throes of a housing crisis," concludes an analysis by the investment bank Salomon Brothers. A 750-square-foot apartment in the outlying New Territories (something akin to Queens in New York City) can cost close to half a million dollars—more than twice what it did even a year ago. Salomon has called this predicament "a potential tinderbox" for social unrest.

Crisis 2: English, the international language of business, is no longer spoken by all Hong Kong businesspeople. Call a Hong Kong executive or even a growing number of the city's investment managers, and there's a good chance you'll hear a short-tempered secretary snap back in broken English, "Him not here. Call back." Remarks Miron Mushkat, chief economist for Asia at Lehman Brothers in Hong Kong, "To be an international finance center, Hong Kong must maintain its split personality of Western and Chinese culture. But it is becoming more inward looking." Investors around the world will get the message that the city is not interested enough in global business to extend the courtesy of the world's most commonly spoken business language. I've seen this happen elsewhere. When an international market center conveys to the investment world that it's not interested, the most impressive portfolios don't stick around to be insulted a second time. They just move on to more inviting locales.

Crisis 3: Hong Kong now has many Asian competitors working to attract foreign investors. Hong Kong is no longer the only game in town. Not long ago if you wanted a presence in Asia, you had to work through Hong Kong. Today rival Asian business centers are beginning to offer the same advantages that for so long formed the base of Hong Kong's appeal. Several of these advantages are discussed in Chapter 5. Not mentioned there is Singapore, which has put a great deal of time and money into upgrading its workers (who speak perfect English) and wooing multinationals with tax breaks every bit as attractive as Hong Kong's. Taiwan is also a rival, and its efforts could soon diminish Hong Kong's historical role as the go-between connecting mainland China and the rest of the world. As *Fortune* magazine recently reported, "Already Taiwan has started its first direct shipments from South China, provided that the goods are bound for other countries—a move that will divert business from Hong Kong's busy but expensive container port."

Crisis 4: Hong Kong faces a serious shortage of skilled talent. I hear this complaint echoed by my own contacts in Asia and in almost every astute analysis I read on the area's financial troubles. The city's higher education system is rapidly expanding, but its graduates are reported to be of very low quality. The fatal flaw, argues Allan Wong, an engineer educated at the University of Wisconsin and now the chairman of Vtech, one of the territory's most successful electronics manufacturers, lies in secondary schools that teach by rote rather than by training young people to solve problems creatively and to communicate clearly in English as well as in Chinese. "Some classes have forty-five to fifty students," Wong reports. "So only those in the front rows can hear the teacher. Consequently, the quality of education goes down."

What does all this say about Hong Kong's future as one of the world's investment capitals? Here's the picture I see.

Due in large part to the economic problems we've already covered and an inflation rate of nearly 10 percent, I predict that more and more Western-owned corporations will flee Hong Kong. Though they may choose to maintain a tiny office space inside a skyscraper where perhaps a hundred other companies keep a base camp cubicle, powerful businesses will choose to conduct the bulk of their research, development, and distribution elsewhere. Vtech's Allan Wong is a pioneer in this exodus. "The sharp rise in costs here is my biggest problem, so we're a virtual corporation with nearly everything based somewhere else." He means that literally. Most of his design engineers work in North America, England, or China, while his products are made in Dongguan, China.

I believe "virtual companies" are the inevitable future for Hong Kong. Thousands of them, most owned and operated by mainland Chinese businesspeople who will confiscate the city as their own semiprivate offshore tax haven. About a thousand Hong Kong businesses are already controlled by Chinese state-owned companies—up from just 400 in 1992. Hong Kong company-owned businesses currently employ 3 million Chinese workers. (That's six times the number of people those companies employ in Hong Kong.)

Don't get me wrong. Global investors will never be shut out of Hong Kong. Like other havens, the financial center will be home to an array of private banks and small businesses that eagerly welcome foreigners with assets to invest in new ventures. Westerners will still be able to make a lot of money in Hong Kong. They'll just be doing it through partnerships with invisible Chinese interests. Instead of purchasing stocks and bonds from major institutions with

Westerners will still be able to make a lot of money in Hong Kong. They'll just be doing it through partnerships with invisible Chinese interests.

household names, Americans, Canadians, and Europeans will join financial forces with brass plate facilities owned by PRC investors with international connections.

I don't see this transformation as a tragedy. If the point is to make money efficiently, legally, and discreetly, then what's to dread? Hong Kong will continue to offer those benefits, but it won't continue to function as a cultural halfway house for Western capitalists smitten with Asian market size. Hong Kong will increasingly become just another city in China. Doing business there will not insulate investors from China. Rather, it will insert them right into the mainland's social, cultural, and economic style.

CHINESE OVERSEAS: THE FIRE IN THE DRAGON'S ROAR

Hong Kong isn't the only place that affluent Chinese keep their money. Researchers tell us, in fact, that there are some 57 million Chinese living outside the mainland, and even the most conservative estimates calculate their wealth at between $2 and $3 trillion. They live mostly in Southeast Asia, but more than 1 million now live in California—the largest Chinese community outside Asia. Fully 90 percent of these "Chinese Overseas" (as they have been nicknamed) are now naturalized citizens of their adopted countries. Only one out of every fifty opts to retain Chinese nationality. Yet, orphaned and dislocated as they may be, the Chinese Overseas are an economic force to be reckoned with. Indeed, they have been called the greatest entrepreneurs in the world. Those are grand words, but I think they may well be deserved.

Let me use some numbers to convey the power these people hold. In 1994 the Chinese-language *Forbes Zibenjia* studied the top 1,000 companies from ten Asian stock markets. Their combined assets totaled $1.14 trillion—that was 89 percent of total market capitalization. More than half those companies (517, to be exact) had a Chinese Overseas as their single largest stockholder. That means ethnic Chinese controlled $541 billion—some 42 percent of the total capital in these ten markets.

The figures become all the more stunning when you stop to consider that Chinese make up only a small percentage of the population in each of the countries where they reside, yet they control an incredible amount of the economy. For example, in Malaysia they represent barely 30 percent of the population but control more than 60 percent of the economy. The numbers elsewhere are even more remarkable. Chinese make up just 3.5 percent of the Indonesian population but control 73 percent of the country's economy. In Thailand Chinese are 10 percent of the population, yet they own 81 percent of all publicly listed companies. And in the Philippines Chinese account for a minuscule 2 percent of the population but control between 50 and 60 percent of the Filipino economy.

What about all the small and midsized companies that constitute 96 percent of the economic life in the Asian-Pacific Economic Cooperation (APEC) realm? Fully 90 percent of them are owned by Chinese Overseas!

If you counted the economic activity of all Chinese Overseas as a country, it would rank third in the world—surpassed only by the United States and Japan. Where do you suppose these investors tend to put most of their money? You got it: venture partnerships and sole business ownerships in mainland China. In fact, the Chinese Overseas already account for slightly more than 80 percent of all foreign investment in China. Even as far back as 1995 estimates put the number of people in China employed by Chinese Overseas businesses at 20 million. A more recent figure is not available, but you can be sure it's increased.

What accounts for these amazing statistics? In his extraordinary book on modern Asia, *Megatrends Asia*, John Naisbitt provides at least a part of the answer. "The Chinese Overseas are not a nation-state, and the vocabulary and concepts used to think about nation-states will not help us understand the phenomenon," he writes. They are, instead:

> a network of networks . . . a new formulation within the framework of the world's economy. All key players among the Chinese Overseas know one another. Their businesses stay singularly apart, but they work together when necessary. They are intensely competitive among themselves and exclude outsiders, especially those not of the same family, village or clan. When crisis arises or a great opportunity presents itself, they will close ranks and cooperate. Chinese business boils down to people and contacts. As one Hong Kong banker puts it, "If you are considered for a new partnership, a personal reference from a respected member of the Chinese business community is worth more than any amount of money you could throw on the table."

The power networks that define the Chinese Overseas are not unlike the universe of Internet users. Using the Internet, you can influence (and even control) people you've never met and places you've never visited. "It is decentralized right down to the individual," Naisbitt explains. "Because of this complete decentralization, the Internet can have as many members as want to join. Similarly, the Chinese Overseas network can get as big as it needs to be to transform Asia's economy."

For Western investors the Chinese Overseas pose a unique challenge. If we are going to profit from financial associations with these people, we've got to begin understanding the way they think. First, we need to realize that they are the quintessential global players. It's been said that they are paving the way for the emergence of a truly international operating model. Long before Americans or Europeans even started to explore offshore havens, the Chinese Overseas were using them. That has given them an important edge. They have enormous sums of money safely tucked away in foreign financial centers. Rich Chinese businesspeople establish their families in comfortable neighborhoods in Vancouver, Los Angeles, or London and—after residing there themselves long enough to qualify for citizen-ship—fly to and from Asia like most of us commute back and forth from work each day, managing their interests from small offices set up in one or more cities in the Far East. Or they stay home and use electronic media to control their collection of profitable business ventures spread throughout the Pacific Rim.

I find it so odd that Western governments (along with most Western investors) habitually think and talk about China in political terms. Elected officials and network news anchors regularly sensationalize the growing military threat of China. Yet half of the mainland's military force is directly engaged in doing business and shows more interest in bottom-line profits than in combat training. Since 1984 China's People's Liberation Army (PLA) has set up more than 20,000 companies with profits of about $5 billion. That makes the PLA the largest and most profitable commercial empire in China. By some estimates as many as half of China's military personnel are involved in nonmilitary, commercial activity. Citicorp has invested in the 999 Pharmaceutical Company, which is part of the PLA's San Jiu Enterprise Group. Other successful PLA businesses include Guangzhou's three-star hotels, the best karaoke bars, the best bus route between Guangzhou and Shenzhen, and Shenzhen's fastest growing securities company. Baskin-Robbins works with a military-run firm to sell its ice cream throughout the mainland. Westerners need to wake up and see not what will happen in China but rather what is already happening.

Bᴜʏɪɴɢ ᴀɴᴅ Sᴇʟʟɪɴɢ ɪɴ ᴀ $10 Tʀɪʟʟɪᴏɴ Mᴀʀᴋᴇᴛ

A new, consumer-minded middle class the size of which the world has never seen is emerging in China. A 1995 Gallup poll reveals that 1 billion Chinese want to become rich and use their money to buy televisions, washing machines, refrigerators, and video cameras. Asked how they intend to acquire this kind of buying power, 64 percent of those polled said they will "work hard and get rich." The old China is gone. In fact, when reminded of it, only 4 percent of mainland Chinese agreed with Mao's famous precept: "Never think of yourself. Give everything in service to society."

Traditionally a country's buying power has been determined by measuring per capita income. To get that figure economists historically converted the value of the country's gross domestic product into U.S. dollars at the official exchange rate. In recent years financial experts have concluded that the resulting figures don't mean much. In 1993, eager to find a more accurate method of measurement, the International Monetary Fund devised a new approach, coming up with what they call "purchasing power parity" (PPP). Put simply, the Fund now calculates how much, say, a gallon of milk, television, or tube of toothpaste costs in other currencies. Calculating China's national output based on this PPP method, China was found to have produced $1.7 trillion in goods and services in 1992—far more than the $400 billion previously estimated. Using modern methods of estimation, some economists have tabbed the country's per capita income at around $4,000. If that figure is to be taken seriously, then China currently has a $4.8 trillion economy. By the year 2000, we're told, per capita income should be at least $6,000 and the economy worth $7.2 trillion—equal to today's entire U.S. economy.

Armed with this information, companies from around the world have tried to set up shop in China and garner even a fraction of its emerging market. Unfortunately, many of them have failed precisely because there's too much competition for the same customers. Talk to Jean C. Monty, chief executive of Northern Telecom Ltd. Since agreeing to a sweeping $130 million investment plan in 1993, Nortel has been wholeheartedly committed to China. To date it has built a factory to make state-of-the-art switches, forged a raft of research-and-development tie-ups with government institutes, and secured a solid foothold in China's $13 billion telecom-equipment markets.

Then why is Monty upset? Because Nortel is barely breaking even. All its major rivals—Lucent Technologies, Alcatel, Ericsson, NEX, and Siemens—have built their own plants. Instead of battling the five competitors that he expected back in 1993, he's up against twelve. "We all built to capacity and killed the price levels," confesses Monty. "That's fundamental economics." Unfortunately, he doesn't see things getting much better any time soon. Neither do executives at McDonnell Douglas, Peugeot, BellSouth, or the Japanese retailer Yaohan—all of whom have been burned on big investments in China.

As you make your way through the global investment world, don't get suckered into believing that the mainland's size and wealth translate into certain profits. For one thing, the communist government—despite all its loosening of the economic sphere—is still in charge. The party rules everything in China and is not overly fond of outsiders. It imposes import duties four times as high as the Japanese. To tap markets such as consumer electronics and automobiles, policy demands that foreign companies manufacture locally and transfer key technologies. And service sectors like banking, media, and telecommunications? They're virtually off limits. Officially, China isn't capitalist. It's a "socialist market economy." That really means a nation saddled with 110,000 overstaffed, inefficient, money-losing state industries.

Then there's the issue of entree into the Chinese marketplace. How do you get your foot in the door? China's business world operates according to complex interlocking circles of personal contacts. Even industrious Chinese are stymied by the exclusionary implications of *guanxi*. It's even more difficult for foreigners to meet and influence the people whose support can ensure success (and whose rejection can foreshadow failure). Of course, you can purchase "red chips"—shares in companies owned by Chinese state ministries or provincial and local governments that are

traded on the Hong Kong exchange. No doubt about it:
They're the highest of the global high flyers right now. The
industrial conglomerate China Everbright International is a
case in point. It's trading at 500 times its 1995 earnings!

China now has three stock markets: Shanghai, Shen-
zhen, and Hong Kong. All three are soaring. If you include
Taiwan's Taipei market, Chinese stock markets are only
going up. Many observers think that Shanghai's stock market
is one of the hottest in the whole world. In 1996 alone shares
on the market were up an impressive 65 percent. But an
interesting fact is that only PRC citizens were able to reap
the 65 percent. Foreigners had to be satisfied with a 40 percent return. To help you understand the discrepancy, I'll
walk you through a brief history of how stock exchanges in
China operate in 1997 (and for the foreseeable future).

First of all, the Shanghai stock market is a baby. It
opened its doors in 1991, more than forty years after the
communists closed down the original Shanghai market. The
notoriously xenophobic government mandated two different
classes of shares: "A" shares for Chinese citizens, "B" shares
for foreign investors. Basically, the B shares are a convenient way for the Chinese to raise foreign capital. Both A and
B shares fluctuate wildly, but A shares trade in U.S. dollars,
while B shares are in the local currency, renminbi.

In terms of size the A market is giant compared to the
B market. By early 1997 the 287 companies on the Shanghai
exchange had a total market capitalization of $15 billion,
while the B market had a total of just $1.9 billion in forty-
three companies. Although there's some overlap of companies in the two markets, shares can sometimes perform very
differently in one than the other. Direct Pacific Financial Services notes that "if the share of Lujiaizui, a large real estate
developer in Shanghai, is rising on the A market, that does
not mean that the B share price will rise as well."

The bottom line is fairly simple if somewhat frustrating:
As a U.S. investor, you should not look for open arms to wel-

Recent history suggests that communist leaders would prefer industrial stagnation over progress spurred by foreign partnerships. Still, fortunes will be made in China—by Chinese investors and outsiders alike.

come you to mainland China. The government is not eager to share its market potential with outsiders. Indeed, recent history suggests that communist leaders would prefer industrial stagnation over progress spurred by foreign partnerships. Still, fortunes will be made in China—by Chinese investors and outsiders alike. If you want to buy into this inevitability, you may be able to purchase Shanghai B shares simply by contacting your current broker and asking if the brokerage company trades on the market. Many do.

While on the phone, ask what your broker knows about particular companies. Just to get the conversation started, here are what I consider (at least for the moment) to be three good bets:

- Consider Erdos Cashmere, the world's largest producer of integrated cashmere with a central base in Inner Mongolia. Its current market capitalization is about $70 million, and shares are selling at just $0.63 apiece.

- There's the Shanghai Lujiaizui Development Company, which has a market capitalization of $354 million with shares going for about a $1 each. Important PRC financial institutions (including the Shanghai Stock Exchange itself) will be relocated soon, igniting a need for real estate developers. I think Lujiaizui's sheer size and well-earned prominence will position it to lead the pack.

- Another company that might be worth holding for the future is the Shanghai Dajiang Group, the largest vertically integrated chicken meat processor in all of China. The company is starting to diversify, and its export sales to Japan are already 30 percent of China's total chicken meat exports to that country.

I think you generally would be better off sticking with the Hong Kong market. Now back in the "motherland's embrace," it will easily remain the preferred capital market for state-run, mainland enterprises. What's more, says top policymaker for China's securities industry, Ma Zhonghi, it will give non-Chinese investors their first real chance to benefit from the strong growth of the mainland economy. The Hang Seng Index for the Hong Kong Stock Market surged 343 percent in 1996.

Because information and situations change so fast, I prefer not to recommend specific stocks. But be forewarned: There are many big losers on the Hong Kong exchange. Far too many Western investors are willing to rush in, pockets wide open, without proper research to back up titillating claims about profit potential. How can you find those few diamonds in the rough? In my view, you should let other people do the sorting for you. Instead of purchasing specific red chips, go through a savvy mutual fund manager who's thoroughly versed in the Chinese and East Asian markets. You can identify such people through conversations with business associates, attorneys, and accountants and even reading magazine racks. Place some phone calls and begin gathering information. Look until you find someone who's enthusiastic but realistic about China.

Perhaps most important, look for a mutual fund that sees the consumer power of China's "chuppies" (that's the mainland's yuppie contingent). By the year 2010 the working wealthy of the PRC will have close to $10 trillion to spend on making that dream come true. One could argue that they'll have an easier time than most realizing their goal. In China, families are still subsidized by the government, so they have more spending power than their incomes might suggest to a Westerner.

Taking a bottom-up approach, here are a few industries destined to do well.

Education

Private kindergartens and elementary schools are popping up all across China in a mad frenzy to prepare children for the challenge of building a solidly middle-class lifestyle for themselves when they reach adulthood. Equally significant: The country is ending the system that assigns every college and university graduate to a job. "Mandatory assignments cannot meet the needs of the market-oriented economy," is how a spokeswoman for China's State Education Commission put it. The new arrangement will force graduates to swap the option of state-sponsored education for the responsibility of finding their own jobs after graduation. This will give rise to numerous private schools—many of them modeled after and owned by Western academic institutions. I believe that an investment in good, responsible, technology-oriented education (at every level) stands to make a lot of people very rich.

Insurance

"In terms of life insurance, China represents the end of all roads," says Andres Kabel, National Mutual Asia's chief executive of finance. Chinese providers are benefiting from the country's newfound wealth, and foreign players have started to watch the market with the look of hungry predators. U.S. and European insurers are among those waiting to pounce. Asia Inc. reports, "In 1992, according to Swiss

Co., 35 percent of the world's $1.47 trillion insurance busi-
ness was written in the United Sates, 31 percent in Europe
and 22 percent in Japan. The rest of Asia represented just
5 percent of the global market. But within 10 years, China
will be the world's biggest insurance market." The veteran
American firm American International Assurance (AIA),
which is a wholly owned subsidiary of American International Group, is already writing new policies at the rate of
55,000 a month. If Prudential, State Farm, and Firemen's are
smart, they'll start teaching their top sales representatives to
speak Chinese. Their stockholders will love them for it.

Leisure Activity

Like every middle-class market, China is fascinated with fun
and sun. With more money than ever to spend on the non-
essentials, mainland residents are discovering the joys of
luxury hotels and fast food dining. There are already 107
McDonald's restaurants in China, including five of the ten
busiest of the chain's drive-through restaurants. McDonald's
opened four new franchises in Beijing in one weekend in the
summer of 1995. The city now has thirty, and the company
plans to open 100 new restaurants in the city by 2003 and
more than 600 nationwide.

Health clubs are the new sensation among Chinese professionals. That creates incredible investment opportunity in
companies that manufacture indoor exercise equipment,
designer workout shoes, clothes, gym bags, and the healthy-
lifestyle products that go with them—everything from gra-
nola bars to vitamin supplements and yoga mats.

Travel is booming throughout much of Asia as the Chinese find it more possible to visit relatives who live far away
or simply to vacation in luxury. For example, more tourists
from China visited Malaysia in 1993 than did tourists from
the United Sates. "I've never seen anything like it," boasts
Brendon Ebbs, senior vice president of Choice Hotels, a U.S.

company and the world's largest midrange chain. "We're seeing our hotels mushroom in all of these countries. Over the next ten years, there is virtually unlimited growth for us in Asia."

Airlines are enjoying similar profits. Ten years ago executive-class cabins were the exclusive domain of Western business travelers and wealthy Americans on vacation. Today Chinese flyers are increasingly the ones sitting in those first-class seats. The International Air Travel Association predicts that Asian traffic (much of it in and out of China) will grow 7 percent each year between 1991 and 2010. Asia will represent 39.2 percent of world traffic in 2000. By 2010 it will have surged to over half! No wonder the people who build and fly planes are smiling.

These are not the only exciting investment vehicles available in China. They just head the list. So you've got your work cut out for you. The mainland is a bit like a pirate's underground den—plagued by danger and mystery, loaded with treasure. As I have suggested before, hire a reputable consultant to help you make your way through the dark cavern.

THE NEW CHINA

I'm writing this book in 1997, a symbolic time for China. In Hong Kong colonial rule has just ended. When Macau returns to China in December 1999, the final chapter of Western domination in Asia will be over and done. For the first time in centuries China will be run entirely by the Chinese. This is more than a ceremonial change. It will have very real implications for us all. Things have already begun to change, and, like delirious bell ringers, the Chinese are anxious to declare from the rafters their autonomy and economic might.

Let's be clear: There's little protection for foreigners investing in China. The communist government heaps heavy demands on outside businesses. Companies are shaken down by local officials, whipsawed by policy swings, railroaded into bad partnerships, and squeezed almost to death for technology. Since they aren't legally allowed to take equity, it's not clear what their rights actually are—or in what form they'll see a return on their money. Many fear that they have been invited in for only the smaller, initial chunk of a project (which requires heavy investment) and not for the later phases, where the real profits will be made. To add injury to insult, foreign businesses are frequently asked to pay for things that Western protocol would term inappropriate. Beijing recently asked one foreign partner to contribute $18 million for the construction of executive offices that will be filled mostly by Chinese staff.

Yet for any global-minded investor China is the last stop on the line. The buck stops here. If you care enough about your own financial security to be reading this book, I predict that China's limitless potential will get the better of you sooner or later. So get prepared!

CHAPTER 7

E-MONEY

The Wonders of the Web

People buy and sell blips on an electronic screen. They deal with people they never see. . . . They sit and look at screens. It's almost like modern warfare.

— FELIX ROHATYN, LAZARD FRÈRES

Y ou have a choice to make as we embark on our collective journey into the brave new age of cyberspace and twenty-first-century investment. Savvy investors can either join the rush to be part of this phenomenal revolution or continue to invest the old-fashioned way, working with experts they know and trust. Whichever way you decide to go, I believe it is critical that you get a good sense of what's going on in cyberinvesting.

First you need to understand that money now moves at the speed of light. In today's world of electronic data transfers, of a rapidly proliferating Internet and instantaneous, twenty-four-hour trading, money has become a photon moving invisibly through the ether of the electrosphere.

In today's world of electronic data transfers, of a rapidly proliferating Internet and
instantaneous, twenty-four-hour trading,
money has become a photon moving invisibly through the ether of the electrosphere.

Five out of every six dollars that move in the world
economy are involved in electronic transfers, say the au-
thors of *Global Dreams*, Richard J. Barnet and John Cavanagh. As they note, "$2 trillion a day travels across the street
or across the globe at unimaginable speed as bits of electronic information." State-of-the-art information technology
now drives economic and financial decisions and moves vast
sums of money at the stroke of a key. Learning how to operate at the velocity of this high-speed world and how to
access reliable information in this fast-moving environment
is vital to your financial survival.

In the past we thought of money as coins and bank
notes. Now I often refer to it as e-money. The vast global networks and computer systems operated by international
banks and trading houses have become the preferred means
of moving assets. We now rely more and more on the speed
of the Internet and the World Wide Web to keep track of the
financial information we require in order to make our life-or-
death investment decisions.

Perhaps it's trite to say, but information is worth as
much as money itself. This has never been more true than
in the financial services industry. In the international arena
you are always looking for that one thing that will give you
an advantage over the next guy. As Barnet and Cavanagh
observe, "Financiers have always profited from advances in
communication. Nathan Mayer Rothschild employed car-
rier pigeons to bring him advance news of the Battle of

Waterloo, and the timeliness of information was literally worth a fortune."

We now have a way to access information unlike anything ever available or even conceivable before in financial history. We have the Internet. Knowing how to use this tool can make the difference between profit and loss. However, as Jamie Kiggen, managing director of Bears Stearns, points out, "There's a lot of wonderful financial information on the Internet if an investor knows what to look for. But taking everything you read on the Net at face value can be dangerous."

We are all familiar with the hype surrounding this modern resource. Many of us are aware that there are already more than 100 million Web sites, with the number sure to grow by leaps and bounds in just the coming months. Eighty million people all over the world use the Internet for various tasks—everything from e-mail to shopping—and every day more and more investors are using the Net to invest online. In fact, serious investors are rushing online. Whether it is in the form of individual investors who like to be self-sufficient, the rapidly proliferating investment clubs modeled after the Beardstown Ladies, or the nearly 500,000 followers of the very popular Motley Fool site on America Online and the Web, investors have turned their attention to cyberspace with a vengeance.

Think of Ken Heaton, a casual acquaintance of mine, who has an Internet-oriented investment club called the "gang of four" based in Ojai, California. He and his friends were hanging out at his house one fine summer day, surfing the Net, when they came across an interesting piece of information about a disk drive computer company based in Utah.

A friend and occasional investor (an East Coast real estate agent with whom they had shared investment information in the past) told the group via e-mail that his mother and father had recently been in Utah on vacation and, driving by the company's main plant, saw that the parking lot was full. Instinctively the "gang of four" knew they had identified something special, a piece of information that could be worth some real money. They huddled and made a decision to get in touch with their brokers. They purchased shares of the company, which were selling at $2 at the time. To their delight, the shares are now at $27. The "gang of four" has since surmised that the company was gearing up to produce a brand-new disk drive.

As Heaton says, "That's the kind of information you won't find on a company prospectus. And that's what so fabulous about the Net: It's immediate; it's ahead of the curve." Heaton's portfolio speaks for itself. Since early 1995 his holdings have grown from $97,000 to $250,000.

Another person who has seen the Net make a huge difference in his portfolio is Bapcha Ramamurthy. As profiled in *Smart Money* magazine, Ramamurthy is one of the "original members of the cult of Internet investors." He started looking at newsgroups on the Net as long ago as 1994 but has since abandoned that and works with a "private e-mail-based investing group of forty people, mainly like-minded 'Usenet refugees.'" Ramamurthy now goes straight to the SEC's Edgar database, where he directly examines 10-Ks, 10-Qs, and insider trading filings on companies he either owns or is seriously looking to buy in the near future.

"It's full disclosure," Ramamurthy says. "Accountability in an online source is a must." Just as important as his methods is the fact that he goes online for only ten to fifteen minutes every day. As he points out, "Time is money." People don't have to be welded to their computers to make money and get information via the Net.

The Net's real value is the tremendous amount of information it holds. For instance, while on the Net you can find out which countries and stock exchanges are hot, which are not, and which are going to be hot or cold in the near future. Beyond that, much of the best information available on the Internet is so fresh and current that it can help put you in the same information league as the big-time financial analysts. Best of all, most of this information is available for

free. If you have Internet access, you're halfway there as far
as the cost of online research and investing is concerned.

My job in this chapter is to help you learn how to best
utilize the Internet in your personal pursuit of wealth. I want
to walk you through some key sites and other electronic
resources that can help you make sound decisions about
global and international investments. Although there is a lot
of content on the Net, it is often out of date, too minimal to
bother with, or simply wrong. Many Web pages, for example,
have not been updated for a year or even longer. A perfect
example is the Web site called the *Detectives Guide to Financial Information*. This supposedly great site hasn't been
updated since the fall of 1994! Old information is the bane
of any investor, but especially the international investor,
who needs to know the latest data at a moment's notice.

Even more frightening is the sobering reality that many
people have been scammed and shortchanged through
bogus information posted intentionally on the Net. In addition, there is a sometimes a steep price to be paid in terms of
lost personal privacy. These are real concerns, and I will
walk you through both the pitfalls and the benefits of the
e-money world. As always, keep in mind that things always
change, and with lightning speed, in the world of electronic
information. I hope this chapter will help you avoid the
worst problems.

Much of the best information available on
the Internet is so fresh and current that it
can help put you in the same information
league as the big-time financial analysts.
Best of all, most of this information is available for free.

Using the Net

The latest, most up-to-date information is the most precious commodity when dealing with the international market. My personal investing experience has shown me that current data makes the critical difference when investing overseas. But is there a place where one can go for the most current information for international investing? Thanks to the wonders of the Web, the answer, for the moment, is simple: http://www.ifc.org or http://www.emgmkts.com.

The latest news on stock markets in the big emerging markets is now just a click away. The International Finance Corporation (IFC) is a member of the World Bank Group. As IFC's home page states, it is "the world's leading multilateral source of loan and equity financing for private sector projects in developing countries."

If you call up the IFC's Web site address (or URL, for Uniform Resource Locator), you immediately go to a home page that shows you a globe in the middle of a box surrounded by various text links. You can click "About IFC" and learn more about the corporation. There are nine other links, including one that says EMDB (Emerging Markets Data Base). If you click the EMDB button, you quickly go to a page that gives you eight more choices from which to select: Weekly Market News, Product Information, IFC Indexes, Frequently Asked Questions, Technical Notes, Special Announcements, Links, and Daily Market Feed.

The Web is a layered medium. Let's say you use Netscape Navigator as your Web browser. You can enter http://www.ifc.org, click, and then have the IFC home page open. Then, by clicking EMDB, you are soon scrolling down the EMDB page and reading that "IFC's Emerging Markets Data Base serves as a vital statistical resource for the international financial community." Within half a minute you have found your way to the number one Web source for reliable and comprehensive information on forty-five stock markets in the world's top developing countries.

Let's say that on the EMDB page you select IFC Indexes. This is what the EMDB page notes: "IFC's Investable Indexes were introduced in March 1993 and are designed to meet the increasingly sophisticated needs of international investors. Adjusted to reflect the accessibility of markets and individual stocks for foreign investors, the IFC Investables offer the ideal performance benchmark for both active and passive investors."

You also have a selection of three time series of emerging market stock data. The Stock Series gives you current data on more than 1,800 stocks in thirty-one emerging markets in Latin America, East Asia, South Asia, Europe, the Mideast, and Africa. If you use this series you will get information on prices, changes in capitalization, trading volume, and valuation ratios. There are also the Index Series and the Market Series.

Let's say you want to check out the IFC Investable Indexes. Click on the link, and up come five pages of tables that include a price index and total return index for the thirty-one main emerging markets in 1988 U.S. dollar terms.

If you decide to see what's been going on with Brazil, for example, you will find out that by using a sample of sixty-eight stocks in that market, IFC has calculated an index of stock market performance that will give you a benchmark that is "consistent across national boundaries." For the international investor this is critical information. By the way, you can also get the Indexes in terms of Japanese yen.

For now let's imagine that you decide to stay with U.S. dollar terms. The Index for Brazil tells you that the Price Index for today was 600.07. It was 592.73 the day before. The one-day percentage change is +1.2, and the year-to-date percentage change is +51.4. Then you look at the Total Return Index, which shows that today it's 802.15; it was 792.34 on the previous day; the one-day percentage change was +1.12, and its year-to-date percentage change was +54.7. Not bad. In fact, of the seven Latin American stock markets analyzed in the IFC Investable Indexes, Brazil seems to be doing the best.

Next you may decide to look at the South Asia Index. It lists six countries: India, Indonesia, Malaysia, Pakistan, Sri Lanka, and Thailand. You can see at a glance that the Indian and Sri Lankan stock markets give the best return, while Thailand's Total Return Index shows that its year-to-date percentage change is -42.3. It is the worst performer in the South Asia group.

This is information an investor can use. It's timely and accurate, exactly what you need to help you make wise decisions. The tables also give you a composite index for the four emerging market regions as well as an overall regional index for Latin America and Asia as a whole. If you go to this site every day for a couple of weeks, you'll begin to get the pulse of these markets. This is invaluable as you chart your investment course on a global basis.

Now, that's what you get by clicking IFC Investable Indexes. You can still go back to the EMDB home page and click Weekly Market News and Daily Market Feed as well as the five other choices to get even more information. It really depends on what you want to find out given your personal investment strategy and plan. And remember: This is but one button you can click on the overall IFC site.

The IFC is just one alternative. Another one that comes highly recommended (and was cited by *Smart Money* magazine as a worthwhile site for economic data on emerging markets) is the Emerging Markets Companion at http://www.emgmkts.com. This site provides extensive links to foreign governments and development banks in different regions. It also posts "relevant business news from all the world," according to *Smart Money*.

If you open the location for the Emerging Markets site you immediately go to the home page. You might look it over and decide to review "Website content." You click there and instantly have the chance to see what's on the whole site. There are headline business news reports from Reuters, Bloomberg, and Bridge Financial News; market summaries;

international business cycle analysis; investment strategies from NatWest markets, and on and on.

You click the Emerging Markets research section and then click country profiles. You are delivered to an extensive list of all the emerging markets. If you click the Czech Republic, up comes a seven-page in-depth report on everything from the economy by sector to the form of government, population, you name it. For sheer volume of useful information this is an A+ site that seems up to the minute.

As I mentioned earlier, current information is the key. Now, with Web sites such as IFC and the Emerging Market Companion, finding a stock market report for Zimbabwe or Portugal is as easy as getting stock information on Microsoft. That's an inarguable plus for the international investor.

Another way to go for information is to take a look at Usenet groups. These groups (called "newsgroups") are basically anything-goes raw information bulletin boards. The information you find here is unedited, unverified, and can verge on the outlandish. There are about twenty to twenty-five investment-oriented newsgroups on the Net, the most popular being misc.invest.stocks. You can also visit misc. invest.funds and misc.invest.technical. If you decide to go to these newsgroups, be warned: You may well find as many as 5,000 messages posted about everything from the latest gossip about high-tech firms in Silicon Valley to news about a new breakthrough pending at a biotech company to miscellaneous items about companies that went out of business quite some time ago.

On the plus side, you can find good information in newsgroups about how other freelance and individual investors are putting together their investment portfolios as well as some solid background on trading and, once in a while, good critiques on financial topics. On the down side, you will get reams of junk e-mail filled with pushy hustles and sell jobs on everything from erotic videos to nutty get-rich-quick schemes. The worst thing about newsgroups is that they are often filled with what I call e-trash about stocks, dubious information being put out on the newsgroups by people who own the stocks.

A friend of mine once posted a notice about a handful of companies in the biotech sector that he thought had great potential. Within minutes he received all types of messages; some people were even nice, but most flamed him. (For the Net neophyte, a "flame" is a put-down message sent anonymously from one person to another via e-mail.)

The key to using newsgroups is to understand that you have to plow through a lot of junk to find something worthwhile. I can say with some experience based on many late nights working with my laptop that the patient and unflappable newsgroupie can find postings from other investors that just might be worthwhile.

If the wild west nature of newsgroups is not for you, you might look into mailing lists, also known as listservs. Probably about fifty to sixty of these have to do with investing. Anyone with a valid e-mail address can log on. If you go to the Web and do a search of either http://www.list.com or http://www.reference.com, you will receive various mailing lists and learn how you can subscribe to them as well as cancel if you feel you need to quit a particular list. Once you see a list you like, such as Greatstocks or Investors, simply send an e-mail message to the listserv or mailing list and let it know that you want to subscribe. From that moment until you decide to quit, you will receive an e-mail message every time a member of the list sends one to the whole group or list. You have the option of sending a message to the whole group by sending it to the listserv's main address. These lists can be time consuming. Be ready to receive a hefty number of daily e-mail messages, sometimes on the order of fifty to a 100 a day.

If mailing lists don't seem like your cup of tea, you can discuss investment topics online in what are called chat rooms, which are very different from mailing lists. A chat room is a place where people can engage in real-time online conversations. You can use a browser such as Netscape Navigator to find a chat room. If you use a specific search engine such as Yahoo, you'll probably need to download some specified software to visit one of the best chat rooms, http://chat.yahoo. com. One problem with chat rooms is that sometimes chatters are impolite or don't stay on the topic of discussion.

You might think getting all this information is great, but how do you actually invest in overseas stocks via the Net? As I noted earlier, it does take some effort to invest internationally.

Buying foreign stocks is still somewhat difficult. Until recently you could either buy stock in those foreign corporations that already listed their shares on a U.S.-based exchange, or you had to trust U.S.-based mutual funds to make the best choices of foreign stocks. Fortunately the Web is starting to provide an alternative. While purchasing offshore stocks from within the United States is still time consuming, one site allows you to trade shares right over the Internet: Electronic Share Information's Web site at http:// www.esi.co.wk.

It's important to learn how to use Internet investment resources, and the best way to learn is to jump right in and start clicking away. At present these resources are research tools for the international investor, not investment media. Someday they will offer overseas online trading, just like domestic electronic brokerage houses. That day has yet to come, but it will.

My advice is this: Learn how to use the Net to help you dig into the fundamentals of online investment and trading. Master the art of investment research that is now available. If you follow this advice you will be there when the Internet explodes with international trading opportunities and tools. Remember, the Internet was created in the United States but is becoming a global resource with a growing international base of users. When that day comes—and I believe it will very soon—you will be ready to take full advantage of it if you begin operating on the Internet now.

Wave of the Future

The world of online investing is exploding. Just a few days ago I was skimming through a slick financial publication when I saw an ad with an eye-grabbing picture of a fierce-looking dog baring its sharp fangs. It got my attention, so I read the tag line: "Don't let high commissions bite your assets." Sounded interesting. I stopped and began reading the whole ad. It said, "Unleash your future with E*Trade. Now you can place trades and access the latest market intelligence through your PC or telephone—around the clock—without paying high commissions."

This aggressive approach is a trademark of E*Trade, an online brokerage house that allows investors to buy and sell stocks for $14.95 per trade. With a click of your mouse you can now access the market without using a broker. E*Trade is part of a new trend toward online trading. The number of online accounts is forecast to grow from about 1.5 million in 1997 to more than 10 million by the year 2001. (For comparison purposes, Americans now have about 60 million brokerage accounts.)

The cyberleader in this latest online frenzy is E*Trade. The president of E*Trade, Christos M. Cotsakos, expects his company to be one of the first electronic financial services firms to hit $1 billion in revenue by the turn of the century. Keep in mind that it only launched its current e-trading business in early 1996. To go from zip to $1 billion in four years is extraordinary.

From Cotsakos's point of view E*Trade is reinventing the financial services industry. As reported on *Communications Wire*, "E*Trade's online services let consumers trade and invest in stocks electronically. . . . The $51 million company is posting a 10 percent growth in its 112,000-strong customer base. E*Trade expects to add mutual fund income securities and full cash management services in the near term, with several initial public offerings over the Internet and underwriting, long term." Keep in mind that when E*Trade went public in August 1996 the stock opened at $10.50. Recently, due to a remarkably strong earnings report, the stock went to $18. Something is happening, and all investors need to know that things will never be the same again in the brokerage world.

With more than 10,000 Internet-based trades per day and "a startling 500 accounts and $8 to $10 million in new assets each day" according to *Fortune* magazine, E*Trade has changed the face of the securities industry. The story of how E*Trade became the cyberleader of online trading or why *Money* magazine named E*Trade the "Best Cyberspace Broker" and *PC Computing* awarded E*Trade its "Most Valuable Product Award" is the story of how the world of investing is going online at the whirlwind speed of a bullet train hurtling through the quiet French countryside.

E*Trade is what is called a secure online trading center. It is very simple to use. To set up your own account, you simply send in your basic personal information plus a check for $1,000 (the minimum balance). The company then sends you a password, and you're ready to trade. Ultimately, the fate of E*Trade and all of online trading will depend on how the Internet shakes out. At this point things look like they're going to continue on an upward growth trajectory.

As Bill Ford, of General Atlantic Partners and an E*Trade member, points out, we will see a migration of more and more trading to the online arena. As E*Trade's Cotsakos likes to say, it's an example of "information and speed changing an industry." I predict that we will see the same type of operation—it might even be an offshoot of E*Trade itself—going global before the end of the century.

To see how all this information technology can be pushed onto the global stage, let's look at a company called Cyberian Outpost. This is a fully transactional online retailer that has jumped into the international market fray by selling computer products on a global basis.

In early March of 1997 Cyberian Outpost kicked off its new international Web site, which takes orders for its products in ten languages, with more languages to be added over the next few months. For globally savvy observers, note that Cyberian also links its new site to Olsen & Associates' "164 Currencies Converter" and makes it possible for customers to track an order from the United States to global outposts.

Founder and president Darryl Peck predicts that his company, which now earns $2 million in revenues per month, will be a $1 billion business within five years. Sound too good to be true? One industry analyst thinks Peck may be thinking too small. Denise Sangster, who heads the Global Channel Consulting Group in Berkeley, California, told the *New York Times* cyber section that Cyberian Outpost "could possibly even go higher."

This will kill the European counterparts. European computer prices are routinely 20 to 30 percent higher than in the United States, and if you can reduce overhead charges of having operations overseas—in effect working as a virtual European company—you're in business." Sangster predicts that like everything else in cyberspace, there will be a royal battle to ensure that Cyberian Outpost continues to grow as an online retail outlet. "It will be a bloodbath," she says. "Everyone will want to protect their domain, and it comes down to not just price but customer service as well. You can't exactly kick the tires and check under the hood when you buy online."

The point is that companies that position themselves to make a successful global reach will be the companies that survive the new cyberreality. Cyberian Outpost is focused on the continuing growth of the international market. It is an example of what can be done to service and ultimately control a significant share of the global market through the use of information technology. It shows investors that the wave of companies going international and online is the wave of the future.

FLIMFLAMS AND THE ONLINE THREAT TO PRIVACY

Cyberspace is amazing. It is now possible for people from all over the world to gather in chat rooms and discuss their portfolio and investment strategies. As cyberinvestors are already finding out, it's great fun and often very helpful to have a sounding board for your ideas and find out how other people are managing their assets. But there is a dark side to the Internet.

Earlier in this chapter I mentioned that wrong or skewed investment information is sometimes posted intentionally on the Net. Even worse, many scam artists have discovered that cyberspace can be a very good place to attract investors to get-rich-quick schemes. One of the most notorious false cyberschemes was the Canadian-based promotion about a diamond mine in Zaire (now the Democratic Republic of Congo). The mine turned out to exist only in the virtual world of cyberspace. There was no real mine.

Investors have to be alert for services and products being packaged as information. If you are not skeptical, you can very easily be lured into a site or financial chat room by the promise of useful information but can end up being the victim of a very risky stock tip put on the Net to help drive up the price of a specific stock for the sole benefit of an anonymous tipster.

When using online investment services and information resources, investors have to remember to check all tips and keep in mind that taking a chance on a tip can be very risky. Be skeptical is my advice to anyone who goes online. Of course, it's sometimes hard to take the time to stop and check out a tip that seems reasonable, because they usually carry a sense of urgency. Also, just being online gives a certain immediacy to the information you are reading.

The key is to be patient. Try following a stock for a while to make sure that you aren't going to be burned.

Just ask Ben Stevenson. I learned about him from a client of mine, a surgeon living in Sarasota, Florida. Ben

owns a small and prospering security alarm firm and decided about two years ago to oversee his own portfolio.
Armed with an AOL e-mail account and a sure sense of what
he wanted from the market, he started using an online brokerage firm. He was out there on the Net scouting for the
best tips and checking out financial information.

After about a year Ben had lost $12,500 of the $18,000
in his portfolio. Ben had spent a lot of time visiting newsgroups and all the latest investor-oriented sites on the Web.
One day he came across a tip from a broker who suggested
he invest in a company headquartered in Los Altos, California (located in Silicon Valley), that wired offices with fiber-
optic lines and set up Ethernet systems for small to midsized companies.

In the past Ben had seen this broker give pieces of
advice about various stocks to an investor newsgroup. They
always seemed to turn into winners. Ben e-mailed back and
forth with the broker and decided that this time he was not
going to sit idly by and see another stock shoot up in value
while he just watched. He ended up purchasing 750 shares at
$14 each. The next day the stock dropped $4.50, and before
he was through with it he had lost nearly $8,000. But it didn't
end there. Ben picked up another supposedly hot tip about
a cellular company in a chat room catering to investors interested in high-tech companies.

At first things went well. Ben bought at $11 and saw the
stock rise to $16 within a week. Then it fell and was soon
hovering at about $8. Any money he had made was lost
within a few weeks. As he said to my client afterward, Ben
thinks that the people in the chat room were all involved
with the company, owned stock, and were promoting it out
of self-interest. Wiser and a bit poorer, Ben has learned to
take every piece of advice on the Net with a big grain of salt.

Aside from misinformation and scams, beware of the
ever-growing threat to your privacy in the new information
economy. While I'm one of the first to celebrate the new
information-driven world and sincerely believe that it will be

the basis of true prosperity, I also know that within every strength lies a major weakness. In today's world of speed-of-light electronic trading and research, individual privacy is being threatened on a scale unlike anything I've ever encountered.

Marketers, researchers, and governments all over the world have an unquenchable passion for collecting personal information. One report in the *New York Times* sees this as a consequence of the need to build new customer bases and develop a wider net of consumers. "It is being spurred and sharpened by powerful market forces and ever more pervasive computer technology," reports the *Times*, "including digital mapping tools and so-called 'data-mining' software that blast commercial value from newly linked data bases of unprecedented size."

In other words, watch out. Information technology, networking, and database linking are developing so fast that it's hard to keep pace with the changes and advances. Did you know that every keystroke you make while on the Internet can be archived and recalled? When you visit a Web site or a chat room you leave tracks called "cookies." Highly organized and expert businesses spend a lot of energy collecting cookies and matching them to personal data. When the businesses put this information all together and cross-reference it against public records they have a data bank of highly personal information.

As the *Times* notes, "The electronic deposits keep growing with the pulse of daily life: telephone calls, check-out counters, ATMs and electronic bridge tolls, the street gaze of security cameras, plastic insurance cards imprinted with Social Security Numbers that have become identity's common currency—and its easy to counterfeit." Everyday transactions become another piece in the puzzle, and little by little you begin to lose control over your own privacy.

"When a clerk puts a supermarket card through the scanner," writes Nina Bernstein in an in-depth and frightening story about the loss of privacy in the *New York Times* cyber section, "a data base links the shopper's identity with the bar code on every item bought. A love of rich chocolate cookies not only can be tracked over time, but matched with an individual's address, age, weight and ethnicity, with marital status and credit standing even with religious ties, to name just a few of the personal facts being bought and sold wholesale in today's booming information market." The great technology that lets us do so much so fast can also turn on us in a millisecond.

The flip side of the brave new world of the information age is a massive and very intrusive interlinked system of personal privacy violation. Did you know that with the help of a Geographic Information System (GIS), a business can feed in the license number from a car and get back the driver's name, address, census tract information, and even demographic labels?

As Bernstein discovered in her investigation, there is a company called Acxiom based in Arkansas that has a series of rooms, like bunkers, "where six robots inside small linked silos match data tapes at 60 miles an hour, while 20 mainframe computers swallow 1.3 billion bytes of data a second. G.I.S. is just part of the information infrastructure."

My point is that you are being watched—not only by the government but also by giant information conglomerates such as Acxiom. Every time you make an e-trade, visit a chat room, send an e-mail, or otherwise conduct any kind of business within the massive information economy, it is being noted somewhere.

THE FUTURE OF ELECTRONIC INVESTING

As I said at the beginning of this chapter, we are on the cusp of a new investment world, and you have a real choice to make. You can go with the flow and move into the impersonal world of e-trading and research, or you can continue

> **M**ore and more the best decisions are be-
> coming split-second ones. Whatever you do,
> know that the electronic way of life—both
> the good and the bad—is here to stay. It's
> not going to wait for you to learn to like it.

to work with your favorite brokers, advisors, and consultants and keep the human touch in your financial life.
There's certainly something to be said for the traditional
approach. Because it's slower, it gives you time to think
through options for not just a matter of seconds but for days.
Conversation rests at the heart of methodical reasoning for
some people, and that's not a bad thing. In fact, I'd be out of
business tomorrow if investors could get all the information they need off a computer screen.

Still, there's the proverbial danger in living like an
ostrich. And there's financial loss involved in waiting too
long to decide. The real question is: How long is too long?
The answer to that question keeps changing. More and more
the best decisions are becoming split-second ones. Whatever
you do, know that the electronic way of life—both the good
and the bad—is here to stay. It's not going to wait for you to
learn to like it. It's going to define financial transfer over the
decades you still have to live and during which you have
the opportunity to prosper. This new world is literally at
your fingertips. Use it, and use it with a healthy dose of skep-
ticism and pragmatic self-interest. If you do, you will profit
from it. Who knows: You might even like training yourself
to travel at the speed of light.

CHAPTER 8

HERE'S HOW YOU DO IT

The ABCs of Going International

I looked at the marketplace and convinced my-self: You're either going to be global or you're going to be nobody.

— JAMES THORNEBURG,
NORTH CAROLINA BUSINESSMAN

A s you may have noticed, I like to tell stories. In fact, the adventures of my clients (and other characters I've met along the way) are one the best facets of my work. Watching the flexibility of the international market wrap around the unique needs of so many different investors— I find it an endless source of fascination. Most of the stories I tell involve people with a long investment future. By that I mean most investors have a lot of time in front of them, years in which to watch the global arena's endless love affairs. One year it's wild about one market, and the next it falls head over heels for another.

I want to begin this chapter with the story of Trevor Abrey, a client I met almost five years ago. Shortly before he came to see me he'd been diagnosed with prostate cancer. So Trevor wasn't willing to count on the luxury of time. He needed to make fast investment decisions, and he needed to make good ones. He also wanted to know the outcome of his portfolio plan, much the way you know exactly how a rosebud will look when it comes into full bloom as you watch the process through time-lapse photography.

When Trevor sat down in my office that first time, he looked anything but ill. An orthopedic surgeon with a very successful Los Angeles practice, he appeared to be in his early fifties, tall, and enviably trim. He carried himself almost like a model and wore clothes to fit the part: imports from his limp linen jacket all the way down to his shoes. He looked so robust and composed I could have approached him for makeover advice. But he confided in me that he was not calm or confident. He was worried. He had married for the first time just a year earlier, and his wife's son had been his best man at the wedding. "They're both counting on me," he said, "and I just won't let them down. If I can't be here in five years, or even in ten, then I need at least to ensure their financial security."

Trevor held a number of U.S. investment vehicles in his existing portfolio, but he was not sure they would be enough. Through various friends and associates he'd learned about the profits to be made in international investments, and he wanted to buy into a handful of emerging Eastern European markets. He had $90,000 to work with, he told me, and he wanted some advice about where and how to begin. His goal was simple (if a bit overly industrious): He wanted to see his assets double before he died.

My initial response was to rattle off the real obstacles he faced as a man with not much time and a lot to do. His biggest problem, I explained, was the various strict limitations placed on the rights of U.S. citizens to purchase foreign equity. In some cases, I said, those restrictions actually are written into the articles of the offshore funds that offer the stock, limiting the holding of shares or units by any person or company. For example, a fund may be physically situated in the Isle of Man, but, for various legal reasons, it may not be sold to or owned by residents of that island.

Most often, though, funds limit the participation of people designated as "U.S. persons." Foreign funds have imposed and strictly enforce this restriction because they don't want to be technically considered a public issuer within the United States. Why? Because if they were, they would be immediately subject to all the rules and regulations of the Securities Exchange Commission (SEC). In other words, if an offshore fund has more than a hundred unit/ shareholders who are deemed "U.S. persons," then that fund must register with the SEC or be found guilty of unlawfully offering foreign equity within the United States.

Of course, there were various solutions to Trevor's problem. He needed official platform within the international market, a recognized mechanism for investing and trading on a global scale. It's somewhat akin to needing a car on the freeway. The automobile is just a machine. It can't think. It can't make judgments about the best routes or worst neighborhoods. As the driver you must be responsible for all those decisions. Still, without a car you simply cannot venture onto a highway on-ramp. In that fast-speed world a car is the only acceptable means of getting from one place to another.

We talked about Trevor's options and ultimately developed a plan that would come as close as possible to meeting his needs. In Trevor's case there was a genuine sense of urgency to implementing the plan. Hopefully, you don't have to work so quickly. Still, I want to spend some time walking you through the different ways in which anyone can trade on the international markets. All the approaches that I'll cover are legal, and each of them has benefits. It's simply a matter of understanding how the approaches are different from one another and then choosing the one that best meets your needs. I'll tell you later which one Trevor chose.

ESCAPING THE U.S. SYSTEM

More than twenty-five years of experience has taught me
that ultimately the lion's share of today's global marketplace
goes to lone wolves—investors who know what they want
and aren't afraid to assume responsibility for their own
financial future.

Carlos and Inga De Santiago are those kind of people.
Unlike Trevor Abrey, who worked hard for everything—his
career, his home, his savings account—the De Santiagos
both come from fairly affluent families. While Trevor was
conservative and cautious, they were aggressive and perhaps even a little impulsive. He was concerned with methodical planning; they were concerned with staying ahead of the
mainstream investment curve.

When I met Inga and Carlos several years ago they were
still in their late twenties, and while the three of us first got
together in Cancún (where they were attending one of my
seminars on international investing), this dynamic duo was
not at all interested in the balmy nights or sun-bleached
sands of the Caribbean. They're both urbanites. Back then
they maintained two residences: a home in Santa Fe and
another in Mexico City, where he grew up. She's from Sweden and one of the most insightful investors I've ever met.
In fact, any time I've dealt with the De Santiagos, it's inevitably Inga who requested the meeting, asked the questions,
and made the decisions.

Carlos is too busy closing deals to be overly concerned
with his portfolio planning. He operates an enormously successful import-export fine art company. In the early 1990s,
as a foreign exchange student at the University of New Mexico, he saw an incredible market for Mexican art throughout the entire American Southwest. What's interesting about
Carlos is that he also thought to create a reciprocal market
in urban Mexico. Today many of the wealthiest executives
and scholars in Mexico City decorate their homes and

offices with the Pueblo Indian art that Carlos sells. The couple met while he was on vacation in Stockholm. They enjoyed a whirlwind romance and were married less than six months later.

Inga contacted my firm and registered for the Cancún seminar session because she had a sizable sum of money with which to play. You see, the De Santiagos walked into marriage with a comfortable cushion on which to sit: $200,000 that they'd received as wedding gifts from relatives and friends. I suspect that Carlos would have been happy to pump the entire amount into his business, but Inga had other plans. As a European, she was accustomed to a less restrictive investment market than what she found here in America, and she wanted far more personal financial freedom than she could have here. When I met her she was determined to escape the constraints of the U.S. banking system. She called to request a meeting, just to outline the various "platforms" they could use to invest globally. Although the De Santiagos had very different needs than Trevor Abrey, they all needed to understand the basic features of each international investment platform. And so do you.

PLATFORM NUMBER ONE: A FOREIGN BANK ACCOUNT

No doubt the simplest way to go global is to establish a foreign bank account. This single act will give you a chance to synchronize the benefits of various banking activities and blend them into a unique profit-making financial strategy. It will also offer you a high level of financial privacy.

As long as you confine your assets to U.S. banks and brokerage houses, your records are open to arbitrary review by monitoring agencies. For example, government officials can gather checks, bank statements, signature cards, loan applications, deposit and withdrawal slips, and all bank communications on you or just about anybody else. What's more, U.S. banks release records in the event of civil litigation, criminal proceedings, SEC investigations, and an IRS audit. By law U.S. banks must report all cash transactions, deposits, or withdrawals in excess of $3,000. Think about that. How many times have you put in or taken out of your account a sum this large or larger? I'm sure you've done it countless times—often just to move money from one account to another. Every one of those times Uncle Sam has been privy to your financial decisions.

If that's not enough to offend your sense of personal privacy, consider this. You are legally obliged to report any cash transfers of money across U.S. borders if they exceed $10,000. My wife and I were once approaching the border, about to drive into Canada, when I noticed that up a ways three entire lanes of cars were being stopped, one by one. My wife laughed about the Canadian government being a bit overdiligent in stopping tourists on their way in for a weekend holiday. But she stopped laughing as we got closer and realized that tourists weren't being stopped by Canadian customs. They were being stopped by U.S. border officials, who wanted a full accounting of how much cash they planned to take out of the country. I don't know about you, but this infuriated me. To deflect attention away from its inability to enforce absurd laws governing the transfer of funds internationally, the U.S. government is now all but

No doubt the simplest way to go global is to establish a foreign bank account. This single act will give you a chance to synchronize the benefits of various banking activities and blend them into a unique profit-making financial strategy.

frisking its own citizens at its borders. You have to ask your-self: Where will such ridiculous excess lead us?

Foreign banks generally let you avoid the high service costs that have become an integral part of U.S. banking. They offer very attractive interest rates, too—typically several points above what you could earn in even the most generous quarters of the U.S. scene. What's more, the longer you keep the money on deposit, the more interest you earn. Checks written from a foreign account allow you to enjoy considerable "float time," usually three or four weeks between the writing of your check and its arrival at the foreign bank for clearing. During that time, of course, you continue to earn interest on the money held in your account. This particular feature of foreign accounts has ever-increasing appeal for Americans, who find that their float time has all but vanished in the face of computerized banking transfers, debits, and credits.

Be forewarned that opening a foreign bank account has some important drawbacks. The single most obvious are that it has no tax saving element and it provides minimal financial privacy.

However, if you're still intrigued by the notion of a foreign bank account and can afford to buy a ticket into this approach, here are a few suggestions.

Select a Country and a Bank

Many reputable directories are on the market, directing you to foreign banks and global fund managers. (See the appendices for a list of referrals.) For more detailed information, read my book *The Complete Guide to Offshore Money Havens.* A lot of people select an institution without ever setting foot inside its doors. That's OK, but whether you visit or only correspond by mail, you need to gather some essential information.

- Does it offer the banking services you require? Not every facility offers every service. Make sure ahead of time that you're getting what you want and need.
- Is it the right size? In general, the larger a foreign bank, the more security it offers. Unfortunately, however, security goes hand in hand with lower interest rates and higher service fees.
- How easy is it to communicate with the bank? Will the bank's officers communicate with you in English? Are local mail, courier, and telephone services up to modern standards? In a country like Switzerland this is an irrelevant question. But in some of the more remote banking centers worldwide it can be a problem. Don't set yourself up for frustration down the line. You want to work with a facility that offers more service than U.S. banks, not less.

Start Conservatively

If you've never had an overseas bank account, begin by opening an account that's denominated in U.S. dollars. Transfer only a fraction of your assets into the account until you're sure you like the arrangement. If, after six months, you're comfortable, you can add to the account or open a different one.

Diversify

Once you feel more surefooted, you should diversify your overseas holdings. Spread out the countries in which you do your banking or at least diversify the currencies in which you invest. (The downside to diversification is that the more you have in one account, the higher the rate of interest you'll earn, and diversifying reduces the size of your account. It's important to ensure that your effective rate of interest is reduced as little as possible.)

Consider a Managed Account

For beginners a managed account is a must. Think about opening a discretionary account—one where your banker has authority to invest your funds on your behalf. Managed accounts are offered for stocks, currencies, debt instruments, commodities, or combinations of these vehicles. Of course, you'll be charged for this service, but you'll get the benefit of an expert advisor. It might be a worthwhile use of money. (By the way, never open this kind of account by mail. You must get to know your fund manager and be sure that person knows you. Only then should you trust your fund manager with your investment money.)

PLATFORM NUMBER TWO: A PRIVATE INTERNATIONAL CORPORATION

Another global investment platform is the private international corporation, or the offshore corporation. If you like the idea of actually running a foreign business, you might want to establish a manufacturing firm abroad and make

If you like the idea of actually running a foreign business, you might want to establish a manufacturing firm abroad and make your million-dollar invention concept a reality.

your million-dollar invention concept a reality. (Believe me, it's been done by people no more experienced at international business than you.)

If you're like most beginners, though, you're less confident about what you'd like to do with a private corporation. You may have absolutely no desire to assemble products or provide services in a foreign country. Most international corporate owners don't. Instead, they want to finalize the incorporation paperwork and then allow the corporation to function as nothing more than their broker in the international marketplace.

The wonderful thing about these private foreign corporations is that they can invest in stocks, commodities, CDs, foreign real estate, and foreign currencies. They can import, export, and serve as holding companies to protect patents and trademarks. All the corporation's activities and trades are done in its name; not in yours. Essentially it becomes your proxy, a phantom agent that accrues the benefits and incurs the liability for your investment choices.

A legally structured, private international corporation once offered the world's best tax-avoidance strategy. The principle behind this benefit was "tax deferral." Every year the corporation's profits were rolled over into the following year's investment pool. Nothing was owed to Uncle Sam until the owner decided to cash out and repatriate the original funds. For many years the private corporation platform provided a completely legitimate way for smart investors to avoid U.S. taxes. "You win by waiting," I used to tell clients who asked me how it worked.

But then the U.S. government figured out what was happening. Of course, the federal bureaucrats didn't like the idea of waiting to get their "fair" share of global investment profits from what it called "incorporated pocketbooks." They developed no fewer than four antideferral rules, each of which imposed harsh economic penalties on investors who deferred tax payment on any corporation deemed to be a Passive Foreign Investment Company (PFIC). To earn this title your international corporation had to either earn at least 70 percent of its income from passive activity or hold at least 50 percent of its assets for the purpose of generating passive income. That rendered virtually every privately held international corporation a PFIC.

The abuse doesn't stop there. Despite these antideferral penalties, U.S. tax authorities provided no formal mechanism by which investors could opt to annually report (or pay taxes on) their profits. On the one hand the IRS said that any investor who deferred tax payment would be penalized for not reporting sooner. On the other hand the IRS made no allowance for annual reporting. In effect the law set up PFIC owners to owe huge penalties at the time they finally chose to cash out of the investment vehicle.

The government's attitude toward PFICs is best understood if we take the example of someone driving through the city of Los Angeles on the freeway system. As you drive through the big sprawling metropolis, you often pass smaller incorporated cities. Let's imagine for a moment that you are stopped for speeding and instead of getting one ticket, you get several. One from each jurisdiction that you drove through including Los Angeles. You can see how unfair it would be to receive a ticket because you drove through Santa Monica and another because you went through Pasadena, then still another because you happened to pass through Long Beach. In the same way, the IRS penalizes PFICs on several counts to the point of rank unfairness.

Reformers have made some slight headway in reversing these contradictory policies. Finally willing to admit that its regulations conflict with one another and impose overlapping penalties that are impossible to enforce, the federal government is beginning to back down. The 1997 Taxpayers Relief Act has proposed that this catch-22 strategy be abandoned. The new law still imposes penalties on any U.S. investor who fails to report private investment corporation profits on an annual basis. However, the law would create a special reporting mechanism for these corporation owners, allowing them to pay their taxes (which are calculated at the same rate as regular income) on a year-by-year schedule.

What's the bottom line? The magical tax benefits once associated with private foreign investment corporations are gone for good. But at least investors won't be corralled into a situation that dictates inevitable monetary penalties just for owning one of these corporations.

Should you decide to pursue this platform option, it's also important to know that you can hire a professional advisory firm to operate your corporation. That means you don't ever have to step a foot outside your own borders to gain the benefits of private corporate ownership in a foreign country. In a sense the corporation is a totally preauthorized operation. Set up properly, to meet your individual needs, it can come complete with a seasoned staff of professionals who know how to help you build and manage your portfolio. If you're already familiar with the international marketplace, you're probably acquainted with several of these management firms. If you don't know how to identify them—and most people don't—talk with any reputable offshore consultant, who will be able to refer you to a number of experts (probably in Vancouver or the Cayman Islands, where many of them are based). Any of them will impress you with the wide range of investment and administrative services they have to offer.

PLATFORM NUMBER THREE: A FOREIGN ANNUITY

More than forty years ago U.S. insurance companies started to worry that business was not looking good. In a word, the market was saturated. People interested in life insurance had already purchased a policy, and while they might take out a supplemental one every now and again, there was no robust future for companies looking to make big money from the natural human instinct to secure old age and pass along assets to heirs.

The insurance giants developed a plan. They lobbied Congress and got some fascinating legislation passed. This new law made it possible for insurance companies to begin offering deferred annuities. If you're not familiar with these investment vehicles, you might want to think of them as special savings accounts with unique benefits. A deferred annuity can help you supplement your retirement savings with growth that is tax-deferred. You can think of an annuity as another financial building block especially when combined with other long-term assets you may already own. Let me be clear about the definition of the type of annuity that I am speaking about here: A deferred annuity is a contract issued by an insurance company that allows you to accumulate money on a tax-deferred basis for long-term goals. Once you're ready to take income from your annuity (this is generally when you can receive money as you need it), you can also turn your annuity's value into a regular stream of income guaranteed by the issuing insurance company. Some annuities must be purchased all at once; others can be paid for on a scheduled basis. Either way they guarantee an income for the rest of the owner's lifetime (or guarantee regular payments to the named beneficiary). The amount of money they pay out depends, of course, on the owner's age, initial lump sum and/or regular contribution size and frequency, and when the income payments are scheduled to begin.

An annuity's most attractive feature is the compound interest it earns. Here's how it works. Imagine that you had just $100 to invest, and you put it into a vehicle that would double your deposit every year. At the end of one year you'd have $200. At the end of the second year your annuity would be worth $400. A year later, $800. And so on until you chose to cash out of the project. Do you know what that $100 would be worth at the end of twenty years? A mind-boggling $50 million! Now that's what I call compounded interest!

Of course, there's no investment on earth that can compound interest at the rate of 100 percent per year. Nevertheless, many lifetime annuities offer 7 percent compounded annually, and that adds up to an impressive profit over time. For example, if you had purchased a single-payment annuity worth $10,000 in 1970 that offered a 4.75 percent annual rate of dividend compounding, it would have been worth more than $13,000 by 1976. Today it would be worth over $35,000! Best of all, by the letter of the law, all that profit would be earned tax free because it's held in the annuity!

You can imagine the delight of U.S. investors when this law went into effect. Impressive, tax-free profits. It was a combination of benefits they found virtually impossible to resist. So they didn't. In their rush to participate they reenergized the entire insurance industry. For years everybody was happy. Then a group of dissatisfied annuitants started to grumble. Why were only the insurance executives making decisions about how annuity money was invested? Shouldn't annuity owners themselves have some say over where and how their assets were put to work? Wouldn't it be worth relinquishing a relatively low, fixed interest rate for a variable one—as long as the annuity owners got to select the investment vehicles for their money? And why not get to choose from the wide array of foreign and emerging market investment opportunities that offered far more impressive performance?

So, the birth of an industry: foreign deferred variable annuities. They are a shrewd move for any investor with long-term profit goals. I'm speaking primarily about retirement. Other long-term goals can apply as well: your kids' college tuition, for example. With the purchase of an annuity from one of hundreds of reputable foreign financial institutions, you get all the benefits that any U.S. insurance company could offer—plus the added bonus of knowing that

> **W**ith the purchase of an annuity from one of hundreds of reputable foreign financial institutions, you get all the benefits that any U.S. insurance company could offer— plus the added bonus of knowing that you get to put your money to work wherever you choose, unencumbered by SEC restraints and regulations.

you get to put your money to work wherever you choose, unencumbered by SEC restraints and regulations. Foreign annuities place you in a position where you have more opportunity to gain a higher growth rate than in the United States. My personal experience with my foreign annuity is that I've been able to see my initial investment double every year. I don't know of a single U.S. investment that is comparable.

More and more Americans are opting for one (or more) of these foreign annuities because they amount to a perfect retirement strategy. They can be used to protect your assets from creditors because the return on them is unavailable for years. They protect you from possible future government attacks on domestic retirement plans, any potential failure of your pension plan, or even the possible collapse of the entire U.S. economy. They also capitalize on the world of global investing.

PLATFORM NUMBER FOUR: A PRIVATE OFFSHORE BANK

If you want the benefits associated with foreign bank accounts, private annuities, and private international corporations, you may want to consider private bank ownership.

For starters, you'd get all bank services at no charge, because you'd be your own customer. All your transactions would be handled in the bank's name, so complete confidentiality is guaranteed.

Of course, for the very cautious, it's possible to use a private bank as a discreet international broker. Essentially, it can be a one-person operation. Using its name rather than your own, you can purchase stocks and commodities from around the world and watch your profits gradually build. For the somewhat more experienced and adventuresome investor, the bank can function as an intermediary for structuring business partnerships and new ventures on virtually any continent. In either case, as long as your profits are housed within the bank, they're maintained completely tax free.

I think it would be a shame to own a bank and do nothing more with it than service your own investment needs. Like any other business, your private bank can become a vehicle for servicing other investors as well. Then it makes money just like any other financial institution. You could advertise in various international newsletters and magazines, promoting the bank's services to customers around the world. As the deposits come in, they will pass through an invisible revolving door—becoming money with which your bank offers loans to foreign (and other smart U.S.) borrowers. Within a matter of just months, the interest generated by those loans will form the basis of a handsome bottom line.

> My personal experience with my foreign annuity is that I've been able to see my initial investment double every year. I don't know of a single U.S. investment that is comparable.

I predict that you'll be ready to expand your range of services after having tasted the profits from these services. For example, once you get enough depositors, you can begin issuing letters of credit and financial guarantees. You can offer back-to-back loans. You can also provide venture capital loans at whatever interest rate the free market will allow—often as much as 10 percentage points above the comparable domestic rate.

What are the drawbacks to bank ownership? Not many. I have tried to provide a thorough examination of the topic in my book *How to Own Your Own Private International Bank*. Many people are initially intimidated by the concept because they fear their own inability to tackle such a project. But, as my book explains, you don't have to tackle it. You can hire a qualified consultant to get you started and then a professional management firm to take over the day-to-day banking operation. I think this is the way for most individual investors to go. Most of my clients, for example, have no firsthand international banking experience. My recommendation is always that they hire a top-notch firm on which they can rely for administrative functions and skilled advice. The firm can also eliminate a second drawback to bank ownership: the risk of choosing an inhospitable global center in which to establish it. All good consultants are well versed in the array of foreign jurisdictions that allow for such facilities, and they'll ensure that you're forewarned about and steered away from any disadvantageous jurisdiction.

The only real drawback to speak of is cost. It will require an initial outlay of approximately $40,000 to establish your banking charter and license. If that is money you don't have—or money you would prefer to put straight into equities and bonds—then you would be better off avoiding this investment vehicle. If, however, you're willing and able to buy a ticket into this world, I can promise you won't regret it.

Carlos and Inga De Santiago sure didn't. Ultimately, an offshore bank in Vanuatu was the international platform they chose for themselves. With that initial $200,000 to get them started, the couple were able to purchase a formal bank charter and license, and they still had plenty left over to make a number of select global equity and fixed-interest investments. They also used some of their funds to promote the South Pacific bank to a select clientele worldwide. By the end of the bank's second year its assets exceeded $1 million. Although retirement was a long way off for them, they had taken a percentage of their profits and purchased two annuities: one a lump-sum package and a second that called for regular contributions. They told me at a recent meeting that they now own a third home. This one is a 5,000-square-foot lodge located in the woods outside Stockholm. The couple anticipate being able to comfortably retire by the time they're forty-five. Inga was expecting their first baby when we talked. I guess they'll celebrate her quinceñera—the gala party that celebrates a young Mexican girl's fifteenth birthday—as extremely wealthy retirees.

It's All a State of Mind

Put simply, foreign markets can give you and your family genuine wealth protection. They offer the freedom to invest in pretty much whatever you please, because, unlike U.S.-based investment (which is plagued by bureaucratic red tape and government scrutiny), foreign investment comes complete with everything. It offers some of the most conservative, low-risk vehicles available anywhere. It simultaneously provides a treasure trove of weird, wacky, and wonderful opportunities—investments that the SEC would never approve but that are entirely safe and potentially lucrative. Indeed, to survive for any time at all, foreign investment options must maintain squeaky-clean reputations and better-than-average performance records. That's why they are the way of the future.

Remember Trevor Abrey? He was the client with too little time—or so he thought. I moved as quickly as I could for Trevor. With some guidance, he chose to purchase one large lump-sum annuity with his wife as the solitary beneficiary. He also bought an ongoing annuity for his stepson. We figured it would build a foundation for the boy, and his mom could continue contributing to it after Trevor's death.

In many ways these two annuities met this client's basic request: to provide for his family. They gave him the peace of mind that comes with knowing for certain that those he loved would be able to mourn for him without undue financial pressure adding more hardship to an already difficult time. Immediately upon his death, the annuity package would provide well over $5,000 a month to his widow. While this is not a huge number; it's far more than many affluent widows find themselves with after the U.S. tax system gets finished with their inheritance.

Hoping to provide a bit more than this basic protection, Trevor also took several thousand dollars and invested in international mutual funds that specialize in Eastern Europe (as he originally requested) and in several East Asian markets (as I strongly encouraged him to consider). In conversation we decided that should the potentially profitable but high-risk European equities bomb out, his Asian stock should provide a comfortable sum that his wife could use to supplement her annuity benefits.

The last time I talked with Trevor, he called me from California to wish me a happy New Year. He was doing far better than one might have expected. Not long after our business was concluded, he had told his wife about the cancer. Together they had used the World Wide Web to research and identify effective holistic treatments. He had decided against surgery but was working with an alternative physician in New York who has had great luck treating prostate cancer. Trevor was feeling healthy. In fact, he said, he was

running five miles a day. And he was looking forward to taking the entire summer off from work. "I'll let the other doctors in the office handle what can't be put off until fall," he
told me. "Life's too short to miss three months with my family in Portugal."

Not bad, I thought to myself as we hung up, especially
for a guy who thought five years ago that he might be dead in
eighteen months.

CHAPTER 9

THE SCHNEIDER APPROACH

Peace of mind is . . . placing your money, assets, and investments—in a dark black hole—legally beyond the reach of financial predators.

— JEROME SCHNEIDER

The great majority of global activity involves business-people and investors who are on the up and up. Most international operators are simply seeking safe harbors for their money and/or legal ways to avoid taxes; they are usually trying to take advantage of profit-making opportunities that are unavailable within the U.S. marketplace. It's hard to argue with the reasoning of such goals.

My advice, then, is to keep your eyes wide open. Check everything twice, three times even, before moving some of your assets into the global arena. But at the same time you must never forget the old adage that he who hesitates is lost. To underline the opportunities and benefits that exist right now in the international investment world, I have come up with an easy way to remember why the global option works so well.

THE FOUR MAGICAL P'S

When all is said and done, there are four major reasons to invest internationally. Profit. Privacy. Protection from excessive taxation. Playground fun. I call them the "Four Magical P's." Together they stand in stark contrast to the U.S. financial environment and constitute an almost irresistible argument for going international.

Profit

For most international investors goal number one is to generate impressive profit. That's because anybody with even modest experience in the U.S. market has learned it offers too little too late. From one year to the next, people watch the possibilities for truly profitable investment shrink. All but 1 percent of Americans have been effectively shut out for good. Experts agree: The fortunes still to be made within our market will go to people already sitting in the board seats of major multinational corporations.

In the international arena there's quite a different story to tell. In less than twenty-five years the world's stock market inventory grew 700 percent, from roughly $1 trillion in the late 1960s to more than $7 trillion by the early 1990s. How much of that market do you suppose is contained within the United States? In 1970 U.S. equities composed fully two-thirds of the world's stock market. By 1997 less than one-third were American. That's nothing short of miraculous. It's like some invisible fairy godmother waved her magic wand and cast a spell of good fortune over most of world and left out the United States. In a few years the global equation has shifted dramatically. Nearly 70 percent of the world's stocks (and more than 55 percent of its fixed income) are currently invested in overseas markets. That means the real money to be made is not about to be made on Wall Street, but within emerging markets all around the globe.

Privacy

What about the other benefits inherent in global moneymaking? Privacy, for example. In Chapter 7 we looked at the revolutionary impact that information technology has made on personal investment. Thanks to the Internet, and various investment-related software, you can join the twenty-first century right now. At any hour of any day you can make, change, or cash out on stock, bond, or venture investments anywhere in the world. Used intelligently, modern technology gives you the ability to take profitable action with lightning speed.

Unfortunately, the information age has a down side. According to one recent analysis, billions of computer files now exist concerning untold millions of us. The collection, storage, and retrieval of information that most Americans assume to be private are big business today. You can rest assured, for example, that at least one credit bureau (more likely several) keeps a file on you. Lenders nationwide routinely pay these businesses to disclose a slew of information about your income, debts, tax liens, judgments, arrests, and convictions. The largest of the data collection firms, TRW, maintains files on some 120 million Americans at any given time.

> **W**isely invested in markets worldwide, your money can earn handsome profits that cannot be confiscated by any branch of government.

As you might suspect, this booming information industry has gone the way of all big business—toward specialization. For example, the Chicago-based Docket-Search Network sells a service called "Physician's Alert," consisting solely of information on patients who have filed civil suits. Its clients, naturally enough, are doctors in high-risk specialties who use the service to help them pick and choose the people they're willing to treat.

But guess what? It's Uncle Sam who weaves the most complex web of information on U.S. citizens. At the moment there are more than eighty federal databases on 114 million people. The state in which you reside probably holds another dozen or so active computer files on you. And the Census Bureau regularly updates its records. Within a matter of minutes it can pump out all your basic data and legally pass along that information to other interested branches of government. Then, of course, there's the Internal Revenue Service. The IRS knows how much you make and where it comes from. The Social Security Administration probably knows more than you do about your employment earnings history. If you served in the armed forces, you're permanently listed in the archives of Veterans Affairs as well as your service branch.

Still, it's not the volume of information that's most frightening. It's the fact that sophisticated technology now makes it easy to do what was impossible just a decade ago: crossmatch information at the touch of a keyboard. A network of fifteen federal regulatory and enforcement agencies routinely mixes and matches data—ostensibly in an effort to detect fraud and waste in both welfare and social service programs. In actuality the network often targets deep pockets: the working affluent who surely can be counted on to owe something to somebody somewhere. The IRS debtor master file, created in 1986, is used to withhold tax refunds from anyone who has defaulted on a federal loan, for example. *Business Week* has reported that Uncle Sam even experimented briefly with buying lists from direct-mail companies just to see if

the spending habits of specific individuals were in sync with
their reported income. While the program has been discon-
tinued, the basic concept behind it is now commonplace
within government. The idea is to spot combinations of data
that characterize people deemed most likely to engage in specific behaviors or activities.

An international financial approach offers you the only
escape from this government-endorsed conspiracy. It also
protects you from frivolous lawsuits. The truth is that the
American judicial system has become something of a witch
hunt—with far too many attorneys willing to work for a
percentage of the damages ultimately awarded to their
clients. In such an environment anybody with "deep pockets" becomes potential prey to unscrupulous lawyers and
the greedy people they represent. If, as a wealthy individual, you are slapped with a substantial judgment, your
entire estate could be wiped out overnight. Years of con-
scientious savings and intelligent investment could be rendered worthless. Just as you can legitimately make more
money overseas than you could ever hope to earn in the
United States, you can look forward to enjoying those foreign profits in an atmosphere of complete confidentiality.
You can benefit from ironclad secrecy laws that strictly forbid any bureaucratic review of your personal financial
records. You can legally safeguard your assets from court
judgments and the overzealous inspection that has become
part and parcel of U.S. banking and investment portfolio
management.

Protection from Excessive Taxation

If there's too little financial privacy left in America, there's
even less tax protection. Things have come a long way since
1776, and they've moved in the wrong direction. It's ironic
to think that this country was born out of history's most successful tax revolt. Until 1913 no income tax was levied

against any U.S. citizen. Today the United States is home to the most complicated and burdensome tax laws in the world. A New York City Tax Committee Report from the late 1960s found even then that this nation's tax code was beyond the understanding of most tax specialists. Since then the government has gained another thirty-plus years' worth of complicated tax legislation!

Remember Ronald Reagan's pledge to simplify the tax code? Remember George Bush in 1988 and his promise of "no new taxes"? How about Bill Clinton's approach to federal deficit busting? Myriad tax increases followed the empty campaign speeches delivered by all three men. Between 1980 and 1988 taxpayers earning $200,000 and above saw their tax liability rise as much as 12.9 percent. It's now ten years later, and nothing is any better.

President Clinton claims that if his policies are followed middle-class Americans will enjoy $111 billion in tax cuts by the year 2002. Yet even he admits that if his predictions about the budget are wrong, then most of those well-publicized tax cuts will be reduced or rescinded. In other words, if Uncle Sam ultimately cannot pay his bills, then your tax cut disappears. Do you trust the Democrats' crystal ball? I certainly don't. How can you trust a president who talks about simplifying the tax code even as he defends a system in which the wealthy pay higher tax rates? Why trust a man who promises lower taxes even after he increased the top income obligation from 31 percent to 39.6 percent?

I also find it difficult to respect an administration that brags about its efforts to reduce the capital gains tax from 25 to 20 percent. I remember, not long ago, when hopeful politicians were promising to reduce what was then a 15 percent capital gains tax. Now we're supposed to be grateful for the chance to fork over just one out of every five inheritance dollars to Uncle Sam. This is just another example of what's happened in every sector of our tax system: Americans have grown so accustomed to abuse that a soft hit suddenly seems like something to appreciate. What ever happened to zero tolerance? When did less abuse start to feel good?

The truth is that most experts are predicting more tax hikes, with a significant jump expected every year through the rest of this century. Income tax alone is now close to 30 percent for middle- and upper-income Americans. That's a staggering financial reality. In addition to higher income rates, a number of other tax hikes have been proposed—all in the effort to pay a bloated bill accumulated by the government through years of excess spending. For an ever-increasing number of other wealthy citizens it has become virtually pointless to work any harder in the hope of earning more because so much of the income increase is extracted and transferred over to the government.

There are ways to escape the complexity and fanaticism of the U.S. tax system. Many places still respect your right to earn and spend your money as you see fit. Countless foreign banks and privately held corporations let you legally move your assets outside the United States and beyond the reach of a government that would insert itself into every aspect of your financial life. Wisely invested in markets worldwide, your money can earn handsome profits that cannot be confiscated by any branch of government. Is it legal? Absolutely. I believe it's more than legal; it's heroic because it reflects the finest spirit of this nation: individual ingenuity and the pursuit of personal betterment.

Playground Fun around the World

Finally, these three compelling attractions—profit, privacy, and tax protection—are available in some of the most breathtaking environments on earth. Whether your personal tastes runs more toward European cities steeped in tradition, Far East capitals that bridge an ancient past with a promising future, or island sanctuaries where sun and sea soothe away your urban worries, global investment can take you to playgrounds beyond your wildest dreams.

Far too many in number to cover here, they are scattered throughout the world, and each offers its own distinct experience.

There's Liechtenstein, a tiny state wedged in the visually stunning mountain valley between Switzerland and Austria. If you love to ski or spend long days reading by the fire of a rustic lodge, this could be a wonderful foreign base of operations for you. There are Luxembourg and Switzerland, both with immaculate European cities as well as centers of art and culture. There are the nearly 100 South Pacific islands collectively known as the nation of Vanuatu. Located near Australia and New Zealand, they combine the beauty of balmy nights with close proximity to markets that are rapidly becoming a revolving door between the East and the West. There are the British Virgin Islands, a chain of sixty small Caribbean islands that's shaping up to be a prime money haven and foreign investment center for the next century. There are the Bahamas, the Netherland Antilles, Aruba, the Cayman Islands, and Singapore.

Take your pick from among these and other centers of global financial activity, because the days of downtown banking are long gone. As we rush toward the year 2000, smart investors are creating an enormous market for customized financial services. More than 200 principalities and nations around the world stand to gain a great deal from responding to that market need. By tailoring financial services to meet the needs of specific investor groups, these faraway sites transform themselves from insignificant hideaways to vital fulcrums of international business activity.

Shall We Meet?

For those of you who are ready to take advantage of the exciting world of international investment, I have some good news. There is help to be had. You may want to try to go out there without any guidance, but I recommend that you work with a consultant. You need someone with the expertise to cover all the steps involved in the process. For help, you can contact my office in Vancouver, British Columbia (see page 185). I am always ready.

I'll be pleased to have a consultation with you. I usually help my clients cut down on the months of research and legwork required to establish an international presence. Whether that means helping them customize an annuity, purchase a private international corporation, set up an offshore asset protection trust, open a foreign bank account, purchase equities and stocks, buy a private offshore bank, or even establish foreign residency, I am ready to lend a hand. I relish the chance to discuss your options based on your specific situation and financial goals. After all, as you can tell from reading this book, I find the world of global investment both enjoyable and satisfying. As your consultant I can limit your risks and arrange initial international contacts to help smooth your transition from the U.S. market to the global investment community.

This is a book about the remarkable moneymaking opportunities available throughout the world. We are in the global age now, and the smart investor is the one who wants to be part of a burgeoning market that makes the U.S. investment scene pale in comparison. I have tried to make you aware of all that is possible in international investment. While the dynamics of international investing are changing by the day, I hope I have managed to give you a sound basis upon which to make one of the most crucial decisions of your lifetime. I also hope I've succeeded in showing you that a global investment strategy will offer financial benefits that will brighten your economic future. There's more economic gain to be had in the international arena than ever before. Global investment is part of today's reality. It's not something that is going to happen: It is happening. It's the vision of a bright economic future. Best of

> **We** are in the global age now, and the smart investor is the one who wants to be part of a burgeoning market that makes the U.S. investment scene pale in comparison.

all, it's legally and affordably available to you today. You can be part of it.

So think about it, but don't think too long. Every day the government closes a few more doors to international profit potential. My advice is to get out there and get started while the laws still allow you to discreetly make a profit and realize a true gain on your investment. When I look at the people who read my books and the clients who have explored investment on the global stage, I can tell you that they are all better off today than they were before we met.

When you're ready to get started, let me hear from you. I'd like to be involved in developing your global investment game plan. I think my experience will allow me to offer some worthwhile pointers. I know I could learn from you by simply observing how you design your own international investment strategy. I'm only a phone call away. Let's talk, because who knows: It could be the start of a great partnership.

Jerome Schneider
Premier Corporate Services, Ltd.
Box 12099-Harbour Centre
Suite 700-555 West Hastings Street
Vancouver, B.C., Canada V6B 4N5
Telephone: 604-682-4000
Fax: 604-682-7700
E-mail: taxhavens@aol.com

IT'S ALL A STATE OF MIND

Sometimes I relax by the pool, sipping a campari and soda, in one of the many island havens sprinkled across the world. Or I look out my hotel room in Zurich at a skyline that looks the picture of urban elegance. I ask myself: What would life be like if every smart, serious, and deserving investor took Trevor Abrey's decisive move—out of the U.S. market and into the international arena? Of course, I'd probably be a lot richer if that happened, since I make my living by helping people make that move.

My own income notwithstanding, I think that the global investment world would be less exciting if it made room for absolutely everyone. As it is, international moneymaking is the secret of today's most creative, independent-minded, and fast-thinking men and women. That's how it stays ahead of the curve in generating impressive profits. That's why it results in a legal escape from personal privacy invasion. That's the reason it continuously reinvents itself to ensure tax protection. Its participants are bold, and they will accept nothing less.

Ultimately, what it takes to make the move out of the domestic scene and into the global market is an ability to see the world differently. We've all been raised to view money as an end in itself. But in the international business realm money is just the means to an end, the ticket required to

> **International moneymaking is the secret of today's most creative, independent-minded, and fast-thinking men and women. That's how it stays ahead of the curve in generating impressive profits. . . . Its participants are bold, and they will accept nothing less.**

build an entirely new life based on profit opportunities emerging at every moment of the day and night all over the planet. To the average investor that sounds like fun, but it ultimately feels like too sophisticated a game. And that's fine. I used to have a friend in college named Jake. Whenever he'd have a six-pack or some homecooked care-package food to offer me, he'd happily share anything I wanted. On those rare instances when I refused his offer, Jake would just smile and say, "OK, that leaves more for me."

That's exactly how I've come to view the international arena. It's there, brimming with opportunity. I offer a taste of it to anybody who'll listen. If they're interested, that's great, and we often begin a long and intriguing professional relationship. If they're not interested, that's great, too. It just leaves more for me. And maybe for you, too.

Appendix A

Umbrella Offshore Funds with More Than $100 Million in Assets

Fund Name and Description	Contact
BAER MULTIBOND SWISS BOND A/D *Julius Baer Multibond Sicav* A fund that invests in fixed-income securities. Denominated in Swiss francs. Assets (as of March 31, 1996, or last fiscal period; quoted in U.S. dollars): $265.09 million Banque Generale Du Luxembourg	Mr. Wilfred Kleiner Julius Baer Investment Funds c/o Banque Generale Du Luxembourg 50 Blvd. J. F. Kennedy L-2951 Luxembourg Phone: 352-4242-3638 Fax: 352-4242-6500 E-mail: info@bgl.lu Web page: http://www.bgl.lu Julius Baer also has a Web page at http://www.juliusbaer.com/menu.html.
BAER MULTISTOCK SWISS STOCK A/D *Julius Baer Multistock* A fund that seeks long-term capital growth. Invests in carefully selected dividend-bearing securities issued by prime companies. Up to one-third of the assets are invested in Liechtenstein. Denominated in Swiss francs. Assets (as of March 31, 1996, or last fiscal period; quoted in U.S. dollars): $113.48 million Banque Generale Du Luxembourg	Mr. Beat Buob Julius Baer Investment Funds c/o Banque Generale Du Luxembourg 50 Blvd. J. F. Kennedy L-2951 Luxembourg Phone: 352-4242-3638 Fax: 352-4242-6500 E-mail: info@bgl.lu Web page: http://www.bgl.lu. Julius Baer also has a Web page at http://www.juliusbaer.com/menu.html.
BBL INVEST LATIN AMERICA *BBL Invest Sicav* Invests in securities issued in Latin America. Selects instruments based on a benchmark of Latin American stock markets. Assets (as of March 31, 1996, or last fiscal period; quoted in U.S. dollars): $175 million Banque Bruxelles Lambert	BBL Direct BBL Renta Fund 52 Route d'Esch L-2985 Luxembourg Phone: 32-2-481-33-40 Fax: 32-2-481-32-10 E-mail: info@bbl.be Web page: http://www/bbl.be/

Free Info Available?	Speak English?	American Clients?	Canadian Clients?	SEC Approved?	Work with U.S. Advisors?
NA	NA	NA	NA	NA	NA
NA	NA	NA	NA	NA	NA
Yes; can be sent to U.S. addresses	Yes	Yes	Yes	No	No

(Continued)

Fund Name and Description	Contact
BBL (L) INVEST HEALTHCARE *BBL Invest Sicav* Invests in securities issued by companies in the health care and pharmaceutical industries. Benchmark is MSCI Health & Personal Care. Assets (as of March 31, 1996, or last fiscal period; quoted in U.S. dollars): $105 million Banque Bruxelles Lambert	BBL Direct BBL Renta Fund 52 Route d'Esch L-2985 Luxembourg Phone: 32-2-481-33-40 Fax: 32-2-481-32-10 E-mail: info@bbl.be Web page: http://www.bbl.be/
BBL RENTA FUND DOLLAR *BBL Renta Fund* Invests in bonds denominated in U.S. dollars. Benchmark is JP Morgan American bonds. Assets (as of March 31, 1996, or last fiscal period; quoted in U.S. dollars): $135 million Banque Bruxelles Lambert	BBL Direct BBL Renta Fund 52 Route d'Esch L-2985 Luxembourg Phone: 32-2-481-33-40 Fax: 32-2-481-32-10 E-mail: info@bbl.be Web page: http://www.bbl.be/
BBL RENTA FUND HARD CURRENCY *BBL Renta Fund* Invests in bonds denominated in currencies that appreciated against the ECU in the last five years (for example, the German mark, the Netherlands guilder, and the Belgian franc). The fund's base currency is German marks. Assets (as of March 31, 1996, or last fiscal period; quoted in U.S. dollars): $140.83 million Banque Bruxelles Lambert	BBL Direct BBL Renta Fund 52 Route d'Esch L-2985 Luxembourg Phone: 32-2-481-33-40 Fax: 32-2-481-32-10 E-mail: info@bbl.be Web page: http://www.bbl.be/

Free Info Available?	Speak English?	American Clients?	Canadian Clients?	SEC Approved?	Work with U.S. Advisors?
Yes; can be sent to U.S. addresses	Yes	Yes	Yes	No	No
Yes; can be sent to U.S. addresses	Yes	Yes	Yes	No	No
Yes; can be sent to U.S. addresses	Yes	Yes	Yes	No	No

(Continued)

Fund Name and Description	Contact
BBL RENTA FUND LUX *BBL Renta Fund* The goal of this fund is income growth, which it obtains with a portfolio that primarily consists of bonds denominated in Belgian or Luxembourg francs or any currency that is legal tender in Luxembourg. Uses the JP Morgan Belgian bonds as the benchmark. Assets (as of March 31, 1996, or last fiscal period; quoted in U.S. dollars): $625.82 million Banque Bruxelles Lambert	BBL Direct BBL Renta Fund 52 Route d'Esch L-2985 Luxembourg Phone: 32-2-481-33-40 Fax: 32-2-481-32-10 E-mail: info@bbl.be Web page: http://www.bbl.be/
BL MULTI-TRUST BOND FB—FLUX A/B *BL Multi-Trust Sicav* This subfund invests in fixed-interest bonds that may also be convertible, variable, and indexed with warrants. Assets (as of March 31, 1996, or last fiscal period; quoted in U.S. dollars): $125.71 million Banque de Luxembourg	Mr. Guy Wagner or Ms. Nicole Neve Banque de Luxembourg 103 Grand Rue P.O. Box 2221 L-1022 Luxembourg Phone: 352-49-924-1 Fax: 352-49-424-3333 E-mail: NA Web page: NA
CITINVEST VIP SELECTOR *Citinvest* This fund invests in a small number of companies located around the world. Companies are chosen on criteria such as cash flow, earnings growth potential, and asset value. The fund's base currency is U.S. dollars. Assets (as of March 31, 1996, or last fiscal period; quoted in U.S. dollars): $192.60 million Citibank (Luxembourg) S.A.	Mr. Michel Hagens Citinvest 58 Boulevard Grande-Duchesse Charlotte L-1330 Luxembourg Phone: 352-45-14-141 Fax: 352-45-14-14-75 E-mail: NA Web page: NA

Free Info Available?	Speak English?	American Clients?	Canadian Clients?	SEC Approved?	Work with U.S. Advisors?
Yes; can be sent to U.S. addresses	Yes	Yes	Yes	No	No
NA	NA	NA	NA	NA	NA
NA	NA	NA	NA	NA	NA

(Continued)

Fund Name and Description	Contact
CREDIS BOND DEM A/B *Credis Bond Fund* Aiming for steady earnings at high rates, this fund invests in DEM denominated notes, bonds, convertible bonds and/or notes, fixed- or variable-interest securities, warrant issues, and warrant certificates on bonds traded on a stock exchange or a regulated market. Assets (as of March 31, 1996, or last fiscal period; quoted in U.S. dollars): $186.3 million Credis Fund Holding (Luxembourg) S.A.	Mr. Roger Miller 5 Rue Jean Monnet P.O. Box 369 L-2013 Luxembourg Phone: 352-43-61-611 Fax: 352-43-61-61-555 E-mail: NA Web page: NA
CREDIS BOND SFR A/B *Credis Bond Fund* Invests in a diversified selection of top-rated Swiss franc bonds, including warrant issues, convertibles, and other securities with fixed or variable rates. Base currency is Swiss francs. Assets (as of March 31, 1996, or last fiscal period; quoted in U.S. dollars): $314.4 million Credis Fund Holding (Luxembourg) S.A.	Mr. Roger Miller 5 Rue Jean Monnet P.O. Box 369 L-2013 Luxembourg Phone: 352-43-61-611 Fax: 352-43-61-61-555 E-mail: NA Web page: NA
FIDELITY FUNDS AMERICA *Fidelity Funds Sicav* Invests in a diversified portfolio of mainly blue-chip U.S. companies, for the purpose of producing capital growth. The benchmark for performance is Standard & Poor's Composite Index. Assets (as of March 31, 1996, or last fiscal period; quoted in U.S. dollars): $397.7 million Fidelity Investments Distributors	Ms. Angela Hauske Kansallis House Place De L'Etoiles B.P. L-2144 Luxembourg Phone: 352-250-404-286 Fax: 352-250-404-375 E-mail: angela.hauske@fid.-intl.com Web page: http://www.fid-intl.com/

Free Info Available?	Speak English?	American Clients?	Canadian Clients?	SEC Approved?	Work with U.S. Advisors?
NA	NA	NA	NA	NA	NA
NA	NA	NA	NA	NA	NA
Yes; can't send to U.S. addresses	Yes	No (if their tax position is in the U.S.)	No	No	No

(Continued)

Fund Name and Description	Contact
FLEMING FF AMERICAN *Fleming Flagship Fund* This fund invests in securities issued by North American companies without specialization in a specific sector or company size. All funds are allocated to the United States. Base currency is U.S. dollars. Assets (as of March 31, 1996, or last fiscal period; quoted in U.S. dollars): $427.4 million Fleming Fund Management (Luxembourg) S.A.	Mr. Hans Heller 6 Route de Treves European Bank & Business Centre L-2633, Senningerberg, Luxembourg Phone: 352-34-101 Fax: 352-34-08-73 E-mail: info@flemings.lu Web page: http://www.flemings.lu

**FLEMING FF AMERICAN
   FLEDGELING**
Fleming Flagship Fund
This fund invests in securities issued by smaller U.S. and Canadian companies. These companies are all quoted on a stock exchange or traded on an over-the-counter market with an average market capitalization of less than $500 million (U.S. dollars). Assets (as of March 31, 1996, or last fiscal period; quoted in U.S. dollars): $233.6 million
Fleming Fund Management
   (Luxembourg) S.A.
	Mr. Hans Heller
	6 Route de Treves
	European Bank & Business Centre
	L-2633, Senningerberg, Luxembourg
	Phone: 352-34-101
	Fax: 352-34-08-73
	E-mail: info@flemings.lu
	Web page: http://www.flemings.lu

FLEMING FF US DISCOVERY *Fleming Flagship Fund* With its goal to achieve long-term capital appreciation, this fund contains a diversified portfolio made up of smaller North American companies with an average market capitalization of $100 million (U.S. dollars). Assets (as of March 31, 1996, or last fiscal period; quoted in U.S. dollars): $202 million Fleming Fund Management (Luxembourg) S.A.	Mr. Hans Heller 6 Route de Treves European Bank & Business Centre L-2633, Senningerberg, Luxembourg Phone: 352-34-101 Fax: 352-34-08-73 E-mail: info@flemings.lu Web page: http://www.flemings.lu

Free Info Available?	Speak English?	American Clients?	Canadian Clients?	SEC Approved?	Work with U.S. Advisors?
NA	NA	NA	NA	NA	NA
NA	NA	NA	NA	NA	NA
NA	NA	NA	NA	NA	NA

(Continued)

Fund Name and Description	Contact
G-BOND FUND G-RENTINBEL A/B *G-Bond Fund* This is a subfund that invests mainly in first-grade bonds that are denominated in Belgian francs. Its goal is to obtain a return that is equal to or greater than the linear Belgian Bond Index. Assets (as of March 31, 1996, or last fiscal period; quoted in U.S. dollars): $348.8 million G-Bond Fund Conseil S.A.	Mr. William de Vjilder 14 Rue Aldringen L-1118 Luxembourg Phone: 32-2-565-39-14 Fax: 32-2-565-53-00 E-mail: NA Web page: NA
G-RENTINFIX BEF & LUF 01/06/99 *G-Rentinfix Fund* Maturing on June 1, 1999, this subfund invests in Belgian and Luxembourg franc bonds. Capital gains and income are reinvested. The final market value will be determined by current market interest rates at valuation date. Assets (as of March 31, 1996, or last fiscal period; quoted in U.S. dollars): $103.99 million G-Retinfix Fund Conseil S.A.	Mr. William de Vjilder 14 Rue Aldringen L-1118 Luxembourg Phone: 32-2-565-39-14 Fax: 32-2-565-53-00 E-mail: NA Web page: NA
G-RENTINFIX BEF & LUF 15/09/99 *G-Rentinfix Fund* This subfund aims to achieve capital appreciation by investing in Belgium and Luxembourg francs bonds with a maturity date of September 15, 1999. Capital gains and income are reinvested. The final market value will be determined by current market interest rates on the valuation date. Funds base currency is Belgian francs. Assets (as of March 31, 1996, or last fiscal period; quoted in U.S. dollars): $333.26 million G-Retinfix Fund Conseil S.A.	Mr. William de Vjilder 14 Rue Aldringen L-1118 Luxembourg Phone: 32-2-565-39-14 Fax: 32-2-565-53-00 E-mail: NA Web page: NA

Free Info Available?	Speak English?	American Clients?	Canadian Clients?	SEC Approved?	Work with U.S. Advisors?
NA	NA	NA	NA	NA	NA
NA	NA	NA	NA	NA	NA
NA	NA	NA	NA	NA	NA

(Continued)

Fund Name and Description	Contact
G-RENTINFIX BEF & LUF 30/6/2001 *G-Rentinfix Fund* This fund invests in Belgian and and Luxembourg bonds with a maturity date of June 30, 2001. Denominated in Belgian and Luxembourg francs, the final market value will be determined by current market rates on the valuation date. Assets (as of March 31, 1996, or last fiscal period; quoted in U.S. dollars): $202.01 million G-Retinfix Fund Conseil S.A.	Mr. William de Vjilder 14 Rue Aldringen L-1118 Luxembourg Phone: 32-2-565-39-14 Fax: 32-2-565-53-00 E-mail: NA Web page: NA
HYPO FOREIGN & COLONIAL PORTFOLIOS FUND *Hypo Foreign & Colonial Portfolios Fund* The objective of this fund is to enable investors to participate in a portfolio consisting principally of securities issued by U.S. companies listed on the U.S. stock exchange or NASDAQ. Investment policy is directed toward achieving long-term capital growth through investment in small and medium companies. Assets (as of March 31, 1996, or last fiscal period; quoted in U.S. dollars): $105.62 million Foreign & Colonial Management Ltd.	Broker Services Exchange House 8th Floor Primrose Street London, EC2A 2NY UK Phone: 44-171-454-1434 Fax: 44-171-628-2108 E-mail: NA Web page: http://www.trustnet.co.uk/grp-perf/f&cmgm0.html (Note: This site explains the fund but is not an official company site.)

Free Info Available?	Speak English?	American Clients?	Canadian Clients?	SEC Approved?	Work with U.S. Advisors?
NA	NA	NA	NA	NA	NA
Yes; will mail to U.S. addresses	Yes	Yes	Yes	No	Yes

(Continued)

Fund Name and Description	Contact
INTER OPTIMUM FRF *Inter Optimum* The assets of this capitalized subfund are invested in securities (specifically bonds whose limits are established by law) in money market instruments. These securities are denominated in French francs. The current benchmark is JP Morgan French Government Bonds. Assets (as of March 31, 1996, or last fiscal period; quoted in U.S. dollars): $102.48 million Banque Nationale de Paris	Mr. Pierre Nguyen or Mr. Agut Tran Rommel 22 Boulevard Royal L-2449 Luxembourg Phone: 33-7-40-74-54-34 Fax: 33-7-40-74-79-43 E-mail: PNguyen@Bnp.fr Web page: http://www.calvacom.fr/BNP
KB BONDS STRONG CURRENCY CAP/DIV *KB Bonds* This subfund seeks to appreciate capital through investments in bonds with strong currency denominations, such as German marks. Assets (as of March 31, 1996, or last fiscal period; quoted in U.S. dollars): $161.05 million Kredietbank	Mr. Chris Sterckx Kredietbank N.V. Arenbergstraat 7, B1000 Brussels, Belgium Phone: 02-546-52-14 Fax: 02-546-59-29 E-mail: NA Web page: NA
KB RENTA DECARENTA A/B *KB Renta* This fund invests in Danish kroner-denominated bonds. The fund is also denominated in Danish kroner. Assets (as of March 31, 1996, or last fiscal period; quoted in U.S. dollars): $109.83 million Kredietbank	Mr. Chris Sterckx Kredietbank N.V. Arenbergstraat 7, B1000 Brussels, Belgium Phone: 02-546-52-14 Fax: 02-546-59-29 E-mail: NA Web page: NA

Free Info Available?	Speak English?	American Clients?	Canadian Clients?	SEC Approved?	Work with U.S. Advisors?
Yes; will mail to U.S. addresses	Yes	No	No	No	No
NA	Yes	Yes	Yes	No	No
NA	Yes	Yes	Yes	No	No

(Continued)

Fund Name and Description	Contact
KB RENTA GULDENRENTA B *KB Renta* This subfund invests in bonds denom-inated by guilder from the Netherlands. Assets (as of March 31, 1996, or last fiscal period; quoted in U.S. dollars): $103.18 million Kredietbank	Mr. Chris Sterckx Kreditbank N.V. Arenbergstraat 7, B1000 Brussels Belgium Phone: 02-546-52-14 Fax: 02-546-59-29 E-mail: NA Web page: NA
MERCURY ST NORTH AMERICAN *Mercury Selected Trust* This subfund invests in higher risk equity investments in North America, Mexico, and Canada. Its primary objective is to enhance capital growth. Biased toward small-cap companies. Assets (as of March 31, 1996, or last fiscal period; quoted in U.S. dollars): $108.30 million Mercury Asset Management	Mr. Jean Michel Rasquin BP 1058 L-1010 Luxembourg Phone: 352-34-20-10-52-52 Fax: 352-34-20-102 E-mail: NA Web page: http://www.trustnet.co.uk/groups/mam.html. (Note: This site provides general information about the fund and the company but is not a company-sponsored site.)
MULTIBOND ACTIBOND DEM A/B *Multibond Fund* This subfund's goal is to obtain capital appreciation. It does this by investing in German government bonds, and especially those bonds that outperform the JP Morgan German Government Bond Index. Assets (as of March 31, 1996, or last fiscal period; quoted in U.S. dollars): $113.60 million CCF Structured Asset Management	Mr. Thomas Ricke 115-117 Avenue des Champs-Elysees 75008 Paris, France Phone: 33-1-40-70-74-00 Fax: 33-1-40-70-75-23 E-mail: NA Web page: http://www.calvacom.fr/ccf/accueil.html

Free Info Available?	Speak English?	American Clients?	Canadian Clients?	SEC Approved?	Work with U.S. Advisors?
NA	Yes	Yes	Yes	No	No
NA	NA	NA	NA	NA	NA
NA	NA	NA	NA	NA	NA

(Continued)

Fund Name and Description	Contact
PARVEST OBLI BELUX A/B *Parvest Sicav* The portfolio for this fund primarily consists of domestic and foreign bonds (many which offer fixed rates) and those Eurobonds issued by prime borrowers that are denominated in Belgian francs. The objective of this fund is to obtain capital gain. Assets (as of March 31, 1996, or last fiscal period; quoted in U.S. dollars): $240.92 million Banque Paribas France	Mr. Edouard de Cournon 10 A. Bld. Royal Luxembourg-Ville L-2093 Luxembourg Phone: 352-46-46-44-19 Fax: 33-1-42-98-12-32 E-mail: NA Web page: http://www.paribas.com:8008/www/homeDb.nsf/viewAllPages/EN1?OpenDocument Also http://www.trustnet.co.uk/groups/mam.html (Note: This site provides general information about the fund and the company but is not a company-sponsored site.)
PARVEST OBLI FRANC A/B *Parvest Sicav* This subfund mainly invests in short-term money market securities denominated in French francs. It also includes fixed-rate bonds issued by prime borrowers. Assets (as of March 31, 1996, or last fiscal period; quoted in U.S. dollars): $188.23 million Banque Paribas France	Mr. Edouard de Cournon BP 141,3 Rue d'Antin 75002 Paris Cedex 02, France Phone: 33-1-42-98-12-34 Fax: 33-1-42-98-12-32 E-mail: NA Web page: http://www.paribas.com:8008/www/homeDb.nsf/viewAllPages/EN1?OpenDocument Also http://www.trustnet.co.uk/groups/mam.html (Note: This site provides general information about the fund and the company but is not a company-sponsored site.)
Pictet C.F. UK VAL *Pictet Country Fund* This subfund invests in British equities. It consists of two parts—one managed in line UK Val's benchmark index (the FT350 Index), the other actively managed. Its goal is to obtain capital appreciation. Assets (as of March 31, 1996, or last fiscal period; quoted in U.S. dollars): $112.44 million Banque Pictet Luxembourg S.A.	Ms. Sally Gadbury 17 Cote d'Eich L-1450 Luxembourg Phone: 44-171-972-6800 Fax: 44-171-972-6800 E-mail: sally_gadbury@pictet.demon.co.uk Web page: http://www.pictet.com/FundsAdm.htm

Free Info Available?	Speak English?	American Clients?	Canadian Clients?	SEC Approved?	Work with U.S. Advisors?
NA	NA	NA	NA	NA	NA
NA	NA	NA	NA	NA	NA
Yes; can't mail to U.S. addresses	Yes	No	No	No	No

(Continued)

Fund Name and Description	Contact
RAIFFEISEN SWISS OBLI A/B *Raiffeisen Schweiz (Luxembourg) Funds* This subfund invests primarily in long-term fixed- and variable-rate instruments denominated in Swiss francs. Seeks high-grade instruments. It follows a principle of risk diversification of at least 90 percent. Assets (as of March 31, 1996, or last fiscal period; quoted in U.S. dollars): $294.31 million Fonds Raiffeisen Suisse (Lux)	U. Fraefel Vontobel Asset Management Todestrasse 7 8022 Zurich, Switzerland Phone: 41-1-283-53-50 Fax: 41-1-283-53-05 E-mail: NA Web page: NA
SBC BOND PORTFOLIO DM A/B *SBC Bond Portfolio* This subfund invests in instruments that are listed on a stock exchange or traded on a regular market. Those instruments could include bonds, notes, convertible bonds, warrant issues, variable interest bearing securities with fixed or variable income, and warrant on issues. Instruments are denominated in German marks. Assets (as of March 31, 1996, or last fiscal period; quoted in U.S. dollars): $1,531.86 million Swiss Bank Corporation (Luxembourg)	Mr. Ignatius Bundi 26 Route D'Arlon L-1140 Luxembourg Phone: 352-45-20-30-560 Fax: 352-45-20-30-378 E-mail: NA Web page: http://www.swissbank.ch/sbcweb/index_e.html

Free Info Available?	Speak English?	American Clients?	Canadian Clients?	SEC Approved?	Work with U.S. Advisors?
NA	NA	NA	NA	NA	NA
NA	NA	No	NA	No	NA

(Continued)

Fund Name and Description	Contact
SBC BOND PORTFOLIO FF A/B *SBC Bond Portfolio* This subfund invests in instruments that are listed on a stock exchange or traded on a regular market. Those instruments could include bonds, notes, convertible bonds, warrant issues, variable interest-bearing securities with fixed or variable income, and warrant on issues. All instruments are denominated in French francs. Assets (as of March 31, 1996, or last fiscal period; quoted in U.S. dollars): $539.12 million Swiss Bank Corporation (Luxembourg)	Mr. Ignatius Bundi 26 Route D'Arlon L-1140 Luxembourg Phone: 352-45-20-30-560 Fax: 352-45-20-30-378 E-mail: NA Web page: http://www.swissbank.ch/ sbcweb/index_e.html
SBC BOND PORTFOLIO HFL A/B *SBC Bond Portfolio* This subfund invests in public or private interest-bearing securities with a fixed or variable interest rate. The base currency is Dutch guilders. Assets (as of March 31, 1996, or last fiscal period; quoted in U.S. dollars): $539.12 million Swiss Bank Corporation (Luxembourg)	Mr. Ignatius Bundi 26 Route D'Arlon L-1140 Luxembourg Phone: 352-45-20-30-560 Fax: 352-45-20-30-378 E-mail: NA Web page: http://www.swissbank.ch/ sbcweb/index_e.html
SBC BOND PORTFOLIO SFR A/B *SBC Bond Portfolio* Invests primarily in notes, bonds, and fixed- or variable-interest securities denominated in Swiss francs. Assets (as of March 31, 1996, or last fiscal period; quoted in U.S. dollars): $2,779.93 million Swiss Bank Corporation (Luxembourg)	Mr. Ignatius Bundi 26 Route D'Arlon L-1140 Luxembourg Phone: 352-45-20-30-560 Fax: 352-45-20-30-378 E-mail: NA Web page: http://www.swissbank.ch/ sbcweb/index_e.html

Free Info Available?	Speak English?	American Clients?	Canadian Clients?	SEC Approved?	Work with U.S. Advisors?
NA	NA	No	NA	No	NA
NA	NA	No	NA	No	NA
NA	NA	No	NA	No	NA

(Continued)

Fund Name and Description	Contact
SBC EQUITY PORTFOLIO NETHERLANDS *SBC Bond Portfolio* This subfund seeks to invest in shares, equity securities (such as participation certificates and shares in cooperatives), dividend right certificates, and warrants issued by public corporations or companies based in the Netherlands. Assets (as of March 31, 1996, or last fiscal period; quoted in U.S. dollars): $447.06 million Swiss Bank Corporation (Luxembourg)	Mr. Ignatius Bundi 26 Route D'Arlon L-1140 Luxembourg Phone: 352-45-20-30-560 Fax: 352-45-20-30-378 E-mail: NA Web page: http://www.swissbank.ch/sbcweb/index_e.html
SCHRODER INTERNATIONAL SELECTION US SMALL COMPANIES *The Schroeder International Selection Fund* Invests in securities issued by smaller companies. These companies are listed on the principal U.S. stock exchange; some securities are traded on the over-the-counter markets. Assets (as of March 31, 1996, or last fiscal period; quoted in U.S. dollars): $126.29 million Schroder International Selection Fund	Mr. John Hall 5 Rue Hohenhoff L-1736 Senningerberg, Luxembourg Phone: 352-34-13-42-202 Fax: 352-34-13-42-342 E-mail: NA Web page: http://www.trustnet.co.uk/groups/schrodr.html (Note: This site provides general information about the fund and the company but is not a company-sponsored site.)
SHARE EURO SELECTION *Share Sicav* With the goal of providing investors with above average returns while preserving capital, this subfund invests in European equities. Assets (as of March 31, 1996, or last fiscal period; quoted in U.S. dollars): $122.85 million Bearbull Asset Management	Mr. Yves Kempf 39 Allee Scheffer L-2520 Luxembourg Phone: 809-323-7376 Fax: 809-326-5625 E-mail: NA Web page: NA

Free Info Available?	Speak English?	American Clients?	Canadian Clients?	SEC Approved?	Work with U.S. Advisors?
NA	NA	No	NA	No	NA
NA	NA	NA	NA	NA	NA
NA	NA	NA	NA	NA	NA

(Continued)

Fund Name and Description	Contact
SKANDIFOND NORTH AMERICAN EQUITY *Skandifond Equity Fund* Emphasizes equities in the Americas (mainly North America, but occasionally Central and South America). Net assets value per unit is expressed in U.S. dollars. Only "A" units are offered. Assets (as of March 31, 1996, or last fiscal period; quoted in U.S. dollars): $123.92 million Skandifond Sweden Bond	Mr. Emile Kremer S-E Banken Luxembourg 16 Boulevard Royal L-2249 Luxembourg Phone: 352-46-1717-239 Fax: 352-22-5550 E-mail: fonder@se.bank.se Web page: http://www.sebank.se/ sebank/fonder/defaulte.htm
SKANDIFOND SWEDEN BOND *Skandifond Bond Fund* Invests in debt securities with a life duration of at least two years. Net asset value per unit is expressed in Swedish kronor. "A" and "B" units are offered. "B" unit holders receive annual dividends. Assets (as of March 31, 1996, or last fiscal period; quoted in U.S. dollars): $309.27 million Skandifond Sweden Bond	Mr. Emile Kremer S-E Banken Luxembourg 16 Boulevard Royal L-2249 Luxembourg Phone: 352-46-1717-239 Fax: 352-22-5550 E-mail: fonder@se.bank.se Web page: http://www.sebank.se/ sebank/fonder/defaulte.htm
SWISS LIFE PROTEUS UK EQUITY *Swiss Life Investment Fund PLC—Proteus* This fund invests in a diversified portfolio made up of shares of large and small U.K. companies. Selects only those companies that have greater than average potential. In addition, derivative instruments may be occasionally used. Its goal is to produce long-term capital growth. Assets (as of March 31, 1996, or last fiscal period; quoted in U.S. dollars): $159.37 million Swiss Life Proteus American (an open-ended investment company with tax-free gross roll-up status in Dublin, Ireland)	Mr. George Pavlou IFSC 1 Harbourmaster Place Dublin 1, Ireland Phone: 44-1732-582-000 Fax: 44-1732-582-001 E-mail: NA Web page: NA

Free Info Available?	Speak English?	American Clients?	Canadian Clients?	SEC Approved?	Work with U.S. Advisors?
Yes; can't mail to U.S. addresses	Yes	No	Yes	No	No
Yes; can't mail to U.S. addresses	Yes	No	Yes	No	No
Yes; will mail to U.S. addresses	Yes	No; can sell to U.S. citizens but not to U.S. residents	Yes	No	Yes

(Continued)

Fund Name and Description	Contact
UBS (LUX) BOND INVEST CHF T *UBS (Lux) Bond Invest Umbrella* This subfund primarily invests in bonds, notes, and similar fixed-interest or floating-rate secured or unsecured investments (including floating-rate notes, convertibles, and warrant issues whose warrants entitle the holder to subscribe to securities). These instruments are issued by public, semipublic, or private borrowers. Denominated in Swiss francs. Assets (as of March 31, 1996, or last fiscal period; quoted in U.S. dollars): $647.19 million Intrag Zurich	Mr. Heinz Kaiser Bahnhofstrasse 45 8021 Zurich, Switzerland Phone: 41-1-235-43-27 Fax: 41-1-235-34-13 E-mail: Heinz.Kaiser@ubs.com Web page: http://www.ubs.com/cgi_bin/ framer.pl?/personal/funds/e_index.htm
UBS (LUX) BOND INVEST DEM T *UBS (Lux) Bond Invest Umbrella* This subfund primarily invests in bonds, notes, and similar fixed-interest or floating-rate secured or unsecured investments (including floating-rate notes, convertibles, and warrant issues whose warrants entitle the holder to subscribe to securities). These instruments are issued by public, semipublic, or private borrowers. Denominated in German marks. Assets (as of March 31, 1996, or last fiscal period; quoted in U.S. dollars): $325.72 million Intrag Zurich	Mr. Heinz Kaiser Bahnhofstrasse 45 8021 Zurich, Switzerland Phone: 41-1-235-43-27 Fax: 41-1-235-34-13 E-mail: Heinz.Kaiser@ubs.com Web page: http://www.ubs.com/cgi_bin/ framer.pl?/personal/funds/e_index.htm

Free Info Available?	Speak English?	American Clients?	Canadian Clients?	SEC Approved?	Work with U.S. Advisors?
Yes; can't mail to U.S. addresses	Yes	Yes	Yes	No	No
Yes; can't mail to U.S. addresses	Yes	Yes	Yes	No	No

(Continued)

Fund Name and Description	Contact
UBS (LUX) BOND INVEST FRF *UBS (Lux) Bond Invest Umbrella* This subfund primarily invests in bonds, notes, and similar fixed-interest or floating-rate secured or unsecured investments (including floating-rate notes, convertibles, and warrant issues whose warrants entitle the holder to subscribe to securities). These instruments are issued by public, semipublic, or private borrowers. Denominated in French francs. Assets (as of March 31, 1996, or last fiscal period; quoted in U.S. dollars): $182.36 million Intrag Zurich	Mr. Heinz Kaiser Bahnhofstrasse 45 8021 Zurich, Switzerland Phone: 41-1-235-43-27 Fax: 41-1-235-34-13 E-mail: Heinz.Kaiser@ubs.com Web page: http://www.ubs.com/cgi_bin/framer.pl?/personal/funds/e_index.htm

Free Info Available?	Speak English?	American Clients?	Canadian Clients?	SEC Approved?	Work with U.S. Advisors?
Yes; can't mail to U.S. addresses	Yes	Yes	Yes	No	No

APPENDIX B

OFFSHORE INVESTMENT
PUBLICATIONS

*Note: Subscription rates are quoted in U.S. dollars (USD),
Canadian dollars (CAD), or British pounds (GBP).*

PRINT PUBLICATIONS

Asia Money
Euromoney Publications p.l.c., 20th Floor, Trust Tower,
    68 Johnston Road, Wanchai, Hong Kong.
U.S. subscription address: American Educational Systems,
    173 West 8th Street, New York, NY 10024 USA
Telephone: 852-529-5009 (in the United States: 800-717-2669)
Fax: 852-866-9046 (in the United States: 212-501-8926)
This trade publication, which is issued ten times per year,
covers the financial market and investment developments in

Asia and the Pacific Rim. Annual subscription: £195 (GBP); foreign subscriptions $295 (USD).

Central European

Euromoney Publications p.l.c, Nestor House, Playhouse
  Yard, London EC4V 5EX UK
U.S. subscription address: American Educational Systems,
  173 West 8th Street, New York, NY 10024 USA
Telephone: 44-171-779-8935 (in the United States: 800-
  717-2669)
Fax: 44-171-779-8541 (in the United States: 212-501-8926)
Issued ten times per year, this trade publication covers the
stock and bond markets, in addition to financial news, in
Central Europe. Annual subscription: £240 (GBP); foreign
subscriptions $435 (USD).

China Banking and Finance

Asia Law and Practice Ltd., 2-F, 29 Hollywood Road, Central,
  Hong Kong
U.S. subscription address: American Educational Systems,
  173 West 8th Street, New York, NY 10024 USA
Telephone: 852-544-9918 (in the United States: 800-717-2669)
Fax: 852-543-7617 (in the United States: 212-501-8926)
This publication contains in-depth updates on regulatory
developments that affect banking and finance in the People's
Republic of China. Written for foreign investors, it is issued
ten times per year. Annual subscription $465 (USD).

The Economist

25 St. James Street, London SW1A 1HG, UK
Subscription address: P.O. Box 1H, Harold Hill, Romford,
  Essex RM3 8EQ UK
U.S. subscription address: Box 58524, Boulder, CO 80322-
  8524 USA
Telephone: 44-171-830-7000 (in the United States: 800-
  456-6086 or 212-541-5730)
Fax: 44-171-839-2968 (in the United States: 212-541-9378)

E-mail: economist@neodata.com
Web page: http://www.economist.com/
Published fifty-one times per year, this newspaper offers comprehensive coverage of worldwide events and trends in finance, politics, and business. Annual subscription price is $125 (USD).

Expat Investor
Tolley Publishing, 2 Addiscombe Road, Croydon, Surrey CR9 5AF UK
Telephone: 44-171-686-9141
Fax: 44-171-760-0588
A bi-monthly bulletin covering investment issues for expatriates.

The Financial Times
149 Tottenham Court Road, London W1P 9LI, UK
U.S. subscription address: FT Publications, Inc., 14 East 60th Street., New York, NY 10022 USA
Telephone: 44-171-873-3000. (in the United States: 800-568-7625)
Fax: 44-171-831-9136 (in the United States: 212-319-0704)
E-mail: circulation @financialtimes.com
Web page: http://www.ft.com
A daily newspaper published Monday through Saturday. Annual subscription: $450 (USD).

The Financial Times' Global Investors' Digest
Capital Publications, Inc., 1101 King Street, Suite 444, Alexandria, VA 22314 USA
Telephone: 800-327-7205
Fax: 800-645-4104
A monthly trade publication providing forecasts and analyses for interest rates, equity prices, and bond prices in twenty-three countries, including all major, minor, and emerging markets. Annual subscription $695 (USD); foreign subscriptions $731 (USD).

Freebooter

The Freebooter, P.O. Box 494, St. Peter Port, Guernsey, GY1 6BZ, Channel Islands

Telephone: 44-171-22-4295

Web page: http://www.freebooter.com/index.html

This bi-monthly newsletter describes itself as a publication "written for those who are serious about protecting their wealth, their privacy and their person." Annual subscription cost is $69 (USD).

Fundline

David H. Menashe & Company,

Box 663, Woodland Hills, CA 91365 USA

Telephone: 818-346-5637

A monthly newsletter filled with graphs and indexes depicting long-term indicators, trading oscillators, selling signals, boundaries, and composites for U.S., international, and gold funds. Annual subscription cost is $127 (USD).

Global Custodian

Asset International, Inc., 125 Greenwich Avenue, Greenwich, CT 06830 USA

Telephone: 203-629-5014

Fax: 203-629-5024

This quarterly is a trade publication for investors and, custodial and operational decision makers in the international investment industry. Annual subscription: $80 (USD).

Global Investor

Euromoney Publications p.l.c, Nestor House, Playhouse Yard, London EC4V 5EX UK

U.S. subscription address: American Educational Systems, 173 West 8th Street, New York, NY 10024 USA

Telephone: 44-171-779-8935 (in the United States: 800-717-2669)

Fax: 44-171-779-8541 (in the United States: 212-501-8926)

Issued ten times per year, this publication covers a wide variety of issues relating to investing around the world. Annual subscription: £230 (GBP); foreign subscriptions $425 (USD).

Global Market Perspective
Elliott Wave International, Box 1618, Gainesville, GA 30503 USA
Telephone: 770-536-0309
This monthly newsletter provides an intermediate to long-term outlook on all major world stock, bond, currency, and gold markets. Also discusses economic and social trends. Annual subscription: $699 (USD); $799 (USD) in Europe; $899 (USD) elsewhere.

Global Markets Newsletter
Lenape Investment Corporation, P.O. Box 724, Morrisville, PA 19067-0724 USA
Telephone: 215-949-0659
E-mail: rsauers@enter.net
Web page: http://www.enter.net/~rsauers/global.htm

Global Shareholder
Investor Responsibility Research Center, 1755 Massachusetts Avenue N.W., Suite 600, Washington, DC 20036 USA
Telephone: 202-234-7500
Fax: 202-332-7500
This quarterly publication reports on U.S. regulations that affect foreign proxies;, shareholder rights;, and developments in Asia, Australia, and Europe. Annual subscription: $100 (USD).

Headliner
Headliner Publishing Company, Ltd., 2nd Floor, 64 Cashel Street, P.O. Box 3762, Christchurch, NZ
Telephone: 64-3-3650301
Fax: 64-3-3654255

Issued every two weeks, this publication covers domestic and international areas of investment. Includes information on New Zealand, Australian, Asian, European, and U.S. stock markets, managed funds, and bonds. Annual subscription: $50 (USD).

Interinvest Review and Outlook
Interinvest Corporation, 84 State Street, 7th Floor, Boston, MA 02109-2200 USA
Telephone: 617-723-7870
Fax: 617-723-1966
A monthly newsletter that discusses international markets. Includes analysis of the U.S. stock market, a commentary on currency, portfolio review, and an international political overview. Annual subscription: $125 (USD).

The International
Financial Times Magazine, Greystoke Place, Fetter Lane, London EC4A IND, UK
Telephone: 44-171-405-6969
Fax: 44-171-831-2181
Web page: http://www.iii.co.uk/ftmags/international/index. html
A monthly magazine covering financial, economic, and political information.

The International Daily Herald Tribune
181 Avenue Charles-de-Gaulle, 92521, Neuilly-sur-Seine, France
Telephone: 41-43-93-00 (in the United States: 212-752-3890 or 800-882-2884)
Fax: 41-43-92-10
E-mail: iht@iht.com

International Money Marketing
St. Giles House, 50 Poland Street, London W1V 4AX, UK

Telephone: 44-171-287-5678
Fax: 44-171-287-5136

Investment International
4 Tabernacle Street, London EC2A 4LU, UK
Telephone: 44-171-638-1916
Fax: 44-171-638-3128
E-mail: chartcom@dircon.co.uk.
A publication thatwhich provides information for people living outside the United Kingdom. Annual subscription cost is £20 (GBP).

Market Progress Executive Report
Toronto Stock Exchange, Exchange Tower, 2 First Canadian
   Place, Toronto GN M5X 1J2 Canada
Telephone: 416-947-4655
Fax: 416-947-4585
Published in Canada, this monthly includes regional and international analyses of equities, options, futures, inter-listed stocks, and five Canadian exchanges. Also includes analyses of market quality. Annual subscription: $133.75 (CAD); prices vary for subscriptions outside Canada.

Myers' Finance Review
Myers Finance and Energy, Inc., 104 S. Freyer Street, Suite
   214A, Spokane, WA 99202-4814 USA
Telephone: 509-534-7132
Fax: 509-534-8054
This monthly publication includes a discussion of the world's political and economic situation, with a strong emphasis on its effect upon international monetary conditions, precious metals, stocks, bonds, and interest rates. Annual subscription: $129 (USD).

Offshore Alert
Lion House, 25 High Street, Thames Ditton, Surrey KT7 0SD,
   UK

Telephone: 44-171-398-4187
Fax: 44-171-398-4186

Offshore Financial Review
Financial Times Magazine, Maple House, 149 Tottenham
    Court Road, London W1P 9LL, UK
Telephone: 44-171-896-2508
Fax: 44-171-831-9136
Web page: http://www.iii.co.uk/ftmags/off/
A trade publication that covers industry changes and fund
performance for financial managers whose clients have off-
shore business. Subscription is free to qualified personnel.

Offshore Investment Magazine
Subscription Department, 62 Brompton Road, Knights-
    bridge, London SW3 1BW, UK
Telephone: 44-171-225-0550
Fax: 44-171-584-1093
Web page and E-mail: http://www.offshoreinvestment.com/
    offshore/about.html
Issued ten times per year, this publication presents current
information regarding offshore incorporation, investment,
domicile, and tax issues. Annual subscription is $270 (USD);
outside Europe the cost is $378 (USD).

Offshore Outlook
GinsGlobe Communications, 1510 Cantera Avenue, Santa
    Barbara, CA 93110 USA
Telephone: 805-682-6318
Fax: 805-563-9528
E-mail: info@offshore-outlook.com
Web page: http://www.offshore-outlook.com/
This publication aims to educate the public about the best
use of offshore financial services. An online version is also
available. Annual subscription: $325 (USD).

Portfolio International
Thames House, 18 Park Street, London SE1 9ER, UK
Telephone: 44-171-896-2508
Fax: 44-171-403-4682

Resident Abroad
Financial Times Magazines, Greystoke Place, Fetter Lane,
  London EC4A 1ND, UK
Telephone: 44-171-405-6969
Fax: 44-171-831-2181
Web page: http://www.iii.co.uk/ftmags/international
A monthly trade publication that reports on all tax and financial issues that are likely to be encountered by residents abroad. Subscription cost is £42 (GBP) in the United Kingdom; £49 (GBP) in the rest of Europe, £64 (GBP) in North Africa and the Middle East, and £78 (GBP) elsewhere.

Return on Investment
Investment Management Publications, Inc., 1 Liberty Square,
  12th Floor, Boston, MA 02109 USA
Telephone: 617-422-5450
Fax: 617-422-0162
E-mail: impubs@aol.com
A bi-monthly trade newsletter that reports on the business of investment management worldwide. Written especially for money management professionals and others involved in this rapidly growing area. Annual subscription: $150 (USD).

South China Morning Post
GPO Box 47, Hong Kong
Telephone: 852-26808661 (in the United Kingdom: 44-171-5873683)
Fax: 852-26808688
Daily newspaper covering finance, economics, and politics in the region.

Spectrum International

CDA Investment Technologies, Inc., 1335 Piccard Drive, Rockville, MD 20850 USA

Telephone: 800-232-6362

Fax: 301-590-1329

This journal is published semi-annually, in two volumes. Included in each volume is information on institutional holdings and ownership of worldwide securities. Includes more than 9,200 equities domiciled in fifty-one countries outside the United States, and over 2,200 institutional trusts and funds in fourteen countries worldwide.

The Wall Street Journal

Circulation Department, P.O. Box 2845, In de Creamer 37, 6401 DH Heerlen, The Netherlands

(U.S. subscription address: 200 Burnett Road, Chicopee, MA 01020)

Telephone: 31-45-576-1222 (in the United States: 800-568-7625)

Fax: 31-45-571-4722

E-mail: webwsj@wsj.dowjones.com

Web page: http://www.wsj.com

A daily publication (Monday through Friday) covering finance and business. Also publishes regional issues throughout the United States, in Belgium, and in Hong Kong.

World Affairs Review

Centre for International Studies Ltd., Bramley House, Woolstone, Cheltenham, Glos., GL52 4RG UK

Telephone: 44-1242-679100

Fax: 44-1242-679101

This monthly newsletter includes updated guidelines on international stock, currency, and precious metals markets. Its aim is to guide internationally-oriented investors. Annual subscription: $175 (USD).

World Investor

Agora, Inc., 1217 St. Paul Street, Baltimore, MD 21202 USA
Telephone: 800-433-1528
Fax: 410-223-2553
This monthly newsletter covers the U.S. and foreign financial markets, and provides an economic outlook. Its recommendations are aimed at investors who utilize two model portfolios—the income and the long-term growth portfolio. Annual subscription: $94 (USD).

ELECTRONIC MAGAZINES AND JOURNALS

Berbiz

Web page: http://www.webcom.com/~wrsl/index.html
E-mail: wrsl@ibl.bm
This e-mail newsletter is published monthly, and available at no charge to individuals who complete an online subscription form. It covers events and changes within the international business sector of Bermuda. Included are press releases and clippings, financial statement releases, and statistical updates. Topics covered include insurance, corporate administration, investment, mutual funds, trusts, and legal issues.

Business Monitor Online

Web page: http://www.businessmonitor.co.uk/index. html
E-mail: feedback@businessmonitor.co.uk
Published by Business Briefing Publishing Ltd., this free online journal is written for professionals and business people involved in international trade and investment. Topics covered include legislation, regulations, finance, offshore finance, market and economic analysis, and worldwide business news.

The Eastern Economic Review Interactive Edition
Web page: http://www.feer.com/
E-mail: webmaster@feer.com
This online newsletter offers a variety of information on Asian investments, current affairs, and business. Although registration is required, access to the site is free.

Euromoney World Link
Web page: http://www.emwl.com/
E-mail: kleigh@emwl.com
The online version of *Euromoney* magazine, this publication offers access to all the articles available in the print edition, along with the ability to search its archives. Past articles/special issues include "Global Investors," "Asian Bonds," and "Emerging Markets." Registration is required for free access to the site's resources.

Global Market Strategist
Web page: http://www.margin.com/cbn/newsletters/GMS index.html# GMSR
An online publication that offers market advisory reports. Includes perspectives on U.S. and global economic and socio-political trends and forecasts. Also covers a technical analysis of U.S. global stock markets, interest rates, currencies, precious metals, and commodities. Free sample available at the Web site. A one-year online subscription costs $297 (USD).

Interactive Investor
The International-Worldwide Guide to Offshore Personal Finance
Web page: http://www.iii.co.uk/ftmags/international/index. htm
An online journal published by Financial Times Magazines. Provides investment and personal finance information from other FT publications, including the *Financial Advisor*, *Product Advisor*, *Investment Advisor*, and *Offshore Finan-*

cial Review. This Web page allows viewers to submit questions (which are answered by financial and investment experts), obtain price quotes on more than 14,000 investments, research investment trusts, and access investment performance tables. Free access.

Investor's Internet Journal

Web page: http://194.6.100.3/~iij/
E-mail: wheelock@discover.co.uk
Subtitled "The Leading Internet Journal for World Stockmarket News," this free online publication provides updated summaries and insights on more than thirty international stock markets.

Jersey Financial News

Web page: http://www.jersey.gov.uk/news/index.html
E-mail: jsyfsd@intl.net
The official online newspaper of the state of Jersey's Financial Services Department. Published two times per year, this journal covers political, financial, and economic news relating to the Island of Jersey.

Martin Pring's Intermarket Review

Web page: http://www.margin.com/cbn/newsletters/MPN
  index.html#PIMR
This online publication covers the major equity indexes, bonds, currencies, and precious metals. Also includes complete asset allocation recommendations for U.S.-based (dollar-based) investors. A free sample is downloadable from their Web site. Price for an annual online subscription is $245 (USD).

Offshore

Web page: http://www.euro.net/innovation/offshore. html
E-mail: offshore@dnai.com
An asset protection publication, produced in the United States by Cornez and Associates. Contains legal, financial,

accounting, and other information of interest to the offshore investment community. Annual subscription price is $20 (USD).

Offshore Funds Directory
Web page: http://www.trustnet.co.uk/
E-mail: mail@trustnet.co.uk
This Web page provides free daily comparative performance data and detailed information covering 600 U.K. investment funds and close-ended offshore and U.S. funds.

Offshore Outlook Online
Web page: http://www.offshore-outlook.com/
E-mail: info@offshore-outlook.com
This journal is the online version of the printed publication *Offshore Outlook*, published by GinsGlobe Communications in Santa Barbara, California, USA. Its stated purpose is to educate the public about the best use of offshore financial services. A number of free archived articles are available from the Web site. Subscription price: $190 (USD) for the online version; $325 (USD) for the print publication.

Worth Online
Web page: http://www.worth.com/
E-mail: subscription@worth.com
This online version of the print magazine includes a variety of articles on the subject of worldwide investing. Recent titles include "Global Investing," and "Expanding Your Fund Horizons." The site is free.

GLOSSARY

ABOVE THE LINE. In accounting, ordinary items of income and expenditure are treated "above the line," which means they are included in determining "net profit." Extraordinary items are treated "below the line."

ACCEPTANCE. When a bank accepts a bill of exchange it signs the bill's face to signify that it will guarantee payment. The acceptance can then be discounted on fine terms. Until recently in London it was particularly desirable that the accepting bank be a member of the Accepting Houses Committee, as the bill could be discounted with the Bank of England.

ACCEPTING HOUSES COMMITTEE. An exclusive group of approximately seventeen U.K.-owned merchant banks whose acceptance of a bill guaranteed that it could be sold to the Bank of England. This privilege disappeared during moves to make London a more international financial center.

ACCOMMODATION ADDRESS. An address to which letters may be directed but where the addressee has no physical presence. Arrangements will normally have been made to forward letters to the addressee at an alternate address.

ACCOUNTS. Every company must keep sufficient records of its transactions for persons to ascertain the company's financial position with reasonable accuracy at any time. These are normally kept at the principal place of business. After the end of each fiscal year the directors are responsible for providing the following financial statements to the shareholders: balance sheet, revenue account, and an auditors' report. In the United States this may also require the filing of the statements with the SEC or another regulatory agency.

ACCOUNTS PAYABLE/RECEIVABLE. U.S. terms for amounts owing by or to a business.

ACCREDITED INVESTOR. As promulgated by the U.S. SEC in Regulation D, a wealthy investor who is not counted as a purchaser/investor in a private or limited offering. Generally, such an investor must have a net worth of at least $1 million or an annual income equal to or greater than $200,000; the investment must be at least $150,000; and it may not exceed 20 percent of the person's wealth.

ACCRUALS. Allowances in accounts for money earned but not yet payable or received. Thus, if a bond pays interest annually at the year end, half of that interest may be accrued in accounts as of June 30.

ACCUMULATION AND MAINTENANCE TRUST. A U.K. device whereby a trust is liable to reduced taxation provided that at least one beneficiary can receive the principal or income on or before the age of twenty-five.

ACCUMULATIONS. The former practice whereby an English trust could accumulate income throughout its perpetuity period. Some common law jurisdictions currently allow the practice.

ACID TEST. The extent to which a company could meet its current liabilities from current assets other than stock. This is an onerous test of liquidity, which may be inappropriate to normal business practice in many industries. Also known as the *quick ratio.*

ACTUARY. A qualified statistician who will calculate the likelihood of various probabilities, such as mortality tables, on behalf of pension funds or insurance companies. Fellows of the British Faculty of Actuaries are designated by the letters FFA after their name. The Institute of Actuaries is at Staple Inn Hall, High Holborn, London WCLV 7QJ.

ADMINISTRATIVE FEE. Money paid to the fund administrator. It's usually a percentage of the fund's net asset value.

ADR (AMERICAN DEPOSITORY RECEIPT). Also, an advance determination ruling obtained upon application to the IRS. Used, for example, to determine if a multinational policy decision is tax compliant.

AD VALOREM. Latin term for "according to value." A variable form of tax that is determined according to the price of the object taxed. An ad valorem tax suits revenue authorities better in times of inflation.

ADVISORY CLIENT. A type of relationship between a person and a broker. Under this relationship the person receives investment advice from the broker but is responsible for the decisions made. Contrasts with an *execution-only relationship*, wherein the client makes all decisions without advice from the broker.

ADVOCATE. The correct designation of a qualified lawyer in some jurisdictions, including the Channel Islands and the Isle of Man. In those islands an advocate acts as both barrister and solicitor; in Scotland an advocate is a barrister only. In civil law jurisdictions an avocat/avvocato/abogado will normally concentrate upon court work, routine work like the drafting of legal documents being carried out by a notary.

AFBD (ASSOCIATION OF FUTURES BROKERS AND DEALERS). A self-regulating organization approved by the United Kingdom's SIB. Correspondence concerning a member should be addressed to AFBD B Section, 5th Floor Plantation House, 4-16 Mincing Lane, London EC3M 3DX.

AG (AKTIEN GESELLSCHAIT). A German public company. The board of directors is elected and controlled by a supervisory board ("Aufsichstrat").

AGENCY BROKER. A situation that occurs in the United Kingdom whereby a broker acts as an agent between the buyer and seller but is not the market maker.

AGENT. One who is dealing on behalf of another, the principal, with the ability to obligate the principal in contract, even though the principal bears the entire financial risk. The status of an agent may be less secure outside a common law jurisdiction.

AGGRESSIVE GROWTH FUND. An investment fund whose primary goal is to seek maximum capital gains. Income is a less important goal. To do this, the fund manager may invest in stocks of fledgling companies, new industries, or companies that are having problems. Other fund managers may use investment techniques like option writing or short-term trading to obtain their primary goal.

AIBD (ASSOCIATION OF INTERNATIONAL BOND DEALERS). A trade organization established with the purpose of standardizing dealings in Eurobonds between its members. Although recognized by the SIB as a "designated investment exchange," it is not a regulatory organization. It publishes a weekly Eurobond "guide," which is principally a price list. Its address is Seven Limeharbour Docklands GB-London E14 9NQ.

AITC (ASSOCIATION OF INVESTMENT TRUST COMPANIES). A nonregulatory industry group that supplies free information on U.K. investment trusts. Its address is 16 Finsbury Circus, London EC2M 7JJ.

ALPHA. (1) The relationship of the specific risk of an equity to the risk of the market as a whole. An alpha value other than 0 indicates an over- or undervalued stock. (2) Equities on the ISE are graded according to marketability, from alpha stocks, where one can deal in volume with any of a number of brokers, down through delta, which are seriously illiquid.

ALTERNATIVE MINIMUM TAX. Under U.S. tax law, a tax at 21 percent on the gross income of individuals or 20 percent for corporations, which is applicable if it would yield more to the IRS than taxing income net of permitted deductions at normal rates.

AMERICAN DEPOSITORY RECEIPT (ADR). A certificate issued by a U.S. bank conferring beneficial ownership of a block of foreign shares held at one of its overseas offices. An ADR is negotiable on a U.S. exchange, and so the device combines the convenience, to a U.S. investor, of a domestic security with the opportunities of overseas investment. In some instances, notably major South African mining companies, ADRs constitute the most liquid form of investment open to foreigners.

AMERICAN STOCK EXCHANGE. The second stock exchange in New York, often referred to as the "Curb." Its address is 86 Trinity Place, New York City, NY 10006.

AMORTIZATION. (1) (U.K. usage) Reduction of the principal of a loan by repaying it in installments, each installment payment including interest. (2) (U.S. usage) Depreciation.

ANNUAL GENERAL MEETING. The meeting at which the shareholders of a company, having received the annual report, can exercise their rights to vote on such matters as accepting the accounts, reappointing directors and auditors, and any other matter on the agenda.

ANNUAL PERCENTAGE RATE (APR). A standardized measure of quoting an interest rate, as required by the U.S. Truth in Lending Act and the British Consumer Credit Act.

ANNUITANT. The beneficiary or beneficiaries (in a last-to-die arrangement) of an annuity who receives a stream of payments pursuant to the terms of the annuity contract.

ANNUITY. A tax-sheltering vehicle. An unsecured contract between the company and the annuitant(s) that grows deferred free and is used to provide for one's later years. All income taxes are deferred until maturing of the annuity. Capital gains and income accumulate tax deferred. Results in a stream of payments made to the annuitant during his or her lifetime under the annuity agreement. Taxes are paid on the income, interest earned, and capital gains, but only to the extent as and when they are received. Currently, there is no annual limit on purchases, but there is no tax credit for purchases. An annuity is not an insurance policy. Annuities have a fixed payment or income stream usually for a term measured by one's life. A tool used in estate planning whereby a person pays a lump sum in exchange for a specific income stream. The income stream then consists of principal, that is, repayment of the purchaser's purchase price, which is tax free, and income in the form of interest, which would be taxable.

AP. Asset protection.

APPRECIATION. A rise in the value of an asset. Also used to signify the rise in a nation's currency value when measured against at least one other currency.

APPROPRIATIONS. Uses for the profits of a company remaining after tax. They are usually either distributed as dividends or added to reserves as retained earnings.

APT. See **asset protection trust.**

ARBITRAGE. To seek to take advantage of price differentials of the same security on different markets by buying on the cheaper one and selling on the other. Arbitrageurs are wholly dependent on receiving prices before their competitors. Occurs frequently in the cash and futures markets, or it can involve options.

ARTICLES OF ASSOCIATION. The rules and regulations whereby the internal affairs of a U.K. company are governed. The equivalent U.S. term is **by-laws.**

ASSESSABLE. A security on which a further call is payable. The U.K. term is **partly paid.**

ASSET. Property of any kind, real or personal, tangible or intangible.

Current assets. Assets readily converted to cash, that is, cash, marketable securities, and accounts receivable.

Fixed assets. Assets of a long-term or permanent nature that may be used in the operation of a business or production of income.

Frozen assets. Assets that are illiquid or otherwise difficult to convert to cash.

ASSET MANAGER. A person appointed by a written contract between the IBC (or the exempt company) or the APT and that person to direct the investment program. It can be a fully discretionary account, or limitations can be imposed by the contract under the terms of the APT or by the officers of the IBC. Fees to the asset manager can be based on performance achieved, trading commissions, or a percentage of the valuation of the estate under her management.

ASSET PROTECTION TRUST (APT). A special form of irrevocable trust, usually created (settled) offshore for the principal purposes of preserving and protecting part of one's wealth offshore against creditors. Title to the asset is transferred to a person named the trustee. Generally used for asset protection and usually tax neutral. Its ultimate function is to provide for the beneficiaries of the APT.

ASSET STRIPPING. Buying a quoted company and then hoping to recover the cost by selling off its constituent parts.

ASSOCIATED COMPANY. One over which a parent company exercises some control, but less than with a subsidiary company. In accountancy, such control is typically taken as being the ownership of at least 20 percent of voting shares and a say in management.

AUTHORIZED CAPITAL. With respect to a corporation or company (IBC), the sum value of the aggregate of par value of all shares that the company is authorized to issue. Also see **flight capital.**

BACK-TO-BACK LOANS. Back-to-back loans are matching deposit arrangements. They may be used to obtain medium- to long-term financing or to solve an exchange control problem. However, in the case of certain tax havens, the function of back-to-back loans is to reduce the taxable base subject to withholding taxes on interest payments by interposing an intermediary subsidiary company between the source of the income and the recipient. For example, an intermediary company located in the Netherlands or the Netherlands Antilles may be interposed so as to take advantage of a favorable tax treaty. In such cases the authorities usually require a certain spread or "turn" on the rates so as to create a small profit that is subject to tax locally.

BALANCE OF PAYMENTS. A system that uses double-entry bookkeeping to track a country's economic transactions with the rest of the world during a specific time period. Divided into three categories: (1) current account, based on external trade in merchandise and services; (2) capital account, which refers to direct and portfolio investments into and out of a country; and (3) capital flows, which occur between the central bank and the foreign central banks.

BANK OF INTERNATIONAL SETTLEMENTS (BIS). Structured like the U.S. Federal Reserve Bank, controlled by the Basel Committee of the G-10 nations' Central Banks, it sets standards for capital adequacy among the member central banks.

BANK SECRECY. In most countries one of the terms of the relationship between banker and customer is that the banker will keep the customer's affairs secret. Staff members are normally required to sign a declaration of secrecy as regards the business of the banks. Where numbered accounts are used, their purpose is to limit the number of persons who know the identity of the client. In certain countries (for example, Switzerland and the Cayman Islands) specific legislation makes breaches of bank secrecy subject to criminal law sanctions. However, in all legal systems (including Switzerland) there are specific cases where the duty of secrecy of a banker is discharged. The exchange of information clause contained in most tax treaties may enable the tax administration of one treaty country to obtain information concerning bank accounts that its residents have in the other country.

BASE RATE. (1) The benchmark lending rate for U.K. banks. In contrast to the "prime rate" quoted by U.S. banks, it is set at a level below which even the most creditworthy customers can hope to borrow. The base rates of the leading U.K. commercial banks sometimes vary for whole hours at a time. (2) A year chosen to act as the basis of comparison for an index number.

BASIS POINT. One hundredth of 1 percent. Thus, a spread of 50 basis points between the bid and offer prices of a bond means that one must pay 0.5 percent more to buy it than one would get from selling it.

BBC (BRITISH BROADCASTING CORPORATION). The major British TV and radio broadcasting company. Its overseas service is financed by the British foreign office. It broadcasts financial reports packed with information five times daily. Information from programs and frequencies of transmission is contained in the monthly magazine *London Calling*, obtainable from P.O. Box 76, Bush House Strand, London WC2B 4PH.

BCCI. See **Bank of Credit and Commerce International.**

BEAR. Someone who expects prices to fall and may therefore sell short securities that he does not already own in the expectation of being able subsequently to buy the same stock at a lower price with which to make delivery. If the price at which he must buy back rises, he is said to be the victim of a "bear squeeze."

BEARER BOND. A bond that can be redeemed by anyone who presents it on the redemption date, regardless of whether that person actually owns the bond.

BEARER SECURITIES. A security, such as a bank note, in which the issuer recognizes the legal owner as the individual who possesses the security. It is also negotiable by the owner.

BED AND BREAKFAST. The device of selling a security with the intention of repurchasing it with the minimum delay in order to establish a tax loss for U.K. CGT purposes. The exercise is invalid if it is impossible for the investor, or for corporate shareowners, to lose.

BELOW THE LINE. In accounting, extraordinary items and appropriations are treated "below the line," which means that they do not form part of net profit.

BENEFICIAL INTEREST OR OWNERSHIP. Not a direct interest but rather through a nominee, holding legal title on behalf of the beneficial owner's equitable interest. Provides privacy and avoids use of one's own name for transactions.

BENEFICIAL OWNER. The true, ultimate owner of anything, who may or may not choose, for reasons of convenience or confidentiality, to conceal her identity behind nominees. The use of nominees does not alter the position of the beneficial owner as regards IRS reporting requirements and liability for taxes.

BENEFICIARY. The person(s), company, trust, or estate named by the grantor, settlor, or creator to receive the benefits of a trust in due course upon conditions that the grantor established by way of a trust deed. An exception would be the fully discretionary trust. The beneficiary could be a charity, foundation, and/or person(s) that or who are characterized by "classes" in terms of their order of entitlement—their hierarchy. Any person for whose benefit, whether or not she knows it, property has been placed in trust. Includes persons with present or future interests, vested or contingent.

BETA COEFFICIENT. A measure of the volatility of the price of an individual security relative to the market on which it is quoted. A beta factor of 1.2 would indicate that the security in question had normally risen or fallen by 120 percent of the overall market movement.

BID PRICE. The price at which a market maker is willing to buy a security, generally including the commission.

BIG BANG. The popular term for the simultaneous endings of fixed rates of commission and single capacity on the ISE on October 27, 1986.

BIG BOARD. A reference to the New York Stock Exchange.

BILL-BROKER. A member of the London Discount Market. Members may be identified by their tradition of wearing a top hat.

BILL OF EXCHANGE. An unconditional order in writing addressed by one person to another to pay a certain sum of money either immediately—a "sight" bill—or at a fixed or determinable date in the future, either to the bearer or to a specified payee. The person who originates the bill, or draft, is the drawer, and the person to whom the instruction is given is the drawee until he signs the bill in acknowledgment, when he becomes the acceptor. Bills are traded on the secondary market, discounted to reflect both the current cost of money and the creditworthiness of the names on the bill.

BILL OF LADING. A document conferring ownership of goods in transit.

BIS. See **Bank of International Settlements.**

BLOCK. A large quantity of equities or bonds, traded in one transaction, usually at the lowest commission rates. In the United States, 10,000 shares or $250,000 worth of bonds would be considered a block.

BLUE CHIP. A security issued by a large, well-established company. Generally, blue chips carry a lower risk of failure than securities issued by smaller or younger companies.

BLUE SKY LAWS. Common name for U.S. states' (as opposed to federal) laws regulating the sale of securities intended to protect investors.

BOARD LOT. A quantity of a security, typically 1,000, that can be traded immediately upon a Far Eastern exchange. Trying to deal in odd lots can be difficult.

BOARD OF TRUSTEES. A board acting as a trustee of a trust or as advisors to the trustee, depending upon the language of the trust indenture. Also see **committee of advisors.**

BONA VACANTIA. Latin term for unclaimed goods, such as the assets of a person who dies without a will, or intestate.

BOND. Evidence of a debt whereby a business or government agency promises to pay the holder a specified amount of interest for a specified time, paying the principal amount at a fixed date. The time schedule of repayment varies with the type of bond. In the United Kingdom, bonds are called "gilts" or "stocks."

BOND ISSUE. The process of selling bonds to the public during a specified time period.

BOND-RATING AGENCY. An organization that rates bond issues, the major agencies being Moody's and Standard & Poors. It should be noted that it is the bond that is rated, not the issuer.

BONUS. A life assurance company that has issued a policy "with profits" will declare annual bonuses in addition to the guaranteed sum, to allow the insured some idea of what she can look forward to. Because these bonuses are guaranteed by the company, it must protect itself against a market crash shortly before the policy matures. It achieves this by deliberately understating bonuses earned during the life of the policy and correcting this with a "terminal bonus" at maturity.

BOOK. A market maker may refer to his portfolio, long or short, as his book. It would make fascinating reading for his competitors.

BOOK COST. The aggregate cost of a holding in a portfolio. The book cost per share will change on a subsequent purchase at a different net price, but not on a disposal.

BOOK VALUE. The value at which assets or liabilities are carried on the accounting books. Also see **net asset value.**

BOOM. A high level of business activity, which usually occurs at the end of expansion of a business cycle. Usually this level cannot be sustained.

BOTTOM-UP APPROACH. An approach to investing whereby the fund manager concentrates on identifying attractive individual securities. Contrast with **top-down approach.**

BOUGHT DEAL. Where an issuing house takes an entire new

issue onto its own books at its own risk. Very convenient for the company that is raising capital but risky for the issuing house.

BOUTIQUE. Any small, specialized brokerage or fund management firm. Boutiques are often established by managers who have previously earned a reputation while working for a "financial supermarket," who prefer to work for themselves within their field of expertise.

BRADY BONDS. Introduced in the late 1980s, these bonds were issued by developing countries to pay off their defaulted loans made on commercial banks. These bonds are often collateralized by claims on the U.S. government.

BRASS PLATE COMPANY. A company that has no physical presence at its registered office other than its name at the outer door. Firms of lawyers and accountants in tax havens often provide registered office facilities to scores of brass plate companies.

BREAKUP VALUE. The value attributable to a company's assets in the event of their forced sale. See also **going concern.**

BRITISH PUBLIC COMPANY. See **PLC.**

BROKER. An agent retained to make bargains and contracts, at a specified compensation, for a principal.

Broker-agent. Person licensed as both a broker and agent.

Broker-dealer. A securities brokerage dealer, usually an NASD member and licensed by the states in which it does business.

Money-broker. One who lends or raises money to or for another.

Real estate broker. One who is licensed to sell real estate of another.

Securities broker. Person who sells securities.

BUDGET SURPLUS OR DEFICIT. The balance on a government's fiscal account after considering its receipts and expenditures for a period of time. A positive balance is called a surplus; a negative balance is called a deficit.

BUFFER STOCK. Quantities of a commodity purchased on behalf of a cartel at a time of apparently depressed prices with the intention of selling at higher prices, thereby smoothing price fluctuations. An admirable aim, which works most of the time.

BULL. Someone who expects prices to rise. A "stale bull" will have bought when he expected prices to rise, have seen them fall instead, and will now be looking to sell into a rally.

BULLET. A loan where all the principal is repaid on maturity, as one that is subject to calls.

BULLION COINS. Coins made from precious metal whose price is determined by the weight of metal contained rather than their numismatic value. Pioneered by the Krugerrand and the Noble in gold and platinum, respectively.

BULL MARKET. Term for a market in which prices are rising or expected to rise.

BUNDESBANK. The West German central bank. It is allowed greater independence of government than is usual in other countries, and it uses that independence to pursue policies consistent with an abhorrence of inflation.

"BUSTED" BONDS. Bonds issued by a nation or corporation that has since defaulted; therefore they are worthless. The issuer will not, however, be able to raise more money on that market until he has come to some arrangement with the owners of the defaulted bonds, so a highly specialized market exists in them.

BUY BACK. An arrangement whereby a firm exporting factory machinery will agree to buy a certain percentage amount of the product of that plant.

BV (BESLOTEN VENNOOTSCHAP MET BEPERKTE AANG-PANKELIJKHEID). The Dutch approximate equivalent to a private company.

BY-LAWS. The rules and regulations whereby the internal affairs of a U.S. company are governed. The equivalent U.K. term is **articles of association.**

BYPASS TRUST. (U.S. trust law) A revocable trust designed to reduce the estate tax payable on assets passing to children on their parents' death. The parents can enjoy the income from the trust during their lifetimes, and they may even be able to draw upon the principal in specific circumstances.

CA. A member of the Institute of Chartered Accountants of Scotland, which is the oldest such institute in the world. Its address is 27 Queen Street, Edinburgh EH2 1LA.

CALL. A demand from a company for payment of all or part of sums unpaid on shares that have yet to be fully paid.

CALL OPTION. The owner of a call option is entitled to buy something from the writer at a predetermined price during the time of the option.

CAPITAL. (1) Assets used for the production of profits and wealth. (2) Owner's equity in a business. Also see **authorized capital** and **flight capital.**

CAPITAL ACCOUNT. The net money flowing into a country for long-term investment plus any sums that need to be borrowed to balance any deficit on current account.

CAPITAL GAIN. The positive difference between the price of an asset and its cost. Contrasts with capital loss, which indicates a negative difference between the price of an asset and its cost.

CAPITAL GAINS DISTRIBUTION. Payments made to the shareholders of mutual funds. The money for these payments come from the profits derived when the fund's portfolio securities were sold. These distributions are usually paid once each year.

CAPITAL GAINS TAX (CGT). (1) A U.K. tax on gains made by "ordinary residents" on profitable disposals, apart from various excluded items, which includes gilts, a designated home, and an automobile for normal use. There is a threshold on profits taken during a fiscal year below which they are excused. CGT corporations pay corporation tax on profitable disposals. (2) A tax on income earned due to the sale of an asset. Measured on a net basis, using the original cost of the asset adjusted for depreciation. Sometimes this cost is adjusted for inflation. The U.S. Tax Reform Act of 1986 provided that capital gains should be taxed at ordinary income tax rates starting in 1988.

CAPITAL GOODS. Durable goods—such as plants, buildings, or equipment—that are utilized in order to produce other goods and services.

CAPITALISM. The economic system that permits anyone with money to employ it as she sees fit, on the argument that the greatest collective good result from individuals trying to advance their private interests.

CAPITALIZATION. (1) The current value of a recurring income or cash flow. (2) The act of computing the value of recurring income or cash flow. A corporation can determine its market capitalization by multiplying the market price of its shares by the number of outstanding shares.

CAPITAL MARKETS. The market in long-dated bonds. Short-dated paper is traded on a money market.

CAPTIVE BANKS. The term *captive bank* is sometimes used to refer to a banking subsidiary set up in a tax haven or financial center that operates principally for the benefit of the members of a multinational group and their customers and suppliers. Such captive banks may also operate as merchant banks and offer commercial banking as well as financing services.

CAPTIVE FINANCE. Financing the sales of a group through a specialist subsidiary, for example, when General Motors Acceptance Corporation finances the purchase of a GM automobile.

CAPTIVE INSURANCE. Insurance with a company in the same group as the insured. This practice can reduce premiums sharply, as the insurer need not pay marketing costs. It may also be able to accumulate reserves against possible losses in a favorable tax environment, although it would be self-defeating to abuse this potential. A captive should reinsure any risk that exceeds its own reserves.

CARAT. Approximately 205 milligrams, or about the weight of the seed of the carob tree which, being remarkably consistent, was used for measuring the weight of precious stones from earliest times. Pure gold is described as 24 carat; 18-carat gold will be 75 percent gold and 25 percent hardening alloy.

CARICOM (CARIBBEAN COMMON MARKET). Consists of fifteen sister-member countries of the Caribbean community. Members include Antigua and Barbuda, Bahamas, Barbados, Belize, Dominica, Grenada, Guyana, Jamaica, Montserrat, St. Kitts and Nevis, St. Lucia, St. Vincent, Surinam, Trinidad, and Tobago. They have set as a goal that in 1997 there will be a single market allowing for the free movement of labor. Conspicuous by their absence are the Cayman Islands and the British Virgin Islands, two major players in international banking and finance.

CARTEL. An agreement among the major suppliers of a good or service to fix its price at an advantageous level. "Antitrust" legislation attempts the difficult task of suppressing this practice.

CASH COW. A business that generates a predictable cash flow, usually through customer loyalty. Deemed desirable by highly leveraged corporate raiders.

CASH FLOW. Cash inflows consist of the proceeds of new issues, trading profits, and depreciation/amortization, less the increase in working capital. Cash outflow goes on fixed assets, dividends, and increases in reserves. Company's cash flow is disclosed in the statement of source and application of funds.

CASH SETTLEMENT. Bargains on the ISE that are due to be settled on the following day—as is usually the case with gilts or bearer securities—are said to be for cash settlement. All stock exchange bargains in Japan, other than bond index futures, are for cash settlement.

CASH SURRENDER VALUE. The sum that an insurance company will be willing to pay on the premature surrender of a life insurance policy. This will be quite small in relation to its future value, especially early in the life of the policy. It may therefore be advantageous to borrow against the cash surrender value.

CERTIFICATE OF DEPOSIT (CD). An investment instrument available through a financial institution. Investors agree to deposit a predetermined amount of money in the financial institution for an established time period (for example, one month, two months, three months, or six months). In return they receive a certificate of deposit. Because they are easily negotiable and generally a safe investment, certificates of deposit usually pay lower rates of interest than riskier investment instruments, such as mutual funds and stocks.

CERTIFIED PUBLIC ACCOUNTANT (CPA). A member of the American Institute of Certified Public Accountants. Generally requires a bachelor's degree in accounting plus two years of public accounting/auditing experience. The offshore counterpart is the chartered accountant.

CFC. See **controlled foreign corporation.**

CLEARING HOUSE INTERBANK PAYMENT SYSTEM (CHIPS). A computerized system for clearing payment of U.S. dollars in New York within the day.

CHARTERED FINANCIAL ANALYST (CFA). A designation assigned to certain investment managers who select securities for sale or purchase.

CIVIL LAW. Law courts in jurisdictions that follow civil law will aim to follow a highly structured legal code to the letter. Common practice is immaterial, and so juries are irrelevant. Cases are decided by an expert judge. Most of the nations of continental Europe and their former colonies are civil law jurisdictions. The expression is also used within common law jurisdictions to distinguish the law governing actions between private parties as opposed to criminal law.

CLASS OF SHARE. A company's regulations may permit it to issue shares of more than one class. For example, it may issue both voting and nonvoting shares. While the holders of different classes of share will be entitled to different treatment from the company, all holders of the same class must be treated identically.

CLEARING BANK. A British commercial bank that is a member of a bankers' clearinghouse, through which checks are cleared.

CLEARINGHOUSE. An institution where members' liabilities to one another are netted out, so that only a final net sum owing need be paid.

CLIFFORD TRUST. A grantor trust whereby the settlor, the creator of the trust, retains the right to regain possess the trust property upon the happening of a specified event.

CLOSED-END FUND. A collective investment scheme that does not undertake to issue and redeem its shares on a regular basis. Because they need not fear a rush of redemptions, the managers can afford to take a longer view when investing. Shares can be bought and sold on the secondary market, usually at a discount to their net asset value. British investment trusts are closed-end funds.

COLD CALLING. An unsolicited telephone call or visit from a salesperson to anyone other than a professional in the financial world, suggesting a financial transaction.

COLLATERAL. Property put up to secure a loan (U.S. usage) or only that put up by a third party to support a guarantee (U.K. usage).

COLLECTIVE INVESTMENT SCHEME. Any arrangement for pooling several investors' funds. The usual U.S. term is *investment company*. The intention is that the pooled fund will be able to achieve economies of scale and a spread of investments that would be beyond the reach of individual investors.

COMECOM (COUNCIL FOR MUTUAL ECONOMIC ASSISTANCE). The Eastern European counterpart to the EEC but differing in the dominance of a single member, the Soviet Union, and in its economic effectiveness.

COMMERCIAL PAPER. Loan notes issued by a commercial company as opposed to a bank. Commercial paper grew in popularity in the mid-1980s on account of distrust of the commercial banks' exposure to LDC lending. The market has never been very liquid.

COMMITTEE OF ADVISORS. Provides nonbinding advice to the trustee and trust protector. Friendly toward settlor but must still maintain independence. In cases where there is too close a relationship with the settlor, the committee can be construed as an alter ego of the settlor.

COMMITTEE OF TRUST PROTECTORS. An alternative to utilizing merely one trust protector. Friendly toward settlor but must remain independent. See also **trust protector.**

COMMISSION. Money paid to an agent for services.

COMMITMENT FEE. Money paid in advance to ensure that a line of credit will be available from a bank throughout a given period. A marvelous investment in a time of monetary stringency.

COMMODITY. A raw material that is reasonably homogeneous and can be freely traded on a commodity market. The market is roughly divisible into metals, soft commodities (agricultural produce, further divisible between food and nonfood items), and fuels. The weather, strikes, and the operation of cartels, among other factors, have a substantial effect on the prices of commodities.

COMMODITY FUND. A fund that invests in companies that operate in the commodities industry or holds commodities such as metals or fuels.

COMMON LAW. The statutory and case law background of England and the U.S. colonies before their independence.

COMMON SEAL. See **company seal.**

COMMON SHARE. U.S. term for **equity.**

COMPANIES ACT OR ORDINANCE. Legislation enacted by a tax haven to provide for the incorporation, registration, and operation of international business companies (IBCs). More commonly found in the Caribbean tax havens. For a typical example, read the Bahamas' International Business Company Act of 1989.

COMPANY. (1) A restricted corporation, that is, an IBC or exempt company. (2) A union or association of persons organized to carry on a business or enterprise. Each country's laws differ as to the requirements for the formation of a company. However, the following are few of the common requirements: maintain a registered office, mailing address, or agent for service of process within the jurisdiction in which it is organized; a minimum of one or two directors; and the filing of articles of incorporation with the jurisdiction. Failure to follow statutory requirements may result in a loss of the shareholders' limited liability for the company's obligation.

COMPANY SEAL. An imprint of a company's name and other information as evidence that the document was executed on behalf of the company. In some jurisdictions applying the seal to a document binds the company as surely as a witnessed signature binds an individual. British companies tend to use their seal in instances where a U.S. company would judge the signature of an authorized officer to be sufficient.

COMPANY YEAR. The accounting reference period or fiscal year adopted by a company for accounting purposes. It will usually be 365/6 days, but different jurisdictions usually allow a longer or shorter company year (within limits) if the company chooses. A company year will not necessarily coincide with a calendar year (January through December).

COMPLETION PROGRAM. An oil or gas drilling partnership that takes over drilling leases where commercial quantities of reserves are known to exist.

COMPLIANCE OFFICER. The person within an institution who is responsible for ensuring that the company's programs, policies, and procedures comply to all requirements of any applicable regulation.

COMPOUND INTEREST. The practice of charging interest on unpaid interest in addition to the principal of a loan or deposit.

CONCERT PARTY. (U.K. expression) A group of ostensibly discrete investors who agree to buy sufficient shares in a company to control it jointly, although none of them will have purchased enough (30 percent) to be obliged to bid for the entire share capital. An officially disapproved practice.

CONSIDERATION. The inducement to enter into a contract, that is, money or price paid or given by one party for the performance of the other.

CONSOLIDATE. An accounting term. To include the assets and earnings of subsidiaries, less minorities, with that of a parent company, to give a true view of the group as a whole.

CONSOLIDATED STATEMENTS. The practice of combining the financial statements of affiliated companies, thus avoiding the necessity of intercorporation debts and profits.

CONSTRUCTIVE TRUST. A trust created by operation of law against one who obtains property through fraud from another.

CONTANGO. (1) The extent by which the price of a future commodity exceeds the price of the physical commodity. This is the usual situation, because of the time value of the future. A negative contango is known as a *backwardation*. (2) Money payable by the purchaser of a security on the ISE to delay settlement for one account period (now rare).

CONTINGENT BENEFICIAL INTEREST. An interest given to a beneficiary that is not fully vested by being discretionary. In theory, since they are inchoate interests, not truly gifting, they are unvested, are not subject to an attachment by the beneficiary's creditor, and are not reportable as an IRS Form 709 gifting.

CONTINGENT FEES. A method of remunerating lawyers whereby the compensation earned by the counsel will be a percentage of any awards won, but nothing if no award is given to the client. The method has the merit of entitling people with a just grievance but moderate means to seek redress at law.

CONTROLLED FOREIGN CORPORATION. (A concept of U.S. tax law) Any corporation in which U.S. persons have owned more than 50 percent of voting stock on any day in the relevant year. This percentage drops to 25 percent in the case of an insurance company writing U.S. risks.

CONVERTIBLE. Used to describe any security that can be converted into another security. The most frequent use is for bonds that can be exchanged for equities in the same company at a predetermined price and within a specific period. A major factor in determining the price of a convertible bond is whether it stands at a premium or discount to the price of the equity; in other words, whether it is cheaper to buy the equity directly or to buy the convertible and convert it, respectively. After a convertible bond has been converted there is no remaining fixed-interest security, in contrast to bonds with warrants.

CORNER. Any person or group of persons who attempts to control the supply of a commodity, so that thereafter she or they can dictate its price, will be trying to corner the market in that commodity. Theoretically this could be achieved by buying sufficient future contracts to become entitled to all production as it is produced.

CORPORATION. See **company.**

CORPUS. The "body," or principal, of a trust.

CORRECTION. A bull's term for a falling market.

COST AVERAGING. Investing an identical sum in a collective investment scheme on a regular basis, thereby ensuring that one buys more when prices are down, and vice versa. For most investors this actually works out more successfully than trying to time markets.

COUNSEL. A barrister or lawyer, especially when giving expert legal advice, or "counsel's opinion."

COUPON. (1) The annual rate of interest payable on a bond. (2) In the case of bearer securities, the coupon is literally a little numbered square of paper that one cuts off and sends to the paying agent. When a sheet of coupons is exhausted one can apply for a fresh sheet by sending a similar clipping, known as a *talon*, to the paying agent.

COVENANT. An arrangement under U.K. tax law whereby someone paying tax at high rate could transfer benefit to a low-rate taxpayer, such as a charity or student, at the expense of the inland revenue. Since 1988 new covenant will obtain this favorable treatment only if they are in favor of charity and capable of lasting for at least four years.

CPA. See **certified public accountant.**

CREATOR. A person who creates a trust. Also see **settlor** and **grantor.**

CREDITORS. The person to whom money is owed.

CUBICLE BANK. A "brass plate" bank, issued with a license to carry on banking business, typically by the authorities of one of the more crowded tax havens, where the actual banking decisions are reached elsewhere an nominally put into effect by local subcontractors, who will often be a firm of accountants.

CURRENT ACCOUNT. (1) The combination of a nation's surplus or deficit of visible trade—physical goods actually imported or exported—and invisible trade. Any deficit on current account has to be made good by inflows to capital account. This poses no problems so long as foreign nations are happy to invest in the deficit nation and the money is used to build infrastructure. (2) A non-interest-bearing account against which checks may be written. A U.K. term. The U.S. equivalent is *checking account.* (3) An offshore personal savings or checking account.

CURRENT ASSETS/LIABILITIES. Although there is no accounting rule distinguishing current from fixed assets and liabilities, items that are likely to change their nature within one year (for example, stock that may turn into debtors or debtors that may turn into cash) are normally treated as current.

CURRENT RATIO. The ratio of current assets to current liabilities.

CUSTODIAN. A bank, financial institution, or other entity that has the responsibility to manage or administer, for a fee, the custody or other safekeeping of assets for other persons or institutions. A trustee that holds the trust assets in his or her name.

DEBENTURES. A bond; the safest form of security to be issued by a company. If security is taken against a specific asset owned by the company it is known as a *mortgage debenture*. If the prior claim is of a general nature only there is said to be a floating charge. The document evidencing the loan is called an indenture in the United States; in Britain there will normally be a deed of trust.

DEBT INSTRUMENT. Any written evidence of indebtedness.

DECK. In U.S. commodities trading, a stack of customer orders carried into the trading pit by a floor broker.

DECLARATION OF TRUST. A document creating a trust; a trust deed.

DEEP-DISCOUNT BONDS. Bonds that are issued at a price well below the price at which they will be redeemed of face principal amount. The *zero-coupon bond* is an example of a deep-discount bond.

DEFAULT. Failure to perform a legal or contractual obligation, for example, failure to repay money when due.

DEFEASANCE. Provision in a debt instrument whereby the contract may be nullified under certain stated circumstances.

DEFICIT FINANCING. Deliberately allowing government expenditures to exceed revenue with the intention of boosting the economy. This will give rise to a public sector borrowing requirement to make up the difference.

DEPLETION. Accounting treatment to allow for the declining value of an oil or gas well (or other wasting assets) as its reserves are extracted. This may be available as a deduction from taxes payable by a drilling partnership.

DEPOSIT ACCOUNT. An interest-earning account maintained by a depositor at a bank or other financial institution. Withdrawals may be limited depending on the amount on deposit and whether recent deposits have "cleared."

Demand deposit. A deposit account against which checks may be written.

Negotiable order of withdrawal (NOW) accounts. A type of demand account maintained by U.S. savings and loan associations.

DEPRECIATION. The loss of value of an asset from all causes. In an accounting application, the charge against profits "above the line" to represent the extent that fixed assets have worn out over the year.

DIRECT INVESTMENT. An investment, usually large in relation to the outstanding capital of the company concerned and with the intention of involving the purchaser in the affairs of the company. Contrast with portfolio investment.

DIRECTORS. The persons appointed or elected by the shareholders who are authorized to manage and direct the affairs of a corporation. In Britain the majority of directors normally are executive officers of the corporation, whereas in the United States nonexecutive directors are more common.

DIRECTORS' REPORT. Part of a British company's annual report, in which various statutory facts, such as the names of directors over the year, must be disclosed. The U.S. equivalent is Form 10-K.

DISCLOSURE. Revealing the truth or any other information that is generally not known. Most jurisdictions will require disclosure of the true identity of the owner of a security who is suspected of having done anything that would be illegal under the laws of that country. Virtually all jurisdictions have enacted legislation to facilitate the tracking down of drug money, and almost all will assist in catching insider traders.

DISCOUNT. An allowance against or reduction in the price of a item. Applied to bonds or other interest-paying securities, it may be considered as the taking of interest in advance. Also, the difference between the market price and the net asset value of an investment company's ordinary shares. Contrasts with **premium.**

DISCOUNT BOND. A bond sold at less than face value.

DISCOUNT BROKER. A stockbroker who offers services at lower costs to the consumer; generally in the form of lower commission rates on sales and purchases of securities.

DISCOUNTED CASH FLOW. Method of evaluating the future returns on a business venture by considering whether the money could not more profitably be placed on deposit or some other investment.

DISCOUNT MARKET. The secondary market in bills of exchange. In London, the practitioners are known as bill brokers.

DISCOUNT RATE. The rate at which a central bank will buy bills of exchange from its member banks.

DISCRETIONARY ACCOUNT. An account where the broker/ manager is vested with the power over a client's account to trade on the account without advance approvals of any specific trans- action, including the selection, timing, and price. While this undoubtedly helps the manager to operate more efficiently, to be of benefit to the parties discretion should not be given or accepted except where the manager has a thorough knowledge of the client's circumstances and objectives.

DISCRETIONARY TRUST. A trust where the trustees may use their absolute discretion in deciding whether to distribute any of the assets to one or more beneficiaries. The trust deed may actu- ally forbid the trustees from distributing to a beneficiary who does something foolish, such as become addicted to drugs or reside in a high-tax jurisdiction. Trustees in common law jurisdictions out- side the United States are usually sympathetic to following a let- ter of wishes, but it is important for a settlor to recall that the operative word is *trust;* if the settlor does not trust the trustees and attempts to restrict their discretion, the effect may be to inval- idate the trust.

DIVERSIFICATION. Spreading an investment portfolio among various countries, securities, or types of investments, thereby reducing risk of loss in any one investment without necessarily lessening potential returns. The risk reduction will be most marked if the markets involved have little correlation.

DIVIDEND. A share of the profits of a company paid to all holders of a class of securities. Dividends on preferred shares are usually paid at a predetermined rate and paid prior to any payment to holders of the company's common stock. Dividends on common stock are generally paid at the rate decided by the company's board of directors.

DIVIDEND COVER. The extent to which a dividend is covered by earnings, and hence its safety. Generally speaking, a company that reduces its dividend cover after a bad year is less likely to take re- alistic steps to remedy the damage than one that cuts its dividend.

DM BLOC (DM). The German deutsche mark, and the currencies of countries that choose to keep their exchange rates roughly steady against the DM, namely the Dutch guilder, the Swiss franc, and the Austrian schilling. The Belgians, characteristically, oscillate between the DM bloc and the Latin currencies.

DOLLAR COST AVERAGING. Investing a regular sum of money in a mutual fund, irrespective of its price and apparent prospects. Since this means that one necessarily buys more shares when prices are low and fewer when they are high, this conservative approach has been shown to be more effective for most people over the long term than trying to predict which way prices will move and buying or selling accordingly.

DOMESTIC. Used to describe business conducted between people resident in the same jurisdiction, as opposed to international or offshore business.

DONOR. A transferor. One who transfers title to an asset by gifting.

DOUBLE TAXATION. Where the same item of income is taxed in two different countries or is taxed twice when in the possession of the same or two different persons. An example of the latter is a corporate dividend that is initially taxed as corporate income, then taxed once more once distributed to a shareholder.

DRAFT. A written order whereby one party (the *drawer*) instructs another (the *drawee*) to pay an amount to a third person (the *payee*).

DUAL CAPACITY. The ability for a single person or firm to act as both principal and agent.

DUAL TRADING. In U.S. commodities trading, the practice where some traders trade for their own accounts as well as for customer accounts.

EARNINGS. (1) Income. (2) An accounting term for profit attributable to equity shareholders. It therefore combines dividends with retained profits. This may increase as a result of good management or following a takeover that required the issue of many new shares.

EARNINGS YIELD. The amount a company earned on 100 units of currency (for example, dollars or pounds) over a period. It is the reciprocal of the price earnings (P/E) ratio. It is directly comparable with the yield on a bond when determining comparative values of equities and bonds.

EC. The European Commission of the European Union (EU).

ECONOMICS. The science, or art, of financial management, originally with respect to single households, now with widespread ("macro-11") as well as local ("micro-11") relevance.

THE ECONOMIST. A British weekly magazine, highly regarded for its articles on economic matters in the world. A companion publication, *Foreign Report,* is available by subscription only and contains matter that is judged unsuitable for general sale. The postal address of *The Economist's* subscription service is P.O. Box 14, Harold Hill, Romford RM3 8EQ, England. Its U.S. address is P.O. Box 50400, Boulder, CO 80321-0400.

ECU (EUROPEAN CURRENCY UNIT). A basket currency containing fixed percentages of European currencies. These percentages are renegotiated every five years; their percentage is based on the size of the economy in the country where the currency is used. Currently, the ECU is dominated by the German mark.

EDGE ACT CORPORATION. A U.S. bank that is chartered under Section 25(a) of the Federal Reserve Act to carry on international business only.

EEC. European Economic Community.

ELECTRONIC FUNDS TRANSFER AT THE POINT OF SALE. A payment and purchase made electronically. A shopper's plastic card will be queried to see if the account can afford the purchase. If it can, the account will be debited, and the shop credited, instantly.

ELIGIBLE. An eligible bill can be presented to a central bank for discounting.

EMERGING MARKETS. According to the World Bank, "emerging markets" are those countries whose economies had a GNP per capita of less than $8,626 in 1993.

ENDORSE. To sign the back of a check or other bill of exchange to confirm that one had good title to it at the time of signing. An endorsement "in blank," that is, without naming a transferee, turns the check into a bearer instrument.

Blank endorsement. Made by merely writing the endorser's name on the back of the instrument without naming the transferee.

Conditional endorsement. Where the endorser annexes some condition to his liability on the instrument.

Qualified endorsement. Restrains, limits, qualifies, or enlarges the liability of the endorser.

Special endorsement. Names the transferee to whom or whose order the instrument is payable.

ENDOWMENT MORTGAGE. A mortgage where interest only is paid during the life of the loan. Simultaneously, payments are made into a life insurance policy that will mature at the same time as the mortgage is due.

ENDOWMENT POLICY. An insurance policy that will mature upon the sooner of a specified number of years or the insured's death. In contrast to term insurance, which costs much less, the policyholder will receive a payment if she survives.

EPS. Abbreviation for **earnings per share.**

EQUITY. (1) Corporation application: the net worth of a business; calculated by subtracting liabilities from assets. In a public company, equity is also the money value of the shares of the company. (2) Real estate application: remaining value of a property after deducting total liens from fair market value. (3) Legal doctrine application: the concept of law that aims to do the fair and just thing rather than simply to "follow the book."

EQUITY KICKER. Feature of a loan agreement whereby the lender will participate in part of the success of the venture to which it is lending in addition to receiving interest and repayment.

EQUITY RISK PREMIUM. The excess of the expected rate of return on an equity index over the risk-free rate of return available from an investment in ninety-day Treasury certificates.

ERISA. The U.S. Employee Retirement Income Security Act of 1974, which governs the funding, vesting, and administration of pension plans.

ESCROW. An instrument, money, or property given by one person to a third person, to be held by that person until the happening of a specified event.

ESOP. Abbreviation for employee stock-ownership plan.

ESQ. Abbreviation for esquire; usually placed after the name of an attorney.

ESTATE. Interests in real and/or personal property.

ESTATE TAX. A U.S. tax imposed upon property transferred at death; applied to the assets in excess of $600,000 in the aggregate.

EU. European Union; replaced by the European Commission (EC).

EUROBOND. Any bond issued offshore, usually by a subsidiary resident in a tax haven, such as Luxembourg or the Netherlands

Antilles, and guaranteed by its parent company. The bonds are usually in bearer form, each having a nominal value of $1,000 or its approximate equivalent in other currencies. Deals are passed through members of AIBD, who may quote lower prices for small bargains. Interest is paid without deduction of tax. The prices of several leading Eurobonds are given in the Monday editions of the *Financial Times* and the *International Herald Tribune*. A complete list is available, at a price, from the AIBD Weekly Eurobond Guide.

EUROCLEAR. The most popular clearing house and custodian for Eurobonds. Located at the Brussels office of Morgan Guaranty Trust Company of New York.

EUROCURRENCY. Any European currency deposited or lent outside its home country.

EURODOLLAR. A U.S. dollar that changes hands offshore rather than domestically.

EURONOTE. Commercial paper of not more than six months' life, issued offshore. Some Euronotes receive a credit rating from Standard & Poors. Eurobonds with less than five years' life are also referred to as *notes*.

EUROPEAN CURRENCY UNIT (ECU). A basket of currencies of the members of the EEC at the time that the contents of the basket were recalculated, weighted according to the size of the national economies. The Spanish peseta and Portuguese escudo are due to be included in 1989. Used in EEC accounts, and increasingly used for bond issues, travelers checks, and so on.

EUROPEAN ECONOMIC COMMUNITY (EEC). The original signatories to the 1957 Treaty of Rome (Belgium, France, Italy, Luxembourg, the Netherlands, and West Germany) have since been joined successively by Denmark, Ireland, the United Kingdom, Greece, Spain, and Portugal. The purpose of the Community is to foster free movement of trade, labor, and capital between member states.

EUROPEAN MONETARY SYSTEM (EMS). The intended system for monetary cooperation between members of the EEC. The most important part already in place is the "exchange rate mechanism" whereby voluntarily participating nations aim to keep their currencies in approximate parity with one another between the occasional realignments of parity bands.

EXECUTIVE DIRECTOR. Any director who takes part in the day-to-day running of a company.

EXECUTOR. The personal representative(s) appointed in a will to carry out its provisions. The executor(s) will be responsible for obtaining probate.

EXEMPT. To release, discharge, waive, or relieve from liability. An Isle of Man exempt corporation, for example, is exempt from Manx taxation other than a flat $250 (1989) fee.

Exempt income. Income exempt from taxation.

Exempt property. Property not subject to taxation or execution of a judgment.

Exempt securities. Securities exempt from registration under federal or state registration.

EXERCISE. An option is exercised when the option's owner demands delivery against payment. This may happen at any time during the life of the option but is normally delayed until late in its life, for cash flow reasons.

EX PARTE. An application for an injunction filed and heard without notice to the other side to protect assets.

EXPAT. An expatriate.

EXPERT COMPTABLE. The French equivalent to a CPA or FCA.

EXPIRE. An option that has not been exercised will expire at the end of its life. If it has no intrinsic value at that point it will expire worthless.

EXPRESS TRUST. A trust that is created or declared in express terms, that is, a writing, rather than arising by process of law, as with a constructive trust.

EXTRAORDINARY ITEMS. Major items of expenditure or, more rarely, revenue that is outside a company's normal line of business and so is unlikely to recur. These items are therefore taken below the line and excluded from earnings calculations.

FACE VALUE. See **nominal value.**

FACTORING. Selling a company's accounts receivable for ready cash, to assist cash flow. The discount at which these debts change hands will reflect how soon the debts are payable, prevailing rates of interest, and the likelihood that the debts will be paid.

FAMILY HOLDING TRUST. A trust that is created specifically to hold the family's assets consisting of real and/or personal property.

FAMILY PROTECTIVE TRUST. A U.K. term. See **Asset Protection Trust (APT).**

FAR EASTERN ECONOMIC REVIEW. The leading English-language weekly magazine covering the economies of South and East Asia, Australia, and the Pacific. Its postal address is GPO Box 160, Hong Kong.

FCA. A fellow of the Institute of Chartered Accountants in England and Wales. An associate, ACA, has passed the same professional examinations but may not have the same experience.

FEDERAL HOME LOAN BANK. The central bank for federally chartered and member state–chartered savings and loan associations.

FEDERAL OPEN MARKET COMMITTEE. The committee responsible for controlling the U.S. money supply.

FEDERAL RESERVE SYSTEM. The central bank of the United States.

FIDUCIARY. Anyone who is put in a position of trust has a fiduciary duty to perform those tasks loyally and in good faith and not to permit any conflict between his duties and personal interests to those of his principal.

FILL. In U.S. commodities trading, the execution of a buy or sell order.

FINANCIAL CENTER. The location of a region's financial institutions. The world's principal financial centers are Tokyo, New York, and London.

FINANCIAL INTERMEDIARIES, MANAGER AND BROTHERS REGULATORY ASSOCIATION (FIMBRA). Previously the National Association of Securities Dealers and Investment Managers, whose membership consists mostly of small firms offering financial advice. A self-regulatory organization approved by the United Kingdom is SIB. Correspondence concerning a FIMBRA member should be addressed to 22 Great Tower Street, London EC3R 5AQ.

FINANCIAL NET WORTH. Total assets less total liabilities.

FINANCIAL STATEMENT. Any report summarizing a person's or business' s financial condition or results, usually consisting of a minimum of a balance sheet and income statement.

FINANCIAL TIMES. The principal British daily newspaper for financial news. Because of the global scope of its reporting and its simultaneous publication in many countries, it can reasonably be considered to be the world's premier business newspaper. Its U.K. address is Number One Southwark Bridge, London SE1 9HL. Its U.S. address is 14 East 60th Street, New York, NY 10022.

FINANCING STATEMENT. In the United States, used by most states to show a creditor's security interest in personal property. Usually maintained by each state's secretary of state office.

FIRST IN, FIRST OUT (FIFO). An accounting theory of valuing inventory that assumes that the oldest items in inventory will be the first to be sold, used, or consumed. In inflationary times this leads to a realistic valuation of remaining stock but overstated earnings, since it will not be possible to replace the inventory as cheaply. Contrast with **LIFO.**

FIRST LIEN. A lien against property that takes priority over all other liens and charges.

FIRST TRUST DEED. A loan secured by a deed of trust against property, which is the **first lien.**

FISCAL YEAR. The 365/366-day period adopted by a state agency, partnership, or corporation for its own accounting purposes. This may, but will not necessarily, coincide with the calendar year, that is, January through December.

FIXED ASSETS. In accounting, assets that can be expected to reappear on the balance sheet in a year's time. U.S. balance sheets often refer more specifically to "property, plant, and equipment."

FIXED CHARGE. A mortgage upon a specific object as security for a loan.

FIXED-INTEREST SECURITIES. Another name for **bonds.**

FIXED-INTEREST TRUST. A trust in which the appointed trustees have no discretion when distributing the trust property among the beneficiaries, in contrast to a **discretionary trust.**

FLAT BOND. One that includes accrued interest in the price.

FLAT MONEY. Monetary system that is not backed by gold or silver.

FLIGHT CAPITAL. Money that flows offshore and likely never returns. Flight is exacerbated by a lack of confidence as government grows without bounds, the cost of government grows out of control, and the federal deficit grows (over $5 billion) without the ability of Washington to cap it; it is precipitated further by increasing concerns over invasion of personal privacy, rampant litigation, and the threats of further confiscatory direct and indirect taxes.

FLOATATION. Issuing shares in a company to the public via a listing on some exchange for the first time.

FLOATING CHARGE. A security given by a company over all of its assets, without specifying any particular asset. This arrangement allows the company to buy or sell assets with complete freedom. Should it get into difficulties, the charge will "crystallize" and attach to specific owned assets.

FLOATING-RATE NOTE (FRN). A security whose interest rate will vary from time to time in accordance with prevailing interest rates or some other external measure. The coupon is most often expressed as being a stated percentage above LIBOR. On the Euromarket these securities are usually issued with a stated fixed coupon and variable coupon determined by a stated interest margin over LIBOR.

FLOOR. The floor of a traditional exchange, such as the NYSE or TSE, is where the brokers and market makers do business with one another face to face.

FLOOR BROKER. In U.S. commodities trading, a person paid a commission to execute customer buy and sell orders.

FLOWER BOND. A U.S. government bond that will be accepted at its nominal value in payment of estate tax.

FOREIGN PERSONAL HOLDING COMPANY (FPHC). Different from a controlled foreign corporation. Discuss with your CPA.

FOREIGN SALES CORPORATION (FSC). A corporation that meets the several requirements of section 927(f) of the lRC and chooses to comply with the complicated administrative burden required can obtain exemption from corporate taxation provided that these derive from a foreign presence and activity.

FORFEITING. Discounting bills that are used to finance the export of capital goods, particularly with reference to trade between Eastern and Western Europe

FORM 10-K. An annual form filed with the U.S. Securities and Exchange Commission by public corporations. Information contained in the form includes financial statements, identities and salaries of directors and certain officers, and a discussion of the filing company's performance and strategies.

FORWARD MARKETS. Markets for dealing in currencies for future delivery. Prices are expressed as an annualized premium or discount to the "spot" price. One- and three-month forward rates for fifteen currencies are quoted in the *Financial Times*.

401(K) PLAN. The section of the U.S. tax code that allows a limited amount of an employee's before-tax salary to be deposited into a tax-deferred retirement plan, where it will accumulate free of tax. Withdrawing funds from a 401(K) plan before the age of fifty-nine and a half years, except in certain cases of hardship, gives rise to a 10 percent penalty.

FPHC. See **foreign personal holding company.**

FPT. See **family protective trust.** Also see **asset protection trust (APT).**

FRAUDULENT CONVEYANCE. A transfer of an asset that violates the fraudulent conveyance statutes of the affected jurisdictions.

FREE CAPITAL. The amount of equity in a company that is available for trading by the public on the stock market. Doesn't include equities held by controlling shareholders.

FRONT-END LOAD. The initial expense to the purchaser buying into an open-end fund. This expense can be as high as 8.5 percent, but the normal fee should not exceed 5 percent. If an investor is introduced by an agent, most of the load will be paid to him as a commission.

FRONT RUNNING. A broker who, upon receiving a large order from a client, first places an order for the broker's own personal account in the expectation that she could close it out at a profit after her client's bargain has moved the market. Definitely not allowed but sometimes difficult to spot if she uses another broker and a nominee account.

FUNDAMENTALS. A term used by economists and analysts to assess the investment prospects of a business, a currency, or a country.

FUND OF FUNDS. An asset trust or mutual fund that invests only in shares of other mutual funds.

FUNGIBLE. Interchangeable; for example, a one-pound note is very like another.

FUTURES. A vehicle that allows the purchase, sale, and delivery of financial instruments or commodities at a future date.

FUTURES TRANSACTIONS. The purchase and sale of commodities, securities, or foreign exchange under detailed contracts that specify the delivery, price, and date of the transaction. Contrasts with spot transactions, which take place on the same day the agreement is reached.

G7 NATIONS. A term used for the seven major industrialized nations of the world, including the United States, Japan, the United Kingdom, France, Germany, Italy, and Canada.

GATT (General Agreement on Tariffs and Trade). Established as an international body in 1945 to encourage free trade as opposed to the ruinous protectionism of the 1930s. It did very well during its first forty years.

GDP (GROSS DOMESTIC PRODUCT). The sum of a nation's private consumption, investment, government expenditure, net stock building, and the surplus of exports over imports. Normally expressed in "constant prices," that is, after allowance for inflation. GDP can be calculated by totaling incomes, output, or expenditure.

GEARING. In the United Kingdom, the addition of debt financing to equity financing. The U.S. equivalent term is leverage.

GENERAL OBLIGATION BOND. (U.S. term) A municipal bond backed by the "full faith and credit" of the issuing municipality rather than the revenue from a specific source.

GEOGRAPHICAL SPREAD. A term that describes the distribution of investments in a fund's portfolio over different parts of the world, usually by country.

GIFT TAX. (U.S. tax) A graduated federal tax on gifts of more than $10,000 to a single person in a year. Gifts between spouses are exempted.

GILTS. British government long-term bonds, issued on the domestic market. Formerly the edges of the certificates were gilded. Gilts are normally dealt for cash settlement on the ISE, which means that settlement takes place on the following day. Gilts are normally registered, but bearer shares do exist in some of the older issues. Interest is normally paid net of tax except upon war loans, but there is a list of stocks that are free of both withholding and inheritance taxes if owned by identified nonresidents of the United Kingdom, while stock purchased on the post office register will receive gross interest.

GLOBAL BOND FUNDS. Funds that invest in debt securities of companies and industries located throughout the world.

GLOBAL DEPOSITORY RECEIPT (GDR). Negotiable certificates that put a claim on company shares traded in the company's own market. Traded on global markets, they are issued at the same time in multiple foreign markets.

GLOBAL EQUITY FUNDS. These funds offer individuals an easy way to invest in companies located abroad while obtaining diversification in their investment portfolio. The fund manager handles all administrative tasks related to the fund such as trading, record keeping, differences in currency, language, time, and investment regulations.

GMBH (GESELLSCHAFT MIT BESCHRANKTE HAFTUNG). The approximate German or Swiss equivalent of a private company or limited liability corporation

GNMA (GOVERNMENT NATIONAL MORTGAGE ASSOCIATION). A U.S. government agency that issues U.S. government–backed mortgage securities. Nicknamed "Ginnie Mae."

GNP (GROSS NATIONAL PRODUCT). The market value of all goods and services produced within a nation during a one-year period, plus the excess of exports over imports.

GOING CONCERN. The value of an operating business and its goodwill, as distinguished from a business that has not yet commenced operations.

GOING PUBLIC. The term used to describe the process by which a corporation raises equity from the public.

GOLD BOND. A bond payable in gold coin or its equivalent.

GOODWILL. The extent to which the cost of an acquisition as shown in a company's accounts exceeds its net asset value. In the United Kingdom goodwill can be written off against reserves, as is done by most companies that can afford to do so. In the United States goodwill has to be depreciated over a period of no more than forty years, with a consequent loss in reported earnings.

GRACE PERIOD. A period during which a borrower is excused some obligation.

GRANDFATHER CLAUSE. Provision in new legislation that excuses those already engaged in the activity that is coming under regulation from complying with the new requirements.

GRANTOR. A person who creates a trust or transfers real property to another entity. In a U.S. grantor trust, the person responsible for U.S. income taxes on the trust. May have a reversionary interest in a trust. The person who settles or creates a trust. The U.K. term is *settlor.* It is possible for a nominee to settle a trust, with the intention that only the nominee's name will appear on the trust deed, even though some other person may subsequently introduce the bulk of the trust's property. This subterfuge is likely to succeed only if it is credible that the nominee grantor should have settled that much property on those particular beneficiaries.

GRANTOR TRUST. A trust created by a grantor and taxed to that grantor (settlor). A trust where the trust property is considered, for purposes of U.S. tax law, to remain in the hands of the grantor and to be taxable accordingly.

GRAVEYARD MARKET. An illiquid market with little potential for recovery.

GRAY MARKET. (1) An unofficial market in a new issue prior to its becoming freely negotiable. (2) The purchase of European automobiles direct from the manufacturers and importing them into the United States for the purchaser's private use.

GRESHAM'S LAW. The theory that bad money drives good money out of circulation; originally applied to the sensible inclination to hold on to a sound coin but to circulate a debased one so that eventually only debased coins remain in circulation.

GROSS. A sum without deduction or set off, that is, without deduction of taxes from a person's income.

GROSS DOMESTIC PRODUCT (GDP). The monetary value of all finished goods and services produced in an economy during a period. Measured annually.

GROSS NATIONAL PRODUCT (GNP). The monetary value of all final goods and services produced by domestically owned resources during a specified period. The items can be used at home or abroad. Measured annually.

GROUP. A group generally includes a parent company and its subsidiaries; may also include affiliates.

GROWTH FUND. A fund designed for individuals whose primary goal is not to obtain dividends from their investment but to increase their capital gains. These funds usually invest in the common stock of well-established companies.

GROWTH STOCK. Shares of a corporation that may carry a higher risk than average equities. They generally score faster rates of return.

GUARANTEE. An undertaking from a third party that a loan will be repaid. In U.K. and U.S. law a guarantee must be in writing to be enforceable. A guarantee may be secured by collateral held in escrow.

GUARANTEED FUNDS. A type of mutual fund—especially popular in Hong Kong—that offers not only the potential of gains but also the guarantee that 90 to 100 percent of the original investment will be returned at a future date.

HARD CURRENCY. Currency whose exchange rate is stable or tends to go up because the country has little or no inflation, or at least lower inflation than other countries.

HARD-CURRENCY BOND FUND. This fund's goal is to achieve capital growth by investing in a portfolio of high-quality bonds and other securitized debt instruments. Usually invests only in bonds issued by countries deemed to be hard-currency countries by the directors. Examples of hard-currency countries often include Germany, Austria, Switzerland, and the Netherlands.

HARD-CURRENCY GROWTH COMPANIES FUND. This fund aims to produce long-term capital growth by investing in companies with two main characteristics: (1) their shares are quoted on a regulated market; and (2) the companies are based in hard-currency countries like Germany, the Netherlands, Switzerland, and Austria.

HEAVY. Said of an investment where a single unit costs a lot of money. This acts as a deterrent to small investors; some companies welcome this, but most avoid it through stock splits. Equity prices in continental Europe tend to be heavier than in the United States or Canada, which are usually heavier than in Britain or Japan.

HEDGE. A strategy that allows an investor to reduce risk by purchasing an investment in opposition to another investment. By doing this, the investor can reduce the risk of loss due to adverse movements in equity markets, share prices, currency rates, or interest rates.

HEDGE FUND. A special type of mutual fund with very few limitations on the type of investments that may be added to the portfolio and very few restrictions on the investment techniques that may be used. These funds often have high minimum investment requirements and pay performance fees to fund managers.

HIDDEN RESERVES. Undisclosed net worth, usually created by undervaluing assets such as real estate.

HIGH-INTEREST BOND. See **junk bond.**

HIGH-NET-WORTH (HNW) INDIVIDUAL. Modern U.S. banking parlance for an individual with more than $500,000 in liquid assets to manage

HIGH-YIELD BOND FUNDS. These funds maintain at least two-thirds of their portfolio in lower-rated corporate bonds (that is, those with a Moody's rating of BAA or lower, or those with a Standard & Poors rating of BBB or lower). Generally, these funds will produce higher yields due to the higher risk associated with these corporate bonds.

HIRE PURCHASE. A system of credit financing popular in Britain prior to the widespread use of credit cards. The purchaser of a consumer durable item would have the use of an object from the date of the commencement of a financing loan, but ownership would remain with the financing company until all principal and interest had been repaid.

HNW. See **high-net-worth (HNW) person.**

HOLDING COMPANY. The definition varies from one legal system to another.

In certain legal systems it implies the holding of a majority or the whole of the equity capital of one or more other companies. In other systems the criterion may be the holding of as little as 5 percent of the equity capital of the subsidiary or simply the holding of shares in other nonrelated companies.

The shareholding qualification may result in the reduction of tax or other consequences either by virtue of the provisions of the domestic system or by virtue of a tax treaty.

The term *holding companies* is sometimes employed more loosely to refer to companies that are used in order to control industrial or commercial companies; to act as investment funds; to finance the other companies in their group by supplying them with funds that they may obtain through the floating of bond issues; or to collect income in the form of dividends, loan interest, or patent royalties and licensing fees.

Often, holding companies are intermediary companies in a group structure and hence are also subsidiaries of their parent companies.

A financial holding company is generally established as the wholly owned subsidiary of a foreign parent company for the purpose of channeling financial transactions such as the issue of debentures or notes in the Eurocurrency market and the taking up of bank loans under the guarantee of such parent.

HOME BANKING. A form of personal banking with enormous potential. Instead of having to visit or write to a bank, customers can conduct most of their business from their home via telephone, television, and a terminal.

HOMESTEAD EXEMPTION. State or federal bankruptcy laws that protect one's residence from confiscation by a judgment creditor or loss in a personal bankruptcy.

HOT MONEY. Used to describe capital that will chase after the highest short-term rates of return. Also called **flight capital.**

HOUSE OF KEYS. The popularly elected lower house of Tynwald, the Manx parliament. It has had twenty-four members since early times, eight of whom represented the Hebrides until they were lost to the Scots in 1266.

HYBRID. A company that is limited by guarantee and also has a share capital. The terms of the guarantee may permit certain benefits to accrue to the guarantor that would normally be considered the prerogative of the shareholders. Hybrid companies are not permitted in all jurisdictions. Jurisdictions that do allow them include the British Virgin Islands and the Isle of Man.

HYPERINFLATION. Unusually high inflation; some experts apply this term to an inflation rate that consistently exceeds 25 percent per month.

HYPOTHECATE. Pledge property to secure a loan. The property remains in the borrower's possession unless he fails to abide by the terms of the loan, whereupon it may be sold.

IBC. A corporation. See also **international business company.**

IFC. See **international financial and banking center.**

ILLIQUIDITY. The absence of easily marketable assets, which may mean that payment liabilities and obligations cannot be met on time.

IMF (INTERNATIONAL MONETARY FUND). A major international organization that establishes monetary policy. Based in Washington, D.C., it was established in 1946 at Bretton Wood, New Hampshire.

INBOUND. Coming into the United States; onshore; such as funds being paid to a U.S. person from an offshore entity.

INCOME EQUITY FUNDS. A mutual fund primarily made up of equity securities from companies with a good record for paying dividends.

INCOME STRIPPING. A term used to describe the transfer of funds from an active corporation to a separate entity at arm's length for the purpose of legally providing a tax deduction charged against the company that requires the reduction or elimination of taxes.

INCOMPLETE GIFT. Where the settlor has reserved the right to add or delete beneficiaries to the trust, it is construed as an incomplete gift. See also **contingent beneficial interest.**

INDEPENDENT TRUSTEE. A trustee who is independent of the settlor. Independence is generally defined as not being related to the settlor by blood, through marriage, by adoption, or in an employer/employee relationship.

INDEXED BOND. A security whose interest rate is adjusted according to the inflation rate.

INDIRECT TAXATION. Any tax on consumption.

INDIVIDUAL RETIREMENT ACCOUNT. See **IRA.**

INFLATION. The resulting higher prices of goods caused by such factors as increased energy costs, higher interest rates, demand exceeding supply, and increased costs of production. The higher prices cause a decline in the purchasing power of money.

INHERITANCE TAX. A tax imposed upon the distribution of property of a deceased person.

INLAND REVENUE. The commissioners of the inland revenue are responsible for collecting tax in the United Kingdom.

INSIDER DEALING/TRADING. The buying and selling of securities by officers and directors of a company while acting on the basis of information not generally available to the public.

INSOLVENT. A person's or company's situation of being unable to pay debts as they fall due.

INSTITUTIONAL INVESTORS. Investors in a domestic market other than foreign, public, or private investors. In particular, the expression includes pension and insurance funds and collective investment schemes.

INSURANCE. A contract that provides for the payment of money by one party to compensate for another's loss. Generally, the insured party must have an interest in the event insured against.

INSURANCE AUTHORITY. The authority responsible for the regulation of insurance companies in the Isle of Man. Its address is 30 Bucks Road Douglas, Isle of Man.

INTANGIBLE ASSETS. Values attributed to a going concern, including goodwill, trademarks, and copyrights.

INTERBANK FUNDS. Money borrowed on a short-term basis (usually overnight) by one bank from another.

INTERBANK RATE. The interest rate applied to funds borrowed between financial institutions. Fed Funds and LIBOR are two examples of interbank rates.

INTEREST. "Rent" for the use of money, that is, interest payable on a loan or receivable on a deposit at a financial institution.

INTEREST IN POSSESSION. (U.K. trust law) If a settlor retains a right to the income of a trust and that income cannot be accumulated, that settlor may derive benefits with respect to capital taxes, particularly if foreign trustees are appointed.

INTEREST RATE. The amount paid by one entity for the privilege of borrowing money from another entity. Usually expressed as a percentage of the amount borrowed and often published as an annual rate.

INTERFIPOL (INTERNATIONAL FISCAL POLICE). The tax crime counterpart to Interpol. The draft convention of mutual assistance in tax matters, which it is proposed should form part of future tax treaties. It allows for automatic exchange of information foreseeably relevant to the assessment and collection of tax between revenue authorities, without obliging them to notify the intended taxpayer in any way.

INTERMEDIATE GOOD. Any item that is resold by its purchaser in its present form or after further processing.

INTERNAL RATE OF RETURN (IRR). The annual return on an investment expressed as a percentage of the original investment and allowing for the fact that revenues generated in the near future are more valuable than revenues received in the distant future.

INTERNATIONAL BANK OF RECONSTRUCTION AND DEVELOPMENT. See **World Bank.**

INTERNATIONAL BUSINESS COMPANIES ORDINANCE. A 1984 ordinance of the British Virgin Islands, subsequently amended, that permits the greatest freedom to companies that do no business and own no land in the islands. Such companies require a registered agent resident in the BVI.

INTERNATIONAL BUSINESS COMPANY (IBC). A corporation formed (incorporated) under a "company act" of a tax haven but *not* authorized to do business within that country of incorporation; intended to be used for global operations. Owned by member(s)/shareholder(s). Has the usual corporate attributes.

INTERNATIONAL FINANCIAL AND BANKING CENTER (IFC). A country identified as a tax haven.

INTERNATIONAL HERALD TRIBUNE. An international

newspaper published in Paris since 1887 and now printed simultaneously in several other countries. Its principal sources of information are the *New York Times* and the *Washington Post*. Its address is 181 Avenue Charles de-Gaulle, 92200 Neuilly-sur-Seine, France. Its U.S. address is 830 3rd Avenue, New York, NY 10022.

INTERNATIONAL MONETARY FUND. See **IMF.**

INTERNATIONAL RESERVES. Assets accepted by central banks to settle payments among themselves. There are four main types of international reserves: (1) gold; (2) special drawing rights; (3) foreign currencies; and (4) short-term government securities denominated in currencies such as U.S. dollars, Japanese yen, and German marks.

INTERNATIONAL TAX PLANNING. The object of international tax planning is to determine, from the tax point of view, whether or not to embark on a project; and, if it is embarked upon or has already been commenced, then to minimize or defer the imposition of the tax burden falling on taxable persons and events and to do so lawfully, in the attainment of the desired business and other objectives, while taking into consideration all relevant tax factors with particular regard to the danger of double taxation and the advantages that may be derived from the interrelationship of two or more tax systems, and in the light of the material nontax factors.

The role of tax havens in international tax planning lies in the possibility of situating a taxable person or a taxable event in a tax haven with a view to displacing the connecting factor with a high-tax jurisdiction and thus permitting a modification in the incidence of tax.

INTERNATIONAL TRUST. A Cook Islands term for a special type of asset protection trust (APT). Governed by the laws of the Cook Islands.

INTERPOL (INTERNATIONAL CRIMINAL POLICE ORGANIZATION). The network of multinational law enforcement authorities established to exchange information regarding money laundering and other criminal activities. More than 125 member nations.

INTER VIVOS. The creation of a trust during a person's (the grantor or settlor) lifetime, as opposed to a testamentary trust.

INTESTATE. A person who dies without leaving a valid will is said to die intestate. Most jurisdictions have laws determining how the estate of an intestate person should be divided among the surviving relatives, for example, first to surviving spouse, then to children, then to parents, and so on.

INTRA VIRES. Latin for "within one's powers" and therefore proper. Contrast with ultra vires.

INTRINSIC VALUE. The underlying value of anything. The intrinsic value of an option to buy shares at $50 when the share price stands at $52 is $2.

INVESTMENT ADVISOR. A company or individual that advises—and sometimes manages—an investment fund's portfolio.

INVESTMENT ADVISOR'S FEE. A fee paid to an individual or company in return for investment advice.

INVESTMENT BANK. A U.S. or Japanese bank that arranges capital for industry. The closest U.K. equivalent is a merchant bank.

INVESTMENT COMPANY. U.S. term for a collective investment scheme. Companies that are governed by the U.S. Investment Company Act of 1940 are obliged to state their specific objectives.

INVESTMENT TRUST. Closed-end U.K. collective investment schemes, regulated by Section 822 of the Income and Corporation Taxes Act of 1988 and the ISE. They are exempted from paying capital gains tax, though selling shares in an investment trust at a profit may give rise to capital gains taxes to a U.K. resident. Their shares usually sell at a discount to net asset value, which periodically prompts bids to take them over and "unitize" them (turn them into unit trusts) so that their selling price will be linked to the net asset value. The investment performance of investment trusts has generally been better than that of unit trusts, but this fact is not widely recognized because brokers usually secure more commission by pushing unit trusts. Free information on investment trusts is available from the AITC. Japanese investment trusts are, by contrast, open ended.

INVISIBLE TRADE. Anything that affects the current account of a nation that cannot be described as freight and so form part of the trade. Examples are international banking, insurance, and shipping services, all of which benefit the City of London, and remittances, which are from expatriate Filipino workers to their families at home.

IRA (INDIVIDUAL RETIREMENT ACCOUNT). (U.S. practice) An individual who is covered by a tax-deferred retirement plan may deduct the lesser between $2,000 and 100 percent of compensation each year from taxable income into an IRA. Once an IRA is established, earnings will compound free of tax, but there is a 10 percent penalty for withdrawing funds before the age of fifty-nine and a half, except in case of hardship.

IRC (INTERNAL REVENUE CODE). The Internal Revenue Code of 1986 of the United States.

IRS (INTERNAL REVENUE SERVICE). The Internal Revenue Service of the Treasury Department is responsible for collecting federal taxes within the United States.

ISE (INTERNATIONAL STOCK EXCHANGE). The International Stock Exchange of the United Kingdom and the Republic of Ireland Limited. The official stock exchange of the United Kingdom and Ireland, on which an unusually large number of foreign securities are quoted. Descended from Jonathan's Coffe Shop of the late seventeenth century. Settlement is usually "for the account." Shares are quoted on the main, USM, or third markets, in descending order of size of company. Its address is The Stock Exchange, Old Broad Street, London EC2N 1HP.

ISSUE. To sell a new security on the primary market, that is, the issuer and the initial buyer.

ITPA (INTERNATIONAL TAX PLANNING ASSOCIATION). A genuine international body embracing all financial advisory professions but excluding present or former employees of any revenue service. The membership address is P.O. Box 134, Sevenoaks, Kent TNl 6SZ, England.

JAPAN ECONOMIC JOURNAL. The leading English-language newspaper on Japanese financial affairs. It is published weekly by Nihon Keizai Shimbun, Inc. Subscriptions are handled by Nikkei Media Marketing Inc., 1-9-5 Otenochi Chiyoda-ku Tokyo 100-66.

JOBBER. A market maker on London's stock exchange before the Big Bang.

JOINT AND SEVERAL. Contracts in which the parties obligate themselves both individually and as a group.

JOINT STOCK. Stock owned by shareholders with limited liability. (U.K. parlance. In the United States it is equivalent to a corporation.) Used to differentiate such entities as a bank from a private bank.

JUNK BOND. Any bond where the strong possibility of a default has been recognized from the date of issue by an exceptionally high rate of interest.

JURISDICTION. A "country" over which a code of laws applies. Thus the United Kingdom comprises England and Wales, Scotland, and Northern Ireland, all three of which jurisdictions have their separate laws and courts of justice.

KABUSHIKI KAISHA (KK). The Japanese equivalent of a public company.

KABUTOCHO. The stock market district of Tokyo.

KEIDANREN. The Federation of Economic Organizations, the most powerful business lobby in Japan.

KEOGH PLAN. (U.S. practice) A self-contributory pension plan for the self-employed to put aside part of their income before tax into a tax-efficient vehicle. Any employees must be given comparable benefits. It is possible to put up to $30,000 into a "defined contribution" plan or sufficient to ensure a $94,023 annual income after retirement, adjustable in line with inflation, although alternative formulas prevent low earners from being allowed the maximum deductions.

KEYMAN. A keyman insurance policy compensates a company if a key executive becomes incapacitated.

KRUGERRAND. A South African gold coin.

LAISSEZ-FAIRE. The capitalist doctrine that an economy will prosper most if its entrepreneurs are allowed to go about their business with minimal interference from government.

LANDESBANK. The central bank for a German land, or province.

LAUNDERING. Changing the character of money received from illicit sources to clean the money.

LAUTRO (LIFE ASSURANCE AND UNIT TRUST REGULATORY ORGANIZATION). A self-regulatory organization approved by the United Kingdom's SIB. Correspondence regarding a member should be addressed to LAUTRO at Centre Point, 103 New Oxford Street, London WCLA 1QH.

LAW SOCIETY. The governing body for lawyers practicing in England and Wales. Any correspondence should be addressed to the Society at 113 Chancery Lane, London WC2A 1PL. The Law Society of Scotland has its offices at 26 Drumsheugh Gardens, Edinburgh EH3 7YR.

LAYERED TRUSTS. Trusts placed in series where the beneficiary of the first trust is the second trust; used for privacy.

LAYERING. May be achieved with numerous combinations of entities. For example, 100 percent of the shares of an IBC being owned by the first trust, which has as its sole beneficiary a second trust.

LBO (LEVERAGED BUYOUT). A buyout strategy in the United States whereby shareholders in an operating company will sell their shares at a price above the previous market price to a group often consisting of insiders who will finance the purchase through debt financing. The group then pays off the loans through the sale of the acquired company's assets.

LEGAL PERSON. A "person" recognized in law as having legal standing to be a party in a legal suit. The term includes individuals and corporations.

LETTER OF ALLOTMENT. Communication detailing an allotment of securities, as after a new issue or rights issue. A letter of allotment can normally be traded on the ISE, free of stamp duty, for cash settlement.

LETTER OF CREDIT. The usual means for an individual to obtain cash abroad. A domestic bank would send a copy of the signature to its correspondent bank in the foreign country and debit the drawer's account the sum drawn.

LETTER OF WISHES. Guidance and a request to the trustee having no binding powers over the trustee. There may be multiple letters. They must be carefully drafted to avoid creating problems with the settlor or true settlor in the case of a grantor trust becoming a cotrustee. The trustee cannot be a "pawn" of the settlor, or there is basis for the argument that there never was a complete renouncement of the assets. Sometimes referred to as a *side letter.*

LEVERAGE. The acquisition of property using a combination of equity and debt financing. The U.K. equivalent term is *gearing.*

LEVERAGED BUYOUT. See **LBO.**

LIABILITY. A debt or other obligation owed by a person or corporation. Its usual forms are accounts and notes payable.

LIBID (LONDON INTERBANK BID RATE). The average of the rates that five major London banks will bid for a $10 million deposit for three or six months.

LIBOR (LONDON INTERBANK OFFERED RATE). The rate of interest given to a first-class bank in the London interbank market when it makes a loan off another member bank within the market.

LIEN. A claim or charge placed against property of another, such as a mortgage, deed of trust, or judgment.

LIFO (LAST IN, FIRST OUT). An accounting convention whereby the cost of sales is calculated with reference to the most recent cost of inventory. The effect, especially during inflationary periods, is to reduce inventory values and declared profits.

LIMITED COMPANY. Not an international business company. May be a resident of the tax haven and is set up under a special company act with a simpler body of administrative laws.

LIMITED LIABILITY. The liability of shareholders in a limited company is restricted to any unpaid calls, if any, on their shares. The liability of the guarantors of a guarantee company is limited to that guarantee. The liability of limited partners in a partnership is set forth in the partnership deed.

LIMITED LIABILITY COMPANY (LLC OR LC). Consists of member owners and a manager, at a minimum. Similar to a corporation that is taxed as a partnership or as an S-corporation. More specifically, it combines the more favorable characteristics of a corporation and a partnership. The LLC structure permits the complete passthrough of tax advantages and operational flexibility found in a partnership, operating in a corporate-style structure, with limited liability as provided by the state's laws. The LLC may be managed by members but need not be. It may be managed by a professional company manager. A caveat is in order: LLCs are very new, without a clear body of case law and firm guidelines. They will generate much income for the legal community until they become an integral part of our tax, business, and legal system.

LIMITED PARTNERSHIP. A partnership where only one general partner need accept unlimited liability; the others are responsible only for a specified investment in the partnership.

LIMIT ORDER. An instruction to a broker to execute a transaction only when a certain price is reached, at that price "or better."

LIPPER. The Lipper Analytical Service of U.S. mutual fund performances is available from the company at 5 Carol Road, Westfield, NJ 07090.

LIQUID ASSETS. Cash, or items that can readily be converted to cash.

LIQUIDATION. See **winding up.**

LIQUIDITY. Of a secondary market; the ease or otherwise of finding a buyer for a large parcel of securities.

LISTED ISSUES OR COMPANIES. Companies or stock issues whose shares are listed on the stock exchange.

LIVING TRUST. Revocable trust, for reduction of probate costs and to expedite sale of assets upon death of grantor. Provides no asset protection.

LLC. See **limited liability company.** Also seen in the form of L.L.C., l.l.c., L.C. (Utah), and l.c.

LLLP (LIMITED LIABILITY LIMITED PARTNERSHIP). Intended to protect the general partners from liability. Previously the general partner was a corporation to protect the principals from personal liability. Under the LLLP an individual could be a general partner and have limited personal liability.

LLOYD'S. The insurance market that began in Edward Lloyd's London coffee house in 1668. It provides a forum where wealthy individuals ("Names") who are willing to accept a remote chance of bankruptcy in exchange for hopes of additional returns from their wealth by making it available to an underwriter who will pledge it as backing for accepting insurance premiums on almost any risk.

LLP (LIMITED LIABILITY PARTNERSHIP). A form of the LLC favored and used for professional associations, such as accountants and attorneys.

LOCAL. In U.S. commodities trading, a trader who trades for her own account, not those of customers.

LOMBARD RATE. The rate at which the Bundesbank will lend to West German commercial banks against top-quality financial assets.

LONDON CALLING. The monthly magazine of the Overseas Service of the BBC, which gives times and frequencies on transmissions as well as program details. Obtainable from P.O. Box 76, Bush House Strand, London WC2B 4PH.

LONG POSITION. Holding more of a given asset or commodity than contracted to deliver in the future. A person or company may use this strategy with the hope that prices will rise and then produce a profit on the assets or commodities once they are sold.

LTD. An abbreviation for the word *limited.*

M1. A narrow definition of the money supply. Included is money in circulation and current accounts or balances at banks that can be used to make third-party payments by the depositor.

M2. A broad definition of the money supply. M2 is made up of all items in the M1 category, plus time or savings deposits located in a country's money market account balances.

MANAGED BANK. A "brass plate" bank, issued with a license to carry on a banking business, typically by the authorities of a tax haven. Normally the actual banking decisions are reached elsewhere and nominally put into effect by a local bank subcontracted for that specific purpose.

MANAGED FLOATING. A policy that allows exchange rates to float based on some limits in the exchange rate. The central bank usually defends these limitations by intervening in the market when necessary.

MANAGEMENT CHARGE. The cost of administering a mutual fund, which is usually charged annually against a fund's income. Currently, this fee is approximately 0.5 to 2 percent of the assets under management. This fee covers the cost of administration and management, share registration, audit expenses, and directors' fees.

MANAGEMENT COMPANY. A firm retained to accept administrative, secretarial, and corporate responsibilities for a corporation, usually incorporated in a tax haven. The location of a management company does not necessarily have to be the company of incorporation or its underlining client company.

MANAGING DIRECTOR. The customary designation of the chief operating officer of a British company, equivalent to the president of a U.S. company.

MANDATE. To instruct a bank or similar institution to treat any agent as addressing the same powers as their client, the principal; for example, a registered shareholder may instruct a company to pay dividends to somebody else.

MAPLE-LEAF. A Canadian coin containing exactly one troy ounce of gold, launched in emulation of the Krugerrand.

MARGIN. (1) The difference between two figures. Thus, a bank's margin is the difference between its cost of borrowing and the rate of interest that it can obtain on lending. (2) A cash sum payable to support a long position in a commodity future; it is normally set at 10 percent of the value of the contract. If the potential liability rises, a **margin call** will be immediately payable. If the client declines to pay the additional money, the position will be closed out (sold) immediately.

MARGIN CALL. Order by broker to client to put up money or securities upon the purchase of a security or fall in price of a stock already purchased on margin.

MARKET CAPITALIZATION. (1) The market value of a company's outstanding share capital. (2) When applied to the exchange or market, the value of all listed shares on the exchange or market.

MARINE INTEREST. Interest charged to a higher than market rate, for the use and risk of money loaned on hypothecation and bottomry bonds.

MARK. Abbreviation for German currency, the deutsche mark.

MARKET. Place of commercial activity in which articles are bought and sold.

MARKET CAPITALIZATION. The number of shares or bonds on a particular issue multiplied by the market price; hence, this would be the cost of buying the whole outstanding issue in the unlikely circumstance that prices did not rise against the persistent buyer.

MARKET MAKER. One who is willing to buy or to sell a security on the secondary market.

MARKET RISK. The extent to which a security can be expected to be more or less volatile than the overall market. The volatility is measured as a **beta coefficient.**

MARKING NAME. A nominee who will attend to the collection of dividends and so on in a foreign jurisdiction.

MASSACHUSETTS BUSINESS TRUST. A business entity where the property is held and managed by trustees for the holders of negotiable certificates of beneficial interest.

MASTER DEED. Recorded main deed of a condominium subdivision granting title to common areas that become part of the deed.

MATURITY. The end of the life of a bond or other form of loan. When not repaid promptly, it is said to be "in default."

MAVERA INJUNCTION. A court injunction preventing the trustee for a trust from transferring trust assets pending the outcome of a lawsuit.

McFADDEN ACT. The usual designation of the Pepper-McFadden Act of the United States, whose purpose is to prevent banks from operating in more than one state.

MEMBER. (1) An equity owner of a limited liability company

(LLC), limited liability partnership (LLP), or limited liability limited partnership (LLLP) or a shareholder in an IBC. (2) Shareholder of a U.K. public company.

MEMBER BANK. A bank affiliated with the U.S. Federal Reserve.

MEMORANDUM. The memorandum of association of an IBC, equivalent to articles of incorporation.

MEMORANDUM OF ASSOCIATION. The rules governing the relations of a U.K. company with foreigners. They must state its name, registered office, and authorized capital and whether the liability of members is limited.

MERCHANT BANK. A bank that specializes in advising companies on raising capital, offers some banking activities and portfolio management for wealthy individuals, pension funds, and collective investment schemes. At their best they act more quickly, decisively, and imaginatively than larger commercial banks; at worst they have snob appeal.

MERGER. The absorption of one corporation by another.

MINORITY SHAREHOLDERS. The shareholders in a company who own so few shares of the company's outstanding shares that they have no control over its management.

MONETARISM. The economic theory that holds that economies are moved by the quantity of money in circulation.

MONETARY BASE. Currency in circulation or held by a central bank. Often includes an adjustment for changes in reserve requirements.

MONEY LAUNDERING. A process of placing "dirty money" into legitimate banks or business transactions to cleanse the money. See also **laundering.**

MONEY MARKET. The financial market for transacting in short-term debt paper.

MONEY MARKET FUNDS. A fund whose portfolio is made of short-term debts. Instruments within the portfolio generally have a duration from overnight to three months.

MONEY SUPPLY. The amount of money in circulation, including funds held by banks and individuals.

MONOPOLY. The position of being the sole supplier of a good or service. Antitrust laws are intended to prevent abuse of this potentially lucrative situation.

MOODY'S. One of the two major U.S. bond-rating agencies. Owned by the Dunn & Bradstreet Corp., its bond ratings can be distinguished from those of Standard & Poor's in that only the first letter is in uppercase. The address of Moody's Investors Service, Inc. is 99 Church Street, New York, NY 10007.

MORAL OBLIGATION BOND. A bond issued by a U.S. municipality or state financial intermediary having the uncertain support of a letter of comfort from the state in question.

MORATORIUM. An agreement between a lender and a borrower to defer repayment of the principal of a loan. This does not oblige the lender to place the loan upon a nonaccrual basis so long as interest is paid as if no default has occurred.

MORGAN STANLEY CAPITAL INTERNATIONAL PERSPECTIVE. The service that first demonstrated the role of computers in international equity evaluation and that, since 1969, has published useful monthly international equity price lists and hugely informative quarterlies on virtually all the marketable quoted companies in the world (2,400 companies in twenty countries were covered in 1989). Their world index of equity price movements, expressed in U.S. dollars, is the longest established, and equal best, such measure. Their Europe, Australia, and Far East (EAFE) index was the first to provide a benchmark against which a U.S. investor could measure the performance of overseas equities. The addresses are 3 Place des Bergues, 1201 Geneva, and 1251 Avenue of the Americas, New York, NY 10020.

MORTGAGE. The transfer of interest in a property as security for a loan.

MORTGAGE DISCOUNT. The difference between the principal amount of a mortgage and the amount for which it actually sells.

MORTGAGE INTEREST RELIEF AT SOURCE (MIRAS). U.K. residents who make interest payments on qualifying mortgages net of relief from the basic rate of income tax.

MOVING AVERAGE. The sum of prices over a given number of days, divided by the number of days, to give an average price over that period. A convincing breakthrough, a moving average is considered to evidence further movement in the same direction.

MUNICIPAL BOND. Bond issued by a U.S. state or local government body. Since 1986 only "public-purpose" bonds (that is, those where private parties stand to benefit from less than 10 percent of the issue) remain exempt from federal tax.

MUTUAL COMPANY. A corporation in which shares are held exclusively by members to whom profits are distributed as dividends in proportion to the business that the members did with the company.

MUTUAL FUND. An open-ended investment company (or unit trust) that pools money from its shareholders and then uses the pooled money to purchase a variety of stocks, bonds, or money market instruments. A mutual fund is obligated to redeem its shares at their current net asset value. This value may fluctuate greatly depending on market conditions.

MUTUAL INSURANCE. A captive insurance company owned by various companies in an industry that, despite competing in trade, agrees that the premiums demanded by the commercial insurance companies are excessive.

NAKED. A naked option obliges the writer to deliver something that she does not yet own, leading to a very exposed feeling if the price subsequently rises.

NAME. (1) A company must acquire an acceptable name before it is incorporated. Such a name must be judged by the authorizing authority not to be misleading, offensive, or illegal. The subjective decision as to whether it is any of these will depend upon the jurisdiction. For example, any member of the British Commonwealth will be much more reluctant to allow words such as "royal" or "imperial." (2) Members of Lloyd's of London are known as Names. They are grouped into syndicates by managing agents.

NATIONAL ASSOCIATION OF SECURITIES DEALERS (NASD). Industry regulatory association formed to regulate the over-the-counter market in U.S. securities in accordance with the Maloney Act of 1938.

NATIONAL ASSOCIATION OF SECURITIES' DEALERS AUTOMATED QUOTATIONS (NASDAQ). The computerized system of dealing in shares in U.S. corporations that are registered with the SEC but not quoted on any exchange floor. Share prices are circulated on "pink sheets" and can be found in the *Wall Street Journal* or *Barron's* magazine.

NATIONAL INCOME. Income derived from the production of GNP.

NEGOTIABLE INSTRUMENT. A financial instrument that may be passed from one owner to the other without need to advise the issuer as to the identity of the owner. A flexible instrument, because the owner is not committed to hold it throughout its full term.

NET. The opposite of gross, that is, excluding something, not always clearly stated.

NET ASSET VALUE (NAV). The market value of a company, that is, the value of the assets remaining after all debt and preference shareholdings have been repaid in full. Comparison of the net asset value per share with the share price indicates the extent to which the share price is backed by assets. Also known as **book value** or **net worth.**

When this term is applied to a mutual fund, it defines the market worth of one share of the fund. This amount is determined by subtracting the fund's liabilities from its assets and then dividing that amount by the number of outstanding shares.

NET WORTH. See **net asset value.**

NEW YORK FUTURES EXCHANGE (NYFE). A subsidiary of NYSE established in 1979 to provide competition with Chicago.

NEW YORK STOCK EXCHANGE (NYSE). The principal stock exchange and a major options exchange. Also known as the **Big Board.**

NOBLE. A Manx coin containing one troy ounce of platinum. Issued by Ayrtor Metals. It was the first platinum bullion coin.

NO-LOAD FUND. A mutual fund that has no front-end load or commission. To the extent that this means that no commission is payable to an intermediary this is to the investor's benefit, but it should not be supposed that anything comes for free, and no-load funds often charge higher recurrent fees or derive benefit from undisclosed sources, such as banking at less-than-competitive rates with a related party.

NOMINAL RATE OF INTEREST. The quoted rate, such as the coupon on a bond, as opposed to the real rate of interest, where adjustment is made for the effect of inflation.

NOMINAL VALUE. The face value of a security, which must be repaid before any remaining assets are distributed between equity shareholders. For example, most British equities have a nominal value of twenty-five pence. This does not mean that shares will necessarily be issued at that price (see **share premium**). Many jurisdictions allow shares to be issued with no par (nominal) value.

NOMINEE. An agreement whereby one person or firm holds shares on behalf of another person or organization.

NOMINEE DIRECTORS. A company's regulations may permit

certain shareholders to appoint directors, known as *nominee directors*. Their appointers might intend that their nominee should represent their interests exclusively, but the responsibility of any director is, by law, to all shareholders equally.

NOMINEE GRANTOR. The disclosed grantor of a trust, into which others will introduce the greater part of the trust property.

NOMINEE SHAREHOLDERS. People who permit their names to be used as the ostensible owners of a security, although the beneficial owners believe that they will always follow their wishes and may require that they execute a contract to that effect. The use of nominees does not alter the position of the beneficial owner in regard to IRS reporting requirements and liability for taxes.

NONACCRUAL LOANS. A bank loan that is not in a current status; that is, the loan is in default. If interest is ninety days or more overdue, the loan will be placed on a "cash basis," which means that interest cannot be credited to the revenue account until it has actually been received. A nonaccrual loan is of significantly less value in a bank's balance sheet than a "performing" loan.

NONEXECUTIVE DIRECTORS. Directors who do not take part in the daily management of a company. Their responsibilities are, by law, identical to those of an executive director.

NONGRANTOR TRUST. Usually an APT created by an NRA person on behalf of the U.S. beneficiaries.

NO PAR VALUE. Shares with no nominal value, each of which evidently entitles the owner to a pro rata share of the equity of the company as a whole. Preferred in Belgium and Canada but, curiously, not allowed in British jurisdictions.

NOTARY. A person authorized to certify legal documents. In civil law jurisdictions notaries carry out most legal work other than appearing in court.

NOTE. A negotiable instrument used to prove that funds have been borrowed for a period of less than five years.

NOVATION. The substitution of an existing contract with a new contract.

NRA. Nonresident (of the U.S.) alien. Not a U.S. person as defined under the Internal Revenue Code (IRC).

NUMBERED ACCOUNTS. A system whereby a bank account, particularly in Switzerland, will be identified by a number only rather than by the owner's true name, with the objective to protect the anonymity of the owner.

OBJECTS. The purposes for which a company is established, as set out in its memorandum of association. If its officers exceed these objects they will be acting ultra vires, that is, beyond the corporate powers. The objects of a trust are its potential beneficiaries.

ODD LOT. Any quantity of a security other than a round or board lot. Thus, a lot of less than 100 shares is sold separately on a U.S. exchange, but with no trouble. A lot of less than 1,000 shares in a Japanese company must normally be sold to that company, with a difficulty that frequently exceeds the value recoverable.

OFF BALANCE SHEET. An accounting category that is not reflected on a balance sheet. For example, although a bank may earn fees from placing fiduciary deposits, those fees do not normally appear on its balance sheet.

OFFER PRICE. The price at which a market maker is willing to sell a share. Also known as the "ask."

OFFICERS. Persons appointed by a company's directors to carry out the mandate of the directors and shareholders. The officers of an unincorporated association are the members of its governing body. The officers of a partnership are its partners.

OFFLOAD. To sell gladly.

OFFSHORE (OS). *Offshore* is an international term meaning not only out of your country (jurisdiction) but also out of the tax reach of your country of residence or citizenship; synonymous with *foreign, transnational, global, international, transworld,* and *multinational,* though *foreign* is used more in reference to the IRS.

Offshore also means any activity that is conducted outside the regulations of a major nation can be said to be carried on offshore. This normally implies that the transactions in question are conducted between nonresidents in a foreign currency. It need not be conducted from an island tax haven; many high-tax jurisdictions allow banks to operate accounts for nonresidents outside the tax treatment and prudent ratios that need to be observed in domestic business. The City of London is the principal offshore financial center.

OFFSHORE CENTER. See **international financial and banking center (IFC).** A more sophisticated tax haven.

OFFSHORE FUNDS. The term *offshore* is employed primarily to refer to the tax havens off the shores of the United States; by extension it refers to any tax haven.

Hence, the term *offshore fund* is used to cover any form of unit trust or mutual fund located in a tax haven or a fiscally neutral country. The majority of offshore funds are open-ended investment companies; however, funds may take any of the forms permitted by the legal system or systems concerned. The more popular locations for offshore funds are Bermuda, the Cayman Islands, the Channel Islands, Hong Kong, the Isle of Man, and Luxembourg.

Offshore funds generally enjoy greater investment flexibility than funds located in high-tax countries. However, there is a growing tendency to require greater disclosure and generally to tighten the regulations governing offshore funds.

The bulk of investors in offshore funds are residents or citizens of high-tax countries, many of which severely restrict the local marketing activities of funds.

OFFSHORE TERRITORIES. Jurisdictions that have low or no tax requirements for investment strategies. Individuals living in other countries may be allowed to invest in funds registered for sale in these areas.

OMBUDSMAN. An independent official to whom supposed grievances can be aired, free of charge. Thus, anyone who feels that he has been treated less than fairly by a British insurance company can complain to the insurance ombudsman at 31 Southampton Row, London WC1B 5HJ. His equivalent in the banking world operates from 5-11 Fetter Lane, London EC4A 1ER.

OMNIBUS ACCOUNT. A special account maintained by a depository institution to provide for funds holding of all funds that may belong to individual customers. This is often used by broker-dealers to commingle funds that may be used for investment purposes.

OPEC. See **Organization of Petroleum Exporting Countries.**

OPEN ECONOMY. An economic system that allows the flow of goods, bonds, money, and labor to and from other nations.

OPEN ENDED. Said of a collective investment scheme where new shares may be issued and existing shares redeemed on demand. A British unit trust is open ended.

OPEN MARKET OPERATIONS. The sale or purchase of government bonds by the central bank. These transactions are undertaken to manage assets or establish monetary policy.

OPEN OUTCRY. In U.S. commodity trading, the practice of shouting bids and offers in a trading pit to assure a public auction for all buy and sell orders.

OPTION. (1) A right to buy (**call option**) or to sell (**put option**) something at a given exercise or striking price within a given period. Traditional options are contracts between two parties, the selling party normally being known as the *writer*, and cannot be traded. (2) An option for which a regular secondary market exists.

ORDER. A broker will usually assume that a client wishes any deal to be made at the prevailing market price straightaway, or once the market opens. Asking the broker to deal "at discretion" may impose a moral duty of care but probably has no legal significance. The alternative is to ask the broker to deal at a preset limit, such as with a stop-loss order. A limit order may hold good for a specified period, or it can be "good until canceled."

ORDER BOOK. Uncompleted orders. (U.K. term; the U.S. equivalent is backlog.)

ORDINARY SHARE. Another name for **equity.**

ORGANIZATION FOR ECONOMIC COOPERATION AND DEVELOPMENT (OECD). Australia, Austria, Belgium, Canada, Denmark, Finland, France, West Germany, Greece, Iceland, Ireland, Italy, Japan. Luxembourg, the Netherlands, New Zealand, Norway, Portugal, Spain, Sweden, Switzerland, Turkey, the United Kingdom, and the United States. Not unlike an association of the richer nations of the Western world.

ORGANIZATION OF PETROLEUM EXPORTING COUNTRIES (OPEC). Its members are Algeria, Gabon, Ecuador, Egypt, Indonesia, Iran, Iraq, Kuwait, Libya, Nigeria, Saudi Arabia, the United Arab Emirates, and Venezuela. In the early 1970s OPEC produced more than half the world's oil and could and did operate as a cartel to force its price upwards.

OS. See **offshore.**

OTC (OVER-THE-COUNTER MARKET). Any market without a regular floor but not necessarily unregulated. The U.S. NASDAQ is well regulated by the SEC.

OUTBOUND. Assets flowing offshore from the United States.

OUTSIDE. Persons not employed by or having financial interest in a company.

OUT TRADES. In U.S. commodities trading, trades that do not match up after trading closes.

OVERALL RETURNS. The total returns from an investment, that is, including capital gains, exchange rate gains, and income.

PACMAN STRATEGY. A defense against an unwelcome takeover attempt that involves the aggressive purchase of shares in the bidding company. As in the video game after which it is named, it is a case of eat or be eaten.

PAID IN SURPLUS. The U.S. term for the amount paid on the issue of new shares in excess of their nominal value. The U.K. expression is **share premium.**

PARENT COMPANY. A company that owns more than 50 percent of the voting capital of another, its subsidiary.

PARTIAL PROFIT TAKING. A technique of portfolio management. After the price of a shareholding has advanced, it is often prudent to sell part of a holding, until the subsequent holding represents no greater percentage of the overall portfolio than it had at the time of purchase. This exercise removes the specific risk of a subsequent reversal.

PARTLY PAID. (U.K. expression) A share on which a call is still outstanding. The U.S. term is **assessable.**

PARTNERSHIP. An association of two or more persons to carry on an enterprise for a profit. In some jurisdictions (Scotland, for example) a partnership is a legal person; in others (for example, England and Wales and the United States) it is not, and individual partners would appear in court to defend each other's actions. Although some "sleeping" partners may be allowed limited liability, there must always be at least one "general" partner with unlimited liability.

General partnership. A partnership in which each partner is a general partner and has personal liability for all partnership debts.

Limited partnership. A partnership with a minimum of one general partner who manages the affairs of the partnership and has personal liability for all partnership debts, and a minimum of one general partner whose liability is limited to its investment but who has little or no say in the management of the partnership affairs.

PAR VALUE. The face value of a company stock.

PASSBOOK. A system of banking whereby ownership of a passbook evidencing a deposit entitles the possessor to make withdrawals. Evidently, this system values confidentiality over any duty of a bank to involve itself in its client's affairs.

PAYING AGENT. The institution, usually one major bank in each relevant financial center, that is charged with collecting, verifying, and paying the coupons from bearer securities.

PENNY STOCK/SHARE. A stock where a single share can be purchased for a few pennies, as contrasted with a "heavy" stock. A disproportionate number of securities frauds perpetrated on investors have involved penny shares, possibly because they appeal to unsophisticated investors who may be uncertain how to seek redress (if, indeed, any is possible).

PERFORMANCE FEE. A fee that is sometimes paid to the managers of offshore funds. The fee often ranges from 10 to 20 percent of a fund's annual gains. Designed to act as an incentive for the fund manager, but it can have drawbacks.

PERMANENT HEALTH INSURANCE. Insurance that will pay a regular income to those too sick to work. A necessity for the self-employed.

PERPETUITIES. The common law rule against perpetuities prevents the transfer of any interest in property, such as a beneficial interest in a trust, being delayed beyond the life of someone living or conceived plus twenty-one years or, alternatively, a stipulated period, such as eighty years. Designed to prevent the indefinite accumulation of income.

PERSON. Any individual, branch, partnership, associated group, association, estate, trust, corporation, company, or other organization, agency, or financial institution under the IRC.

PERSONAL ACCOUNT (PA). A broker who is dealing for his own benefit, or for that of his wife or infant children, is said to be dealing PA.

PHYSICAL COMMODITIES. Tangible goods that one can actually see and touch, as opposed to futures.

PINK SHEETS. The pink-colored sheets on which U.S. brokers quote prices for OTC stocks and ADRs.

PLACING. A method of selling newly issued securities in a company to a limited number of persons, usually institutional investors. Much cheaper than a public offering, but care must be taken not to infringe on **preemption rights.**

POINT. A fee equal to 1 percent of the principal amount of the loan.

POISON PILL. Any device introduced by the managers of a company to make the company unattractive to anyone who intends to acquire it. Poison pills tend to relate more closely to the job security of existing management than to the best interests of either shareholders or employees.

PORTFOLIO INSURANCE. A strategy whereby stock index futures are used to reduce the risk of investment.

PORTFOLIO INVESTMENT. Investment in securities—usually quoted as a passive investor, seeking only returns, as opposed to direct investment.

PORTFOLIO MANAGER. See **asset manager.**

POUND. The highest unit of currency in the United Kingdom.

POUR-OVER WILL. Provision in a will that directs the distribution of property into a trust.

PREEMPTION RIGHTS. Rights of first refusal by existing shareholders on any new securities of the same or another class that may be issued by a company in the future.

PREFERENCE SHARE. Class of stock giving its holder a preference to either receipt of dividends or repayment in case of dissolution. Also see **preferred shares.**

PREFERENTIAL TRANSFER. A disposition of an asset that is unfair to other creditors of the transferor.

PREFERRED (or PREFERENCE) SHARES. Shares in a company that must be repaid at their full par value on the winding up of a company before equity shareholders are entitled to anything. Preferred shareholders are generally entitled to dividends even though no dividends are being paid on the common shares. In Europe they are more often identified by the par value payable on redemption, and the annual dividend is expressed as a percentage of that par value. Preference shares may be redeemable at a fixed future date whether or not the company is to be wound up then. If so, they differ from bonds only in respect of tax treatment in the company's books. Preferred shareholders do not share fully in the fortune of the company unless their shares are also convertible, and they choose to convert.

PREFILING NOTICE. Mailed by the IRS to parties (taxpayers) who are believed to be participating in fraudulent trust programs.

The notice requests that the receiver seek professional counsel before filing their next tax return.

PREMIUM. (1) Any excess over apparent worth; for example, if a share with a par value of $1 is issued at $2. (2) The consideration paid to an insurer by the insured for insurance coverage or by the purchaser of an option.

PRICE/BOOK VALUE RATIO. The total market capitalization divided by the total book value of a company. Also known as *net worth* when book value accounting methods are used.

PRICE/EARNINGS RATIO. The quotient of an equity share price divided by the earnings per share. This is a good measure of the relative cheapness of different shares in the same sector and market, but care should be taken when comparing P/E ratios of dissimilar companies or quoted on different markets. The most informative P/E ratio, the current share price divided by future earnings, is the most difficult to calculate.

PRICE INDEX. A way of measuring prices based on consumer or purchaser purchases, domestic output, and wages. This index is constructed as a weighted average of the individual prices and stated relative to a base year.

PRIMA FACIE. Latin term for "on the first view." A fact presumed to be true unless evidence to the contrary is admitted.

PRIMARY MARKET. Market where the issuer sells directly to an investor.

PRIME RATE. The best borrowing rate charged by U.S. banks to their most creditworthy borrowers.

PRINCIPAL. (1) The original sum borrowed or deposited. The principal of a trust is the property originally introduced and any substitutions but not the income earned thereon. (2) Anyone who uses her own money to buy or sell a security (as opposed to an agent).

PRIVATE BANKING. Offshore banking services for high-net-worth (HNW) persons.

PRIVATE BANK. The ancient form of a bank where the owner or owning partners are willing to pledge their entire fortunes that every depositor be repaid in full. The need for ever more capital has led most private banks to be replaced by joint-stock banks. In normal current usage *private banking* is used as a marketing term by any bank that plans to charge more to customers who want the personal service that is traditional with private banks.

PRIVATE COMPANY. A company that does not offer its securities to the general public. Reporting requirements are generally less onerous for public companies.

PRIVATE LIMITED PARTNERSHIP. Under U.S. law, a limited partnership with no more than thirty-five limited partners (apart from accredited investors) that does not need to be registered with the SEC.

PRIVATE PLACEMENT. The sale of securities to persons other than the general public, usually to fewer than thirty-five unaccredited persons and without general advertisement. Does not require a prior review by the SEC.

PRIVATE VARIABLE ANNUITY. A financial instrument issued *not* by an insurance company or other firm that regularly issues annuities. This instrument provides a means of deferring taxes on appreciated property, with the exception of real estate, in exchange for a contract that will obligate the annuity issuer to make payments to the annuitant beginning at retirement and ending at death.

PRIVATIZATION. A 1980s term for the sale of a state asset to such members of the general public as could afford to buy it, normally at favorable terms.

PROBATE. The legal process for the distribution of the estate of a decedent. Proving to a court of law that a will is valid.

PRODUCTIVITY. A method of measuring the output achieved based on the resources used.

PROFIT AND LOSS ACCOUNT. The British term for the statement showing income and expenditure for a particular period. The U.S. expression is *income statement*.

PRO FORMA. Latin term for "as a matter of form." Thus, a bidding company may suggest pro forma accounts for a group following an intended acquisition.

PROMISSORY NOTE. An unconditional promise in writing made by one person to another and signed by the maker, promising to pay a certain sum of money on demand or at a fixed or determinable date in the future, either to the bearer or to a specified payee. A bank note is an example of a promissory note, payable to the bearer on demand.

PROPER LAW. The law of the jurisdiction that the parties to a contract agree should determine any future disagreements among them. It is best to specify the jurisdiction in question before entering into the contract.

PRO RATA. Latin term for "in proportion."

PROSPECTUS. Required by U.S. law, this document invites the public to subscribe to a new issue of a security or a mutual fund. It gives specific details on the company issuing the security. In the case of a mutual fund, it describes the fund's portfolio; the fund's investment strategies and objectives; its shareholder policies; a description of the fees charged; and a list of the fund managers, trustees/custodians, and any advisors. In the United States prospectuses are generally reviewed by the SEC prior to the start of sales. In some jurisdictions a prospectus might be called *product particulars, offering memorandum,* or *scheme particulars.*

PROTECTIONISM. Any measure to protect domestic industry from foreign competition. As with all restraints on competition, it works to the eventual impoverishment of the consumer.

PROTECTION OF ASSETS TRUST. A trust that is intended to protect the grantor's property for the sake of someone other than the grantor (for example, the grantor's spouse and children) in the event of a financial calamity, such as a huge award against him for professional negligence. If he were aware of an impending claim when he granted the trust it would be voided as fraudulent; indeed, the longer a trust has been in existence the less likely it is that a court would seek to invalidate it. As a practical matter, it would be considerably more difficult to seize assets from a foreign trust.

PROTECTOR. A person who may be appointed to guide trustees in carrying out their duties in accordance with the wishes of the grantor. The position is not normally covered in trust law, and therefore the protector's powers and responsibilities should be detailed in the trust deed. If they are excessive there is a real risk that a court would determine that the protector was the effective trustee and the named trustees were no more than administrators. It may be reassuring, however, for a grantor to know that a third, sympathetic, party could replace a recalcitrant trustee.

PROVISIONS. A charge to revenue accounts to allow for an expected loss of profits; for example, a bank might make provisions against the possibility that some of its LDC loans may have to be written off.

PROXY. An agent appointed to vote at a general meeting on behalf of a registered shareholder, unless the shareholder opts to turn up and vote.

PROXY STATEMENT. Information required by the SEC to be given to shareholders as a prerequisite to solicitation of proxies for a security subject to the requirements of the SEC.

PRUDENTIAL RATIOS. The ratios that a bank, and its regulatory authority, will scrutinize to verify that it is not overtrading. The liquidity ratio will establish that it should be able to meet any demand for cash. The capital ratio will show that it could bear a reasonable amount of bad debt without becoming insolvent. The free capital ratio shows if it could do so without having to sell off fixed assets.

PUBLIC COMPANY. Any company that has offered its shares for sale to the public.

PUBLIC LIMITED PARTNERSHIP. (U.S. law) A limited partnership that has been registered with the SEC and therefore need not limit the number of investors to whom partnership interests are sold.

PURCHASING POWER PARITY. An approach to determining what exchange rates should be by comparing relative rates of inflation over a past period on the grounds that currency of the more inflationary nation should be the weaker.

PURE EQUITY TRUST. A special type of irrevocable trust marketed by promoters. The trust assets are obtained by an "exchange" of a certificate of beneficial interest in return for the assets, as opposed to traditional means, such as by gifting.

PURE TRUST. A contractual trust as opposed to a statutory trust, created under the common law. A pure trust is one in which there must be a minimum of three parties—the creator or settlor (never grantor), the trustee, and the beneficiary—and each is a separate entity. A pure trust is claimed to be a lawful but not proven, irrevocable, separate legal entity.

PURPOSE TRUST. A specialized trust that is established under British Virgin Islands, Isle of Man, or Bermuda legislation that provides for a trust to be established with specific purposes and objectives. Often used for aircraft-financing transactions and shareholding purposes. Enabling law provides for a trust enforcer.

PUT OPTION. An option to sell at a stated price within a determined period.

QUALIFIED REPORT/OPINION. An opinion rendered by a company's independent auditors.

QUALIFIED TERMINABLE INTEREST PROPERTY TRUST. A trust that transfers interest to a spouse for life but permits that the assets be distributed to someone else on the spouse's death. The first provision avoids gift and estate taxes; the second allows against the spouse remarrying unsuitably.

QUICK RATIO. Another term for *acid test;* calculated by dividing total current assets by total current liabilities.

QUORUM. Sufficient persons present, in person or by proxy, to validate a meeting.

QUOTED COMPANY. Any company where bid and offer prices for its shares are quoted on a stock exchange.

RA. Reluctant American. *Caution:* Also *resident alien* in other literature, but not in this book.

RANDOM WALK. A theory that there is no logical pattern to share price movements. They will respond only to unexpected events.

RATE OF RETURN. The earnings obtained from an investment. Usually expressed as a percentage of the value invested. Published as an annual rate.

REAL ESTATE. Land and everything permanently affixed to it.

REAL EXCHANGE RATE. The exchange value of a currency, after its adjusted for its relative purchasing power. A rise or fall in the rate indicates the currency's value is rising or falling, respectively.

REAL RATE OF INTEREST. The nominal rate of interest, less an allowance for the rate of inflation. Thus, if a bond has a coupon of 8 percent, and it is assumed that inflation will average 5 percent over the remaining life of the bond, the real rate of interest is 3 percent.

REAL RATE OF RETURN. The actual return yielded by an investment after accounting for inflation.

RECESSION. Defined in the United States as being two successive quarters of declining GNP.

RED CHIPS. Companies controlled by mainland Chinese interests, which are also listed on the Hong Kong Stock Exchange. Traditionally, this has been the main way that an individual or company could buy into mainland government and industry without investing in Chinese incorporated companies.

REDEEMABLE SHARES. Shares that may be redeemed in accordance with a company's articles of association.

REDEMPTION. The repayment of a security. In the case of a bond, this will normally be at its par value. Redemption will normally be at the end of its permitted life, but it may be earlier if individual bonds are liable to early redemption if they are drawn by ballot, or if some condition affecting the issue of a bond, such as the absence of withholding tax, is breached.

REDEMPTION DATE. The date when a bond will be repaid. Contrasts "irredeemable" or "perpetual" bonds, which may never be repaid. Sometimes the issuer may redeem (or "call") a bond earlier than the maturity date.

REDEMPTION FEE. A fee paid by a shareholder when redeeming shares.

RED HERRING. A preliminary prospectus that is designed to test reaction to a proposed stock issue. It contains most relevant information other than the suggested price.

REGIONAL BANK. A commercial bank that restricts its business to a specific area of the country. There are many regional banks in the United States, largely because of the McFadden Act, as well as in Germany and Japan. In the United Kingdom new regional banks tend to be taken over by larger banks, as were their predecessors.

REGISTER. The register of international business companies (IBCs) and exempt companies maintained by the registrar of a tax haven.

REGISTERED OFFICE. The official address of a company within the jurisdiction in which it is registered. The name of the company must be displayed at the entrance. Documents delivered to a company's registered address can be assumed to reach that company's officers.

REGISTERED SECURITIES. Securities that carry the name of the owner on a certificate. Dividends will be paid to the registered owner at that address unless the owner has mandated that they be treated otherwise. The company will not accept any transfer of the security without the registered owner's authority. Companies usually refuse to acknowledge that a registered holder is holding the security on trust for another beneficial owner.

REGISTRAR. The registrar of companies, a governmental body controlling the formation and renewal of companies created under their company act.

REGULATED. Funds that do not have SIB recognition and therefore cannot be actively marketed to private investors in the United Kingdom.

REHYPOTHECATION. The U.S. practice whereby a broker may lend a client's stock certificates in her possession as security for bank loans in her own name or to cover short positions. The circumstances under which she may do so are governed by the SEC. Few other jurisdictions permit this practice under any circumstances.

REINSURANCE. Insurers laying off some of their risks with other, usually specialist, insurers, particularly including syndicates at insurance companies.

REINVESTMENT PRIVILEGE. An option available to shareholders of a mutual fund or unit trust. Under reinvestment privilege, dividends and capital gains are automatically used to buy new shares. There is no sales fee or commission charge for this transaction.

REMITTANCE. Money sent home by an expatriate worker.

REPAYMENT MORTGAGE. One where the principal is amortized over the life of the loan. Contrast with **endowment mortgage.**

REPURCHASE AGREEMENTS ("REPOS"). Arrangements where a U.S. institution, usually a securities firm, which is in a long position on a bond may sell it to a cash-rich institution while undertaking to repurchase it at a price that will ensure a profit to the bank at a future date.

RESERVES. An accounting term for net worth in addition to the proceeds of issuing equity. The principal source as reserves is a surplus on revenue account. This would be available for distribution as dividends even after an unprofitable year (although it would be unwise to do so unless directors were confident that the down year was an aberration). Other reserves, such as those arising from a revaluation of fixed assets, may be *undistributable* (U.K. term; the U.S. term is *restricted surplus*).

RESIDENCE. Residency gives rise to taxation upon income and is subject to complex rules. Almost any country will subject any person who spends more than 182 days of a fiscal year within it to income tax. Much shorter periods may render an individual liable to tax, especially if there is any indication that that person keeps a home in the country concerned.

RESOLUTION. A decision reached by shareholders in general meeting. Ordinary resolutions may be passed by a simple majority of those voting.

REVENUE ACCOUNT. The U.S. term for the account showing a corporation's income and expenditure over an accounting period. The U.K. term is *profit and loss account.*

REVENUE RECONCILIATION ACT OF 1995. Proposed changes to the Internal Revenue Code affecting foreign trust reporting, among other changes.

RIGHTS. The right to buy additional, new shares at issue in proportion to existing holdings. Typically, rights will be offered at a slight discount to the current share price to encourage their being taken up. Unless the issue is at a deep discount, it will normally be underwritten, so that the issuing company can be certain of receiving its money. Rights not taken up are generally sold in the market, and any premium obtained is credited to the shareholders concerned. Evidence of entitlement to rights comes in a letter of allotment.

RISK ARBITRAGEUR ("ARB"). A phenomenon of the mid-1980s on Wall Street, arbs would buy large amounts of stock in a company for which a bid had just been or was about to be announced. Subsequent investigation revealed that the phenomenal success of some arbs in spotting bid victims at just the right time was connected to information provided by company insiders.

ROMAN LAW. The system of law that derives from ancient Roman law rather than the later British common law or the Napoleonic civil law. It distinguishes Scottish from English law and Portuguese from Spanish law by attaching more importance to the head of a household than is common in later patterns of law.

ROUND LOT. A quantity of shares divisible by 100, good for delivery on a U.S. exchange. Contrast with **odd lot.**

ROYALTIES. A percentage of sales paid to an inventor, author, or owner of mineral rights. Royalties receivable from abroad might be enhanced at the after-tax level by careful financial structuring.

RULE 144. Issued by the U.S. Securities and Exchange Commission, this regulation covers the sale of restricted securities.

RULE AGAINST PERPETUITIES. A legal limit on remote vesting of assets in the beneficiaries. May be void ab initio (from the beginning), for a fixed term, or determined on a "wait and see" basis.

RUNNING YIELD. The annual income from a bond at a particular price, ignoring the "pull to redemption." Thus a bid with a coupon of 10.0 percent that is standing at par (100 percent) will yield exactly 10.0 percent, but if the price of that same bond falls to 90.0 percent its running yield will rise to 11.1 percent (10.0/0.90). See also **yield**.

SA. See **Société Anonyme**.

SALES. (Accounting term) Goods sold during the account period, net of sales tax and—in consolidated accounts intragroup sales— whether or not payment has been received.

SALES CHARGE. A fee that an individual pays when purchasing shares in a mutual fund or unit trust that is being sold by an agent or broker. This fee may also fund the initial setup fee. This fee may be collected upon the initial purchase of the sales or after the shares are redeemed. This fee is usually included in the quoted offering price.

SAMURAI. Yen bonds issued on the TSE by foreign borrowers.

SANDWICH. Borrowing one currency to make deposits in one or more other currencies, in the hope that the combination of exchange rate gains and interest received on the deposit(s) will exceed the cost of borrowing. Opportunities for successful sandwich spreads are often most apparent with the benefit of hindsight.

SARL (SOCIÉTÉ ANONYME RESPONSIBILITY LIMITED). The closest French equivalent to a private company, but with some characteristics of a partnership.

SAVINGS. The difference between income and expenditure. Since both figures are large it is misleading to suppose that the residual can be calculated very precisely. Nevertheless one can safely say that nations where households save much of their income, as in Northeast Asia, tend to grow richer than those where more is spent. Savings must be matched by other parties' dissavings. It is usually companies and governments that borrow. If domestic saving is insufficient to meet the demand for money it must be attracted from abroad, of capital account.

SAVINGS BOND. (U.S. practice) Series EE bonds are issued at a discount, to mature in twelve years (earlier issues mature after ten years). No state or local tax is ever payable, and federal tax can be deferred by switching into Series HH bonds (which pay interest at 3 percent every six months). A person can invest up to $15,000 in Series EE bonds (the redemption value of which will be $30,000) in a year. Gifting the money to buy Series EE bonds to a child is very tax efficient.

SCHEME. In the United Kingdom any plan intended to achieve a strategic aim can be called a scheme, without opprobrium. In the United States there is a strong presumption that any "scheme" would flout the law.

SEAL. A mechanical device for imprinting an engraving. See also **company seal.**

SEC (SECURITIES AND EXCHANGE COMMISSION). Established in the United States in 1934. Immensely powerful, the SEC supervises all aspects of the securities industry. Registered companies, that is, any that are quoted in a stock exchange or have assets of $1 million or more and at least 500 shareholders, must submit a Form 10-K annually. The extensive information contained is available to the public.

SECONDARY MARKET. (1) A market whereby securities are traded after their initial placement but still during the issuing period. When applied to the stock market this term is used for the securities market outside of the organized exchanges. (2) The market for any transaction between owners of a security other than the issuer; arises subsequent to a primary issue.

SECRETARY. The chief administrative officer of a company. May also be a director.

SECURITIES AND INVESTMENT BOARD (SIB). The agency designated to handle most aspects of the control of investment business in the United Kingdom. It is only an agent of the department of trade and industry and as such lacks the full authority of the U.S. SEC. Most day-to-day business of regulation has been delegated to the SROs, but an organization may be registered with the SIB itself. If so, any complaints should be addressed to the SIB at 3 Royal Exchange Buildings, London EC3V 3NL.

SECURITY. (1) Cover for a loan, which the lender could possess if the borrower fails to repay. (2) A certificate of ownership of a bond or equity. Because of their liquid nature securities came to be preferred as security by bankers. The expression has since been extended to "the securities industry" to cover the markets in equities and bonds but excluding commodities and futures. (3) Share and debt obligation of every kind, including options, warrants, and rights to acquire shares and debt obligations.

SEGREGATED ACCOUNT. A series of special accounts established at a depository institution designed to protect the segregation of customer funds in a separate account. Funds may be swept out of this account into an omnibus account for investment purposes. See also **omnibus account.**

SELF-REGULATORY ORGANIZATION. (U.K. term) An organization whose rule book has been approved by the SIB as giving investors equivalent protection to its own regulations. Once approval has been obtained, all members of that SRO may carry on an investment business in the United Kingdom within their "scope." In the United States all securities and commodities exchanges, NASD, and the municipal securities rule-making board are designated as SROs.

SELL SHORT. A term used for the strategy whereby one sells an asset that he does not own with the intention of buying the asset later at a lower price. Traders who take advantage of this strategy are known as "bears."

SEPARATE MAINTENANCE. Like alimony, but ordered while the parties are still married and no divorce is pending; they are merely separated. If a divorce case is pending the support order is really "temporary alimony," but the difference between the two is minor or nonexistent.

SETTLE. (1) To create or establish an offshore trust. Done by the settlor (offshore term) or the grantor (U.S. and IRS term). (2) To pay for something purchased, usually simultaneously as delivery is made. (3) To introduce property (assets) into a trust.

SETTLEMENT. The process whereby a payment is made toward an obligation. For example, cash is paid for securities.

SETTLOR. (1) One (the entity) who creates or settles an offshore trust. (2) (U.K. term) One who settles property in trust during her lifetime. The U.S. term is **grantor.** If the property is not transferred until the settlor's death, the trust will be a "will trust," and the donor will be more correctly described as the "testator."

SFAs. Statements of financial accounting standards, issued by the financial accounting standards board for the guidance of U.S. accountants.

SHARE. A right to participate in a company, as defined more exactly in its regulations. Much the most frequent class of share is the common (U.S. usage) or ordinary (U.K. usage) share, entitling the owner literally to a share of that company's equity.

SHARE CERTIFICATE. A certificate from a company's registrar confirming that the possessor is entitled to the rights of holders of that class of share (bearer securities) or that the registered owner is on the company's register as owning that many shares of that class. Although entry on the register is more important than possession of the certificate, a registrar will normally require indemnification before issuing a duplicate certificate.

SHARE PREMIUM. The British term for the amount paid on the issue of new shares in excess of their nominal value. The U.S. expression is **paid in surplus.**

SHARK REPELLENT. A measure adopted by a corporation to deter takeover attempts.

SHARP. In the United States it is complimentary to call an astute lawyer "sharp." In Britain it would suggest that that lawyer is scarcely one step ahead of the law.

SHELF COMPANY. A company that is formed by nominees and then kept "on the shelf" of a professional firm until a client requires a company in a hurry. Buying a shelf company allows a person to obtain a company within minutes, as opposed to a few days; it emphatically does not allow directors to predate corporate resolutions. Some jurisdictions require the future ownership of a company to be established before it is formed. This precludes shelf companies but not "secondhand" companies. It is normally desirable to form a new company, if time allows, to be certain that an existing company has never contracted liabilities. It can take as long, or longer, to change the name of a company as to form a new one.

SHELF REGISTRATION. Since 1982 U.S. companies have been able to obtain blanket approval for possible new issues over the next two years and then to leave them "on the shelf" until needed. This has speeded the process of actual issues considerably.

SHELL COMPANY. A quoted company that has virtually no assets (for example, a form plantation company whose estates have been expropriated) and possesses nothing beyond boardroom furniture and a little cash in its country of incorporation. It is often cheaper to purchase the entire outstanding share capital of a shell company than to register a new company for quotation.

SHORT POSITION. (1) To be short of anything is to have sold more of it than one has bought. Sooner or later the position will have to be closed at a price not for the fainthearted. (2) A negative balance of an individual's net holdings of an asset.

SIB. See **Securities and Investment Board.**

SIDE LETTER. Same as a **letter of wishes.**

SIMPLE INTEREST. Interest paid on the principal of a loan or deposit only, that is, without compounding interest on unpaid interest. Bonds pay simple interest; banks calculate compound interest except over short periods; most jurisdictions require that this be done at least semiannually. Interest on Sterling or Irish Punt deposits is normally calculated on the number of calendar days elapsed, divided by 365. Interest on deposits in other currencies is usually calculated on the basis of twelve months of thirty days each, divided by 360.

SINGLE-PREMIUM DEFERRED ANNUITY (SPDA). (U.S. practice) Tax will be deferred on money put into an SPDA until distributions are taken. There will be an additional 10 percent penalty if distributions are taken before the age of fifty-nine and a half. Unlike an IRA, there is no limit on annual investment in an SPDA, but neither is there any offset against income tax on funds introduced.

SINKING FUND. A system predating the regular "rolling over" of debts. The borrower would set aside sufficient money each year to be able to repay the principal of a loan upon its maturity.

SIPC (SECURITIES INDUSTRY PROTECTION CORPORATION). Provides up to $500,000 insurance protection for your U.S. stock brokerage account.

SMELL TEST. An expressive U.S. concept. There may be nothing technically wrong with any of the details of a tax-avoidance scheme, but would you feel comfortable with the revenue authorities investigating it? If not, think again.

SOCIÉTÉ ANONYME (SA). The French or Belgian form of public company or limited liability corporation. Requires a minimum of seven shareholders. A notable difference between an SA and a U.S. or U.K. company is that an SA has a fixed maximum life of not more than ninety-nine years. An important characteristic of an SA is that the liability of the shareholder is limited up to the amount of the capital contribution.

SOFT COMMISSION OR SOFT DOLLARS. A system that originated in the United States whereby a broker will pay for a service that a fund manager obtains from a third party, such as a pricing service, provided that the commission that the broker receives stays at a certain level, normally at least three times the cost of the service. The practice is justifiable, but it is also wide open to abuse in a period when little dealing is justified and therefore not much commission ought to be generated.

SOFT CURRENCY. Currency that is weak and therefore a less desirable means of payment. Countries that have soft currencies tend to have depreciating currencies or frequent currency devaluations. They may also have difficulty making balance of payments. Contrasts with hard currency.

SOFT LOAN. Any loan made on favorable terms to the debtor, usually for political reasons.

SOGO. A Japanese regional bank.

SOLICITOR. The branch of the U.K. legal profession that deals with the public on day-to-day matters. Solicitors must hold a practicing certificate issued by the law society and insurance against professional negligence. Complaints against a solicitor can be referred to the Solicitors Complaints Bureau, Portland House, Stag Place, London SWLE 5BL.

SOLVENT. A business is solvent if it is able to meet its liabilities as they fall due. It may nevertheless face liquidity problems.

SOTHEBY'S. Long-established London auction house that publishes indices of the prices of different forms of art reached at their auctions. An aggregate index is divided into four categories of paintings and two each of ceramics, silver, and furniture. These are shown in its monthly *Art Market Bulletin*. Sotheby's address is 34-35 Old Bond Street, London WlA 2AA.

SOURCE AND APPLICATION OF FUNDS. A statement now required in U.K. and U.S. accounts showing what it says. It is reassuring if one can note that a company is building up its liquid assets.

SOVEREIGN RISK. The risk that a nation will default on its foreign debt.

SPARBUCH. An Austrian numbered savings account.

SPECIAL CUSTODIAN. An appointee of the trustee in an APT.

SPECIAL DRAWING RIGHT. A payment medium and reserve asset issued by the International Monetary Fund. Used for transactions among the central banks in its membership. Its value is recalculated every five years based on the relative share of world GNP of five major nations. It is therefore the best approximation of a world currency. The SDR equivalent of sixteen major currencies appears daily in the *Financial Times*, two days late. The SDR equivalent in U.S. dollars appears in the *Wall Street Journal* of the following day.

SPECIAL INVESTMENT ADVISOR. An appointee of the trustee in an APT.

SPECIALIST. A member of a U.S. stock exchange who is willing to deal as a principal. Specialists play an important part in maintaining a two-way market.

SPECIAL RESOLUTION. A resolution passed by at least 75 percent of those voting at a meeting of shareholders who have been given at least twenty-one days' notice required for various important decisions, such as a change to the company's regulations.

SPECIFIC DUTY. An indirect tax that does not vary with the price of the goods being sold. Contrast with **ad valorem.**

SPECULATION. Gambling on any exchange.

SPLIT TRUST. A closed-end fund with more than one class of share: for example, one where one class of shareholder is entitled to all the income and another to no income but all the capital gains. Both classes thereby achieve gearing in pursuit of their primary objective. Split trusts must have a final date, in the run up to which the discount on capital shares to their net asset value will fall sharply.

SPONSOR. The company that provides the initial cash when creating a mutual fund or unit trust. Money from new shareholders is used to reimburse the sponsor for the cost of starting the fund.

SPOT PRICE/RATE. The price for immediate payment and delivery.

SPOT TRANSACTION. A transaction whereby cash payment is made and delivery taken immediately on an instrument or a good (such as a security, a foreign currency, or a commodity traded on exchanges). Contrast with **futures.**

SPREAD. (1) The difference between bid and offer prices. (2) See **straddle.**

SPREADING. In U.S. commodities trading, the purchase of one futures contract and the sale of another in the hope that subsequent price changes will yield a profit.

SRO. See **self-regulatory organization.**

SSAPS (STATEMENTS OF STANDARD ACCOUNTING PRACTICE). Statements issued by the Accounting Standards

Committee for the guidance of accountants in the British Isles and Ireland.

STAG. A person who buys shares in a new issue, often on borrowed money, in the expectation of being able to sell them at a quick profit when dealings commence in the secondary market.

STAGFLATION. First used in the 1970s, this term describes the large one-time increases in prices coupled with the occurrence of a recession.

STAMP DUTY. A long-established U.K. tax on documents. Share certificates will hopefully be replaced by electronic data leading to the introduction of an alternative stamp duty reserve tax raise the sale revenue.

STANDARD & POORS. One of the two major international bond-rating agencies headquartered in the United States. Its highest bond rating is AA, but a bond with an AA rating will normally be considered of "investment" grade. The address for Standard & Poors is 25 Broadway, New York, NY 10004. Its London office is at 19 S. Swithin's Lane, London EC4N 8AD.

STANDARD DEVIATION. A measure of the "scatter" of observed results about the mean, found by squaring the differences from the arithmetic mean, dividing by one less than the number of observations and taking the square root of the result. This is necessary in order to establish standard error.

STANDARD ERROR. The divergence of the majority of historic observations of the movement of a stock relative to a market from the prevailing trend (its **beta coefficient**). A wide divergence irritates a tidy mind, as it is "unsystematic."

STATUS QUO. Latin term for the condition as it stands at present.

STATUTE OF LIMITATIONS. The deadline after which a party claiming to be injured by the settlor may no longer file an action to recover damages.

STATUTORY. That which is fixed by statutes, as opposed to common law.

STERLING. The currency of the United Kingdom. Named after the small star ("starling") featured on the silver pennies first tainted in about 775. About 240 could be made from a pound of silver. The Normans introduced an intermediate coin, the shilling, worth twelve pennies. In 1971 the historic system of #.s.d (libra, solidus, denarius, from the equivalent roman coins) was replaced

by a centimalized pound of 100 "new" pence, with immediate inflationary effects.

STOCK. (1) Securities issued in a consolidated form, permitting
subdivision, as opposed to shares. (2) The U.K. term for what
Americans call inventories, that is, goods for sale.

STOCKBROKER. An agent on a stock exchange.

STOCK DIVIDEND. A dividend in the form of stock rather than
cash.

STOCK EXCHANGE. A marketplace for the secondary trading in
equities and bonds.

STOCK SPLIT. Occurs when one share of stock in a company is
surrendered to the company in exchange for additional shares in
the company. Generally, there are no tax or accounting ramifica-
tions other than reflecting on the company's books a different par
value and number of issued shares. The purpose of a split is to
facilitate wider trading in the security.

Reverse stock split. Where more than a number of issued shares
are combined to result in a lesser number of shares.

STOP-LOSS ORDER. An order to close out a position if the price
goes against one, if possible (which it usually will be). Any person opening a short position without stop-loss protection would
be very foolish. A stop-loss order can also prevent one from obsti-
nately retaining a long position when one has clearly misread the
market. In insurance a stop-loss policy can limit exposure. Thus a
member of Lloyd's might buy "stop-loss protection" for losses
greater than $100,000 but less than $250,000 in any year.

STRADDLE. Opening a long and a short position in the same commodity simultaneously. A conservative way of playing the market.

STREET NAME. A U.S. nominee that will be known to a buying
broker, thus expediting settlement and delivery.

STRIKING PRICE. The price at which an option may be
exercised.

SUBORDINATE. If there is a pecking order determining the
sequence in which a company will pay off its debt instruments,
subordinate (or junior) issues will not be repaid until unsubordi-
nated (or senior) debt has been repaid in full.

SUBPART F. Section of the U.S. Revenue Act of 1962 that ren-
ders U.S. shareholders liable to pay tax on the undistributed
income of a controlled foreign corporation.

SUBSCRIBERS. (1) The signatories to a company's memorandum of association who indicate thereby that they wish to become the first members of that company. (2) Initial investors purchasing interests or shares in a private or public offering.

SUBSIDIARY. One company that is controlled by another, either because the parent owns more than 50 percent of its voting shares or because it is able to appoint a majority of the directors for some other reason. As a general principle of British law, directors of other companies in a group may not come to the rescue of a stricken subsidiary unless it can reasonably be claimed that to do so was in the interests of members of the assisting company and not simply of the group as a whole. Banking supervisors nowadays seek to obtain firm assurances from a parent bank that they would support an insolvent foreign subsidiary.

SWAPS. Transactions where two parties exchange currencies and/or interest flows for a specified principal sum and period. Thus each may borrow in the market where they are best known and so can get the finest rate and then swap their loans for one denominated in another currency that they actually need. Interest rate swaps occur between those who feel that rates will rise and so seek fixed-rate coupons and those who believe that they will fall and so are willing to exchange fixed-rate bonds for floating-rate bonds.

TABLE A. The standardized articles of association that a British company may adopt. The U.K. Table A is contained in the regulations made under S.8(1), The Companies (Tables A to F) Regulations 1985 S.I. No. 805, as amended. The Manx Table A is contained in the more easily remembered companies (Memorandum and Articles of Association) regulations 1988, which is bound together with the companies acts 1931 1986. Copies can be purchased from the library government offices of Bucks Road Douglas.

TAKEOVER. A change in the control of a company.

TAX AVOIDANCE. Structuring one's affairs in such a way that the incidence of tax will be minimized. This is quite legal.

TAX-EXEMPT SECURITY. (U.S. practice) A bond that is exempt from federal and (within its home state, at least) state and local taxes. Commonly called *municipals,* although not necessarily issued by a municipality. Only "public purpose" bonds have enjoyed this "triple exemption" since 1986.

TAX HAVEN. An international banking and financial center providing privacy and tax benefits. A nation that has little or no taxes on businesses doing business there. Almost all countries are havens from some tax or other; for example, U.S. and U.K. banks do not deduct tax from interest on deposits made by nonresidents. The term is used pejoratively by some frustrated taxing authorities. The Australian authorities publish a list of tax havens, and any Australian dealing with these will incur suspicion of tax evasion.

TAX PLANNING. Structuring affairs in such a way as will minimize tax liability.

TAX REGIMEN. The local tax treatment of income tax, foreign source income, nonresident treatment, and special tax concessions that, when combined, form complex issues.

TAX TREATY. An arrangement between the revenue authorities of two countries to ensure that residents of either need not pay tax at any higher rate than that required by the more demanding country.

TCI. Turks and Caicos Islands.

TELECOMMUNICATIONS. A computer-guided communications system that expedites payments between member banks.

TERM INSURANCE. Insurance that will guarantee payment only if the life assured dies within the term of the policy. Nothing is payable if the person survives. Since this is pure insurance, as opposed to an endowment policy that is simultaneously a form of saving, it is much the cheaper. Very useful for wage earners who marry young or to cover the period during which another tax, such as U.K. inheritance tax following a gift, would be payable on death.

TERM LOAN. A loan for a fixed period of time.

TESTAMENTARY TRUST. One that is created by a will, as opposed to an inter vivos trust.

TIME VALUE. The premium paid for an option less its intrinsic value.

TOMBSTONE. A newspaper advertisement announcing the managers and underwriters of an issue of securities. Commonly used to commemorate an offering on the Euromarket.

TOP-DOWN APPROACH. The approach to investing where the desired spread of the portfolio will be decided first, and suitable securities to achieve that spread are selected second. Contrast with **bottom-up approach.**

TOTAL RETURN. The return gained from the investment. Calculated by combining dividends or interest received with any capital gain or loss.

TRACING. A process by which a court may "trace" the ownership of joint property or separate property to its origins to make a determination as to what fraction of it is marital or nonmarital. Some states consider all joint property to be marital; others trace the ownership to make that determination.

TRADE BALANCE. The difference between the value of the goods exported by a country and those goods that were imported. Usually applies only to goods and excludes services. To obtain a positive balance of trade, a country must export more goods than it imports.

TRADITIONAL OPTION. An option for which no regular secondary market exists.

TRANCH. A bond series issued for sale in a foreign country.

TRANCHE. A slice. A big loan may be brought to the market in digestible tranches.

TRANSACTION ADVICE. Notification from an agent to his principal of the terms under which a bargain has been struck. Sometimes known as a *contract note*.

TRANSFER. Passing ownership of a security from the seller to the buyer.

TRANSFER AGENT. The organization hired by a mutual fund/ unit trust to prepare and maintain records that relate to the shareholder accounts.

TRANSFER PRICING. Arranging that at least one intermediary, low-tax, or nil-tax country is involved between the partial manufacture of a product in one high-tax country and its eventual sale in another. Part of the profit will stay behind in the tax haven. As so often with tax planning, this works only as long as the planner is not so greedy as to deny commercial logic.

TRANSMISSION. Shares will be transmitted to the personal representatives (for example, the executors) of a deceased person after the registrar has sighted evidence of the granting of probate.

TRAVELERS CHECK. A nineteenth-century invention whereby a bank client's account is debited with the cost of a check that can subsequently be cashed anywhere in the world after duplicating the signature written at the time of issue. In the meantime the bank issuing the check, often American Express, enjoys the free deposit of the money.

TREASURY BILL. A short-dated negotiable bond issued by treasury departments of the United States or United Kingdom. An extremely safe investment: The yield available on ninety-day Treasuries is commonly taken as a proxy for "risk-free" investment when compared with the returns available from more dangerous instruments.

TREASURY BOND. A medium- or long-term debt obligation issued by the U.S. Treasury. Maturity is usually longer than five years.

TREASURY STOCK. In the United Kingdom this refers to gilts. In the United States it refers to shares in a company bought by the company to increase earnings per share or to frustrate a hostile bidder. The latter practice has only recently become legal in the United Kingdom, and it is much less common.

TREATY SHOPPING. Structuring international business in such a way as to derive maximum benefit from tax treaties.

TRUE SETTLOR. The true grantor is not the true settlor, and his or her identity is kept private by the trustee. See also **grantor trust.**

TRUST. An entity created for the purpose of protecting and conserving assets for the benefit of a third party, the beneficiary. A contract affecting three parties, the settlor, the trustee, and the beneficiary. A trust protector is optional but recommended, as well. In the trust the settlor transfers asset ownership to the trustee on behalf of the beneficiaries. An equitable obligation imposing on one or more trustees a duty of dealing with property under their control for the benefit of the beneficiaries, who may enforce that obligation. It should be noted that the obligation arises in equity; therefore a trust is not a suitable vehicle for use in a civil law jurisdiction. There has to be property, meaning any kind of asset, in a trust, but the person introducing that property, who is known in the United States as the grantor and in Britain as the settlor, need not necessarily be identified, or a nominee may be used. There must be one or more trustees, who may be individuals or corporations. The grantor may also be a trustee and/or a beneficiary. If the trust is for the benefit of ascertainable individuals it is a private trust, and any action against the trustees would be brought by one or more beneficiaries. When the trust is for the benefit of the public at large, as with a charitable trust, an action would be brought by government officers. A private trust must have "objects," or intended beneficiaries, without which it will fail. If it is no longer possible to benefit the original objects of a public trust the courts may appoint a substitute beneficiary, under the doctrine of "cy pres." If the trustees have discretion when distributing trust property among the potential beneficiaries it is known as a discretionary trust; otherwise, it is a fixed-interest trust. U.S. practice allows for revocable trusts. These would be a waste of time and money under British law, but the significance of parting with the trust property irrevocably must not be underestimated by the grantor. In the Middle Ages trusts, then known as "uses," were a bone of contention between the Crown and subjects as they were used to avoid having to pay feudal taxes upon the death of a landowner. The conflict continues.

TRUST DEED. An asset protection trust document or instrument. More properly known as a *trust instrument*, it is the document that establishes the identity of the first trustees, the objects of the trust, and the initial trust property. It will normally detail the way in which the trust is to be administered. In the absence of specific instructions the trustees will be able to refer to statutory legislation in those jurisdictions that possess it; it is therefore sensible that the law governing a trust should be that of a jurisdiction possessing modern trust legislation. Express trusts, that is, trusts that are formed deliberately, usually have a trust deed, and a signed deed is essential in many jurisdictions if the trust is to own land.

TRUSTEE. A person totally independent of the settlor who has the fiduciary responsibility to the beneficiaries to manage the assets of the trust as a reasonably prudent businessperson would do in the same circumstances. Shall defer to the trust protector when required in the best interest of the trust. The trustee reporting requirements shall be defined at the onset and should include how often, to whom, and how to respond to instructions or inquiries; global investment strategies; fees (flat and/or percentage of the valuation of the trust estate); anticipated future increases in fees; hourly rates for consulting services; seminars; client educational materials; and so on. The trustee may have full discretionary powers of distributions to beneficiaries. The person or persons appointed to administer a trust. A minor may not serve as a trustee. A trustee is obliged to administer the trust prudently, to comply strictly with the terms of the trust, and not to benefit from the trusteeship except to the extent, if any, that is permitted by the trust deed. A person may decline to serve as a trustee, but once a person has accepted to serve she cannot normally resign until a successor has been signified his willingness to replace her. The requirement for prudence may be waived if all the potential beneficiaries are of legal age and sound mind and sign a form indemnifying the trustees from doing something that the beneficiaries all want but that disturbs the trustees. The ban on benefiting from a trusteeship would make it very difficult to find a professional trustee such as a trust corporation to serve unless the trust deed entitled them to reasonable fees. This would be a pity, as much difficulty can be avoided if the first named trustee, to whom correspondence will normally be addressed in the first instance, is a professional trustee.

TRUST ENFORCER. A person appointed by the settlor to oversee the trust on behalf of the trust. In many jurisdictions local trust laws define the concept of the trust protector. Has veto power over the trustee with respect to discretionary matters but no say with respect to issues unequivocally covered in the trust deed. Trust decisions are the trustee's alone. Has the power to remove and appoint trustees. Consults with the trust's legal advisor.

TRUST INDENTURE. A trust instrument such as a trust deed creating an offshore trust.

TRUST PROTECTOR. A person appointed by the settlor to oversee the trust on behalf of the beneficiaries. In many jurisdictions local trust laws define the concept of the trust protector. Has veto power over the trustee with respect to discretionary matters but no say with respect to issues unequivocally covered in the trust deed. Trust decisions are the trustee's alone. Has the power to remove the trustee and appoint trustees. Consults with the settlor, but the final decisions must be the protector's.

TRUST SETTLEMENT DOCUMENT. See **trust deed.**

TURNOVER. Another word for **sales.**

TURNOVER RATIO. The total value of shares traded during a specified period of time (often one year) divided by the market capitalization for the same period.

UCITS (UNDERTAKINGS FOR COLLECTIVE INVEST-MENTS IN TRANSFERABLE SECURITIES). Adopted in 1985 by the EC, this directive allows collective investment schemes authorized in one member EC state to be marketed in another member state after a two-month notice. The SIB is responsible for overseeing the U.K. marketing activities of UCITS funds. Investors are protected under the U.K. Investors Compensation Scheme.

ULTRA VIRES. Latin for "beyond one's powers." It will be more difficult for outsiders to claim against a company if they could have established from its laws/memorandum of association that its officers were acting ultra vires, although common law jurisdictions are increasingly likely to consider the equity of such a case. The opposite of ultra vires is **intra vires.**

UMBRELLA FUND. A series of offshore funds that permit a limited number of switches between individual subfunds with little or no charges. Consequently, provided that the subfunds follow the separate markets in which they are invested fairly closely, an investor can vary investments with reasonable confidence that the results will be similar to switching between the individual markets. The deferral of U.K. capital gains tax that such funds once enjoyed was ended by the 1989 budget.

UNDERWRITER. (1) A company or organization that distributes mutual funds' shares to broker/dealers and investors. (2) A company bringing a new issue to the market will have to fix the offer price in advance. It is possible that some adverse development between the pricing and the issue dates will deter investors. It is therefore customary to offer various large investors an underwriting premium for agreeing to accept the stock at the issue price. In the United States the underwriter will normally take the stock onto its own books and aim to sell it at a profit. In the United Kingdom the underwriter will not be called upon to buy the securities unless other purchasers cannot be found. Since underwriting premiums usually constitute "easy money" for fund managers, the less experienced ones sometimes forget the real risks involved. (3) An agent for a syndicate at Lloyd's who literally writes his name at the foot of a policy to signify acceptance of all or an indicated part of that risk. Part of the skill of a Lloyd's broker is to know the "lead" underwriters whose prior acceptance of a risk will encourage subsequent signatories.

UNIFORM PARTNERSHIP ACT (UPA). One of the uniform

type of laws adopted by some states or used as a baseline for other states.

UNIT TRUST. An open-ended British collective investment scheme. The rights of shareholders are protected by a trust deed. Unit trusts secured a major advantage over investment trusts in the 1960s and 1970s because their open-endedness made them suitable as investments to underlying insurance policies, and the insurance companies were able to boast the unit trust manager's performance, whereas the actual managers of unit or investment trusts were constrained when advertising. Unit trusts are exempted from capital gains tax when dealing in securities, although selling units at profit may give rise to a charge.

UNIVERSAL LIFE INSURANCE. (U.S. term) A life assurance contract that combines low-cost term insurance with a savings account. Tax is deferred on income and gains realized within the savings portion. Premiums can be varied.

UNLIMITED COMPANY. A private company whose shareholders accept unlimited personal liability for its debts. It may therefore be appropriate to hold shares in an unlimited company through a holding company with limited liability. An unlimited U.K. company is not obliged to file account on public record unless it is the subsidiary or holding company of a limited company.

UPA. See **Uniform Partnership Act.**

UPSTREAMING. The process of retaining earnings offshore through the billing process.

URL (UNIVERSAL RESOURCE LOCATOR). World Wide Web address composed of a combination of letters, numbers, and punctuation.

USC. United States Code.

U.S.D or U.S.$. U.S. dollars.

VALUE ADDED. The value that is added to intermediate goods at a given stage of production. Equals the revenues from sales of goods and the change in the value of the inventory value less the cost of the goods.

VALUE DATE. The date from which money will earn interest in a bank account. This will normally be later than the entry date because the funds must first be cleared. In securities transactions value date is an alternative term for settlement or delivery date.

VARIABLE ANNUITY. An annuity in which you select the investment program that suits your future needs. The ultimate payback is a function of how well your program performs during the intervening period before the maturity of the annuity. A life assurance annuity contract whose value is not fixed but will vary with that on an underlying portfolio of securities. The return to the owner may also be linked to movements in the portfolio.

VARIABLE LIFE INSURANCE. (U.S. term) Insurance that combines term insurance (a death benefit) with a savings account, which can be switched between bond, equity, and money market funds. Tax is deferred within the policy, and distributions are taxed as income only to the extent that they exceed premiums paid. Unlike universal policies, which they otherwise resemble closely, the annual level of premiums is fixed.

VARIATION OF TRUSTS. It is possible to vary a trust deed if all the potential beneficiaries are adult, are of sound mind, and wish the change to be made. Otherwise permission has to be obtained from the courts. British courts, when considering such an application, will consider the interests of the beneficiaries before those of the inland revenue.

VELOCITY OF CIRCULATION. The rapidity with which money changes hands. Calculated by dividing the GDP/GNP by the money supply.

VENTURE CAPITAL. Capital committed to an unproven venture. The initial startup money is referred to as *deed money* and entails the greatest risk. If the project gets off the ground it may require additional finance at the "mezzanine level" before the company is finally brought to the market and the venture capitalist can enjoy handsome rewards. Experienced investors in venture capital situations typically reckon on turning away nine out of every ten proposals that are brought to them, and then they expect as many failures as successes from the selected investments. Even so, one cannot lose more than all of one's investment, but a really successful venture will multiply it many times over.

VETTING. The process used by the offshore consultant for qualifying the prospective client to determine if that person is a good candidate for offshore asset protection; as in to "vet" the prospective client.

VOLATILITY. A term that describes a security's tendency to rise and fall in value relative to market conditions. Volatility ratings are usually calculated after three years of market pricing.

WALL STREET. The street that runs where the wall defending lower Manhattan Island, and subsequently famous buttonwood tree, once stood. Now the home of the NYSE and a byword for the capitalist system in the United States.

WALL STREET JOURNAL. The premier U.S. financial daily newspaper. Its circulation office for the United States is at 200 Burnett Road, Chicopee, MA 01020, and for Europe is at P.O. Box 2845, 6401 DH Heerlen, The Netherlands.

WAREHOUSE RECEIPT. Bearer document conferring ownership of a pile of commodities, usually a lot, sitting in an approved warehouse. The accounting for prepaid charges and insurance tends to be complicated.

WAREHOUSING. The illegal practice of buying more shares in a company than is permitted by the regulations of the stock exchange on which it is quoted but disguising the fact by holding them through several nominee names, not one of whose holdings exceed the permitted limit.

WARRANT ISSUE. An instrument that enables the holder to purchase shares or participation certificates at a predetermined price within a specified period from the issuing company.

WEB. The World Wide Web (WWW).

WHITE KNIGHT. A bidder preferred by management, who emerges after a company has already received an unwelcome takeover bid. A white knight who had bid first would doubtless have been cast as a dark knight.

WILL. The written expression of a person's wishes as to how her property should be distributed by her executors. It should normally be signed in the presence of two witnesses who are not themselves, or their spouses, beneficiaries under the will. The existence of a will avoids the problems of intestacy. A person may have more than one will, relating to different assets, but any direction relating to a particular asset will be invalidated by a subsequent will. Alterations to a will may be made by codicils witnessed in the same way. Property that has been put into a trust no longer belongs to the grantor and so cannot be bequeathed in a will.

WINDING UP. The closing down, dissolution, and final distribution of the assets of a company. The assets are distributed among the company's creditors, including federal and state taxing authorities, employees if any unpaid wages are due, and partners or shareholders.

WINDOW DRESSING. Prettifying one's balance sheet in time for the end of the company year. Many treasurers and fund managers would rather realize a loss on a security than have it appear among their assets at below book cost at balance sheet date. Banks sometimes own more such assets as will soothe their regulatory authorities at their year end than at other times.

WITHHOLDING TAX. A tax withheld on some payments to foreign holders of a security or, less often, a bank deposit. It is often equivalent to the standard rate of taxation in the country concerned. Residents of a country with a double taxation agreement can usually set the tax against their domestic tax liability. No taxing authority can impose withholding tax on Eurobonds.

WORKING CAPITAL. Current assets less current liabilities. A company with a negative working capital may well have to raise fresh funds by borrowing or from shareholders.

WORKING DAY. A day on which business may be conducted. There are five working days in a calendar week that contains no holidays.

WORLD BANK. Formed to be the bank lender and technical advisor to the developing countries, utilizing funds and technical resources from the member nations (the depositors). The headquarters are in Washington, D.C.

WORLD BANK. The International Bank for Reconstruction and Development (World Bank) is the sister organization to the IMF (they are linked by a tunnel under Washington's H Street). The bank began by financing the reconstruction of postwar Europe. Now it serves effectively as an investment bank for the Third World. It is to the credit of its management that its securities are always rated AAA grade.

WRITER. A person who sells an option is normally known as the *writer.* If a writer undertakes to sell something that he owns he is known as a covered writer. This is conservative. If he undertakes to sell something that he does not own he is known as an uncovered or naked writer. This is a high-risk strategy, and the writer will be obliged to put up considerable margin.

WRITER TO THE SIGNET. A member of an ancient society of solicitors in Scotland. They have the exclusive privilege of preparing crown writs.

YANKEE BOND. A dollar-denominated bond issued in the United States by a non-U.S. company.

YELLOW SHEETS. Yellow sheets on which the National Quotation Bureau lists prices of U.S. bonds that are traded over the counter.

YEN. The currency of Japan. Its subdivisions into 100 sen and 1,000 rin would be of greater practicality if the yen were to be redenominated, presumably by making one "new" yen equivalent to 100 "old," as is regularly mooted.

YIELD. The annual return on an investment, expressed as a percentage. The yield to redemption or maturity (the same thing) combines the running yield with the "pull to redemption." Thus, a bond that has a 10 percent coupon and exactly one year of remaining life will sell at 98.2 percent when interest rates are at 12.0 percent, that 12.0 percent being composed of 10.2 percent running yield and 1.8 percent pull to redemption (100.0–98.2 percent).

YIELD CURVE. The difference between short-term and long-term interest rates. If the former are lower the yield curve is said to be positive; if not it is negative. Study of yield curves will show, for example, that either short-term rates are likely to rise or long-term rates are likely to fall.

ZEBRAS (ZERO COUPON EUROSTERLING). Bearer or registered accruing securities. Gifts from which the interest has been stripped, so creating **zero-coupon bonds.**

ZERO-COUPON BONDS. Bonds that pay no interest. Sold at a discount on their face value, they are later redeemed at face or par value. They have therefore to be issued at a considerable discount in order to generate a yield to maturity competitive with a conventional bond. "Zeros" have the merits of no income collection costs and a certain yield to maturity. (Calculations for a conventional bond have to assume that interest rates will have remained constant until income comes to be reinvested.) The fact that no coupons are presented for payment means that a forged zero may not be detected until maturity; it is therefore additionally sensible to hold them through Euroclear or Cedel.

INDEX